MARVEL STUDIOS

AVENGERS
INFINITY WAR

PRELUDE

COLLECTION EDITOR: JENNIFER GRÜNWALD
ASSISTANT EDITOR: CAITLIN O'CONNELL
ASSOCIATE MANAGING EDITOR: KATERI WOODY
EDITOR, SPECIAL PROJECTS: MARK D. BEAZLEY
VP PRODUCTION & SPECIAL PROJECTS: JEFF YOUNGQUIST
SVP PRINT, SALES & MARKETING: DAVID GABRIEL

EDITOR IN CHIEF: C.B. CEBULSKI
CHIEF CREATIVE OFFICER: JOE QUESADA
PRESIDENT: DAN BUCKLEY

MARVEL'S AVENGERS: INFINITY WAR PRELUDE TPB. Contains material originally published in magazine form as MARVEL'S AVENGERS: INFINITY WAR PRELUDE #1-2, INFINITY #1 and THANOS ANNUAL #1. Second printing 2018. ISBN 978-1-302-90943-7. Published by MARVEL WORLDWIDE, INC., a subsidiary of MARVEL ENTERTAINMENT, LLC. OFFICE OF PUBLICATION: 135 West 50th Street, New York, NY 10020. Copyright © 2018 MARVEL. No similarity between any of the names, characters, persons, and/or institutions in this magazine with those of any living or dead person or institution is intended, and any such similarity which may exist is purely coincidental. **Printed in the U.S.A.** DAN BUCKLEY, President, Marvel Entertainment; JOHN NEE, Publisher; JOE QUESADA, Chief Creative Officer; TOM BREVOORT, SVP of Publishing; DAVID BOGART, SVP of Business Affairs & Operations, Publishing & Partnership; DAVID GABRIEL, SVP of Sales & Marketing, Publishing; JEFF YOUNGQUIST, VP of Production & Special Projects; DAN CARR, Executive Director of Publishing Technology; ALEX MORALES, Director of Publishing Operations; DAN EDINGTON, Managing Editor; SUSAN CRESPI, Production Manager; STAN LEE, Chairman Emeritus. For information regarding advertising in Marvel Comics or on Marvel.com, please contact Vit DeBellis, Custom Solutions & Integrated Advertising Manager, at vdebellis@marvel.com. For Marvel subscription inquiries, please call 888-511-5480. **Manufactured between 4/4/2018 and 4/16/2018 by QUAD GRAPHICS SARATOGA, SARATOGA SPRINGS, NY, USA.**

10 9 8 7 6 5 4 3 2

MARVEL STUDIOS

AVENGERS
INFINITY WAR

PRELUDE

MARVEL STUDIOS' AVENGERS: INFINITY WAR PRELUDE #1
BASED ON THE **CAPTAIN AMERICA: CIVIL WAR** SCREENPLAY
BY CHRISTOPHER MARKUS & STEPHEN McFEELY
WRITER: **WILL CORONA PILGRIM**
ARTIST: **TIGH WALKER**
COLORIST: **CHRIS O'HALLORAN**
LETTERER: VC'S TRAVIS LANHAM
COVER ART: RYAN MEINERDING
EDITOR: MARK BASSO

MARVEL STUDIOS' AVENGERS: INFINITY WAR PRELUDE #2
WRITER: **WILL CORONA PILGRIM**
ARTIST: **JORGE FORNÉS**
COLORIST: **CHRIS O'HALLORAN**
LETTERER: VC'S TRAVIS LANHAM
COVER ART: RYAN MEINERDING
EDITOR: MARK BASSO

FOR MARVEL STUDIOS
EXECUTIVE, PRODUCTION & DEVELOPMENT: TRINH TRAN
PRESIDENT: KEVIN FEIGE

AVENGERS CREATED BY STAN LEE & JACK KIRBY

MARVEL STUDIOS' AVENGERS:
INFINITY WAR PRELUDE #1

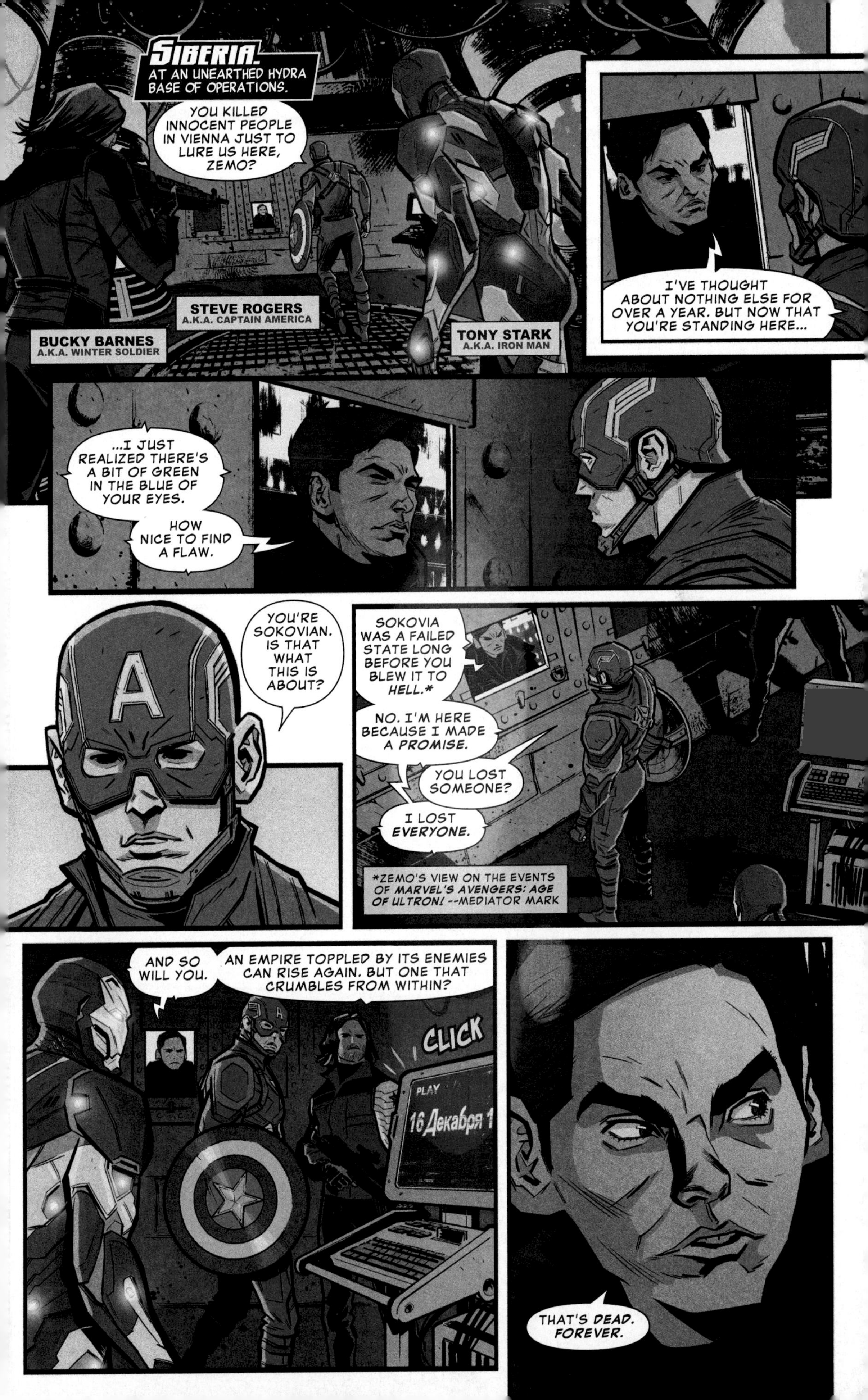
SIBERIA.
AT AN UNEARTHED HYDRA BASE OF OPERATIONS.
YOU KILLED INNOCENT PEOPLE IN VIENNA JUST TO LURE US HERE, ZEMO?
BUCKY BARNES A.K.A. WINTER SOLDIER
STEVE ROGERS A.K.A. CAPTAIN AMERICA
TONY STARK A.K.A. IRON MAN
I'VE THOUGHT ABOUT NOTHING ELSE FOR OVER A YEAR. BUT NOW THAT YOU'RE STANDING HERE...
...I JUST REALIZED THERE'S A BIT OF GREEN IN THE BLUE OF YOUR EYES.
HOW NICE TO FIND A FLAW.
YOU'RE SOKOVIAN. IS THAT WHAT THIS IS ABOUT?
SOKOVIA WAS A FAILED STATE LONG BEFORE YOU BLEW IT TO HELL.*
NO. I'M HERE BECAUSE I MADE A PROMISE.
YOU LOST SOMEONE?
I LOST EVERYONE.
*ZEMO'S VIEW ON THE EVENTS OF MARVEL'S AVENGERS: AGE OF ULTRON! --MEDIATOR MARK
AN EMPIRE TOPPLED BY ITS ENEMIES CAN RISE AGAIN. BUT ONE THAT CRUMBLES FROM WITHIN?
AND SO WILL YOU.
CLICK
PLAY
16 Декабря 1
THAT'S DEAD. FOREVER.

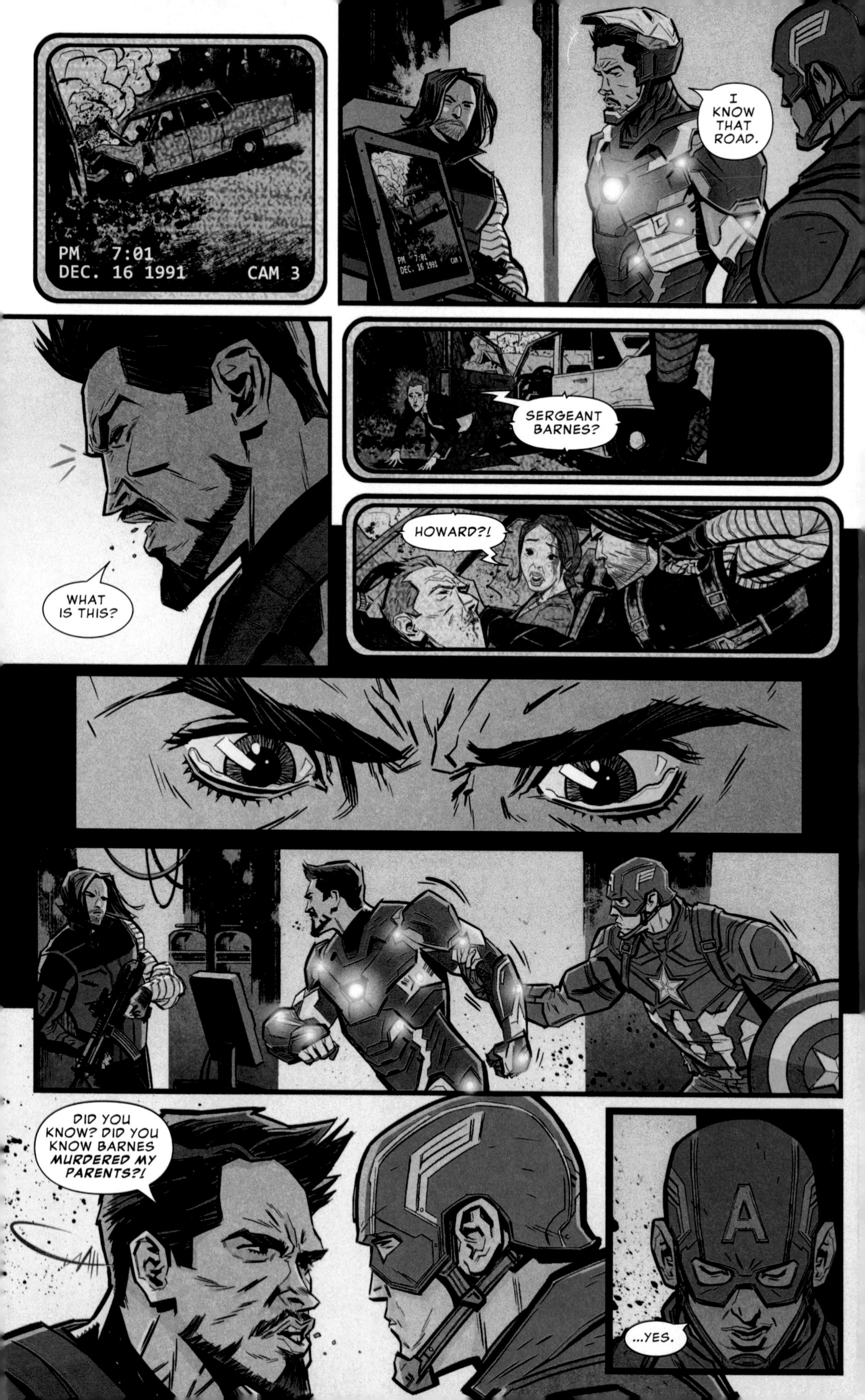
PM 7:01
DEC. 16 1991 CAM 3
I KNOW THAT ROAD.
WHAT IS THIS?
SERGEANT BARNES?
HOWARD?!
DID YOU KNOW? DID YOU KNOW BARNES *MURDERED* MY PARENTS?!
...YES.

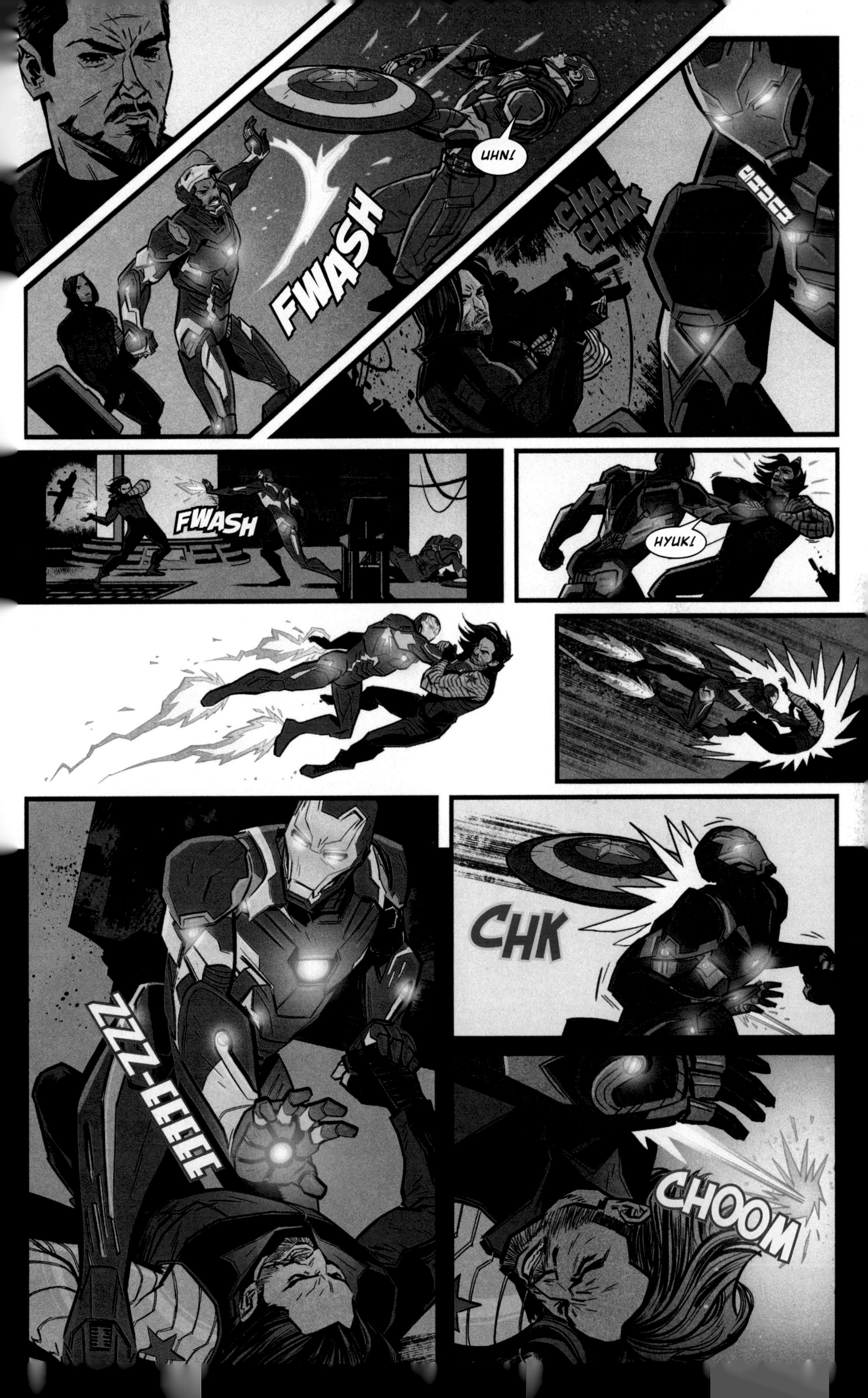
UHN!
FWASH
CHA-CHAK
FWASH
HYUK!
ZZZ-EEEEE
CHK
CHOOM

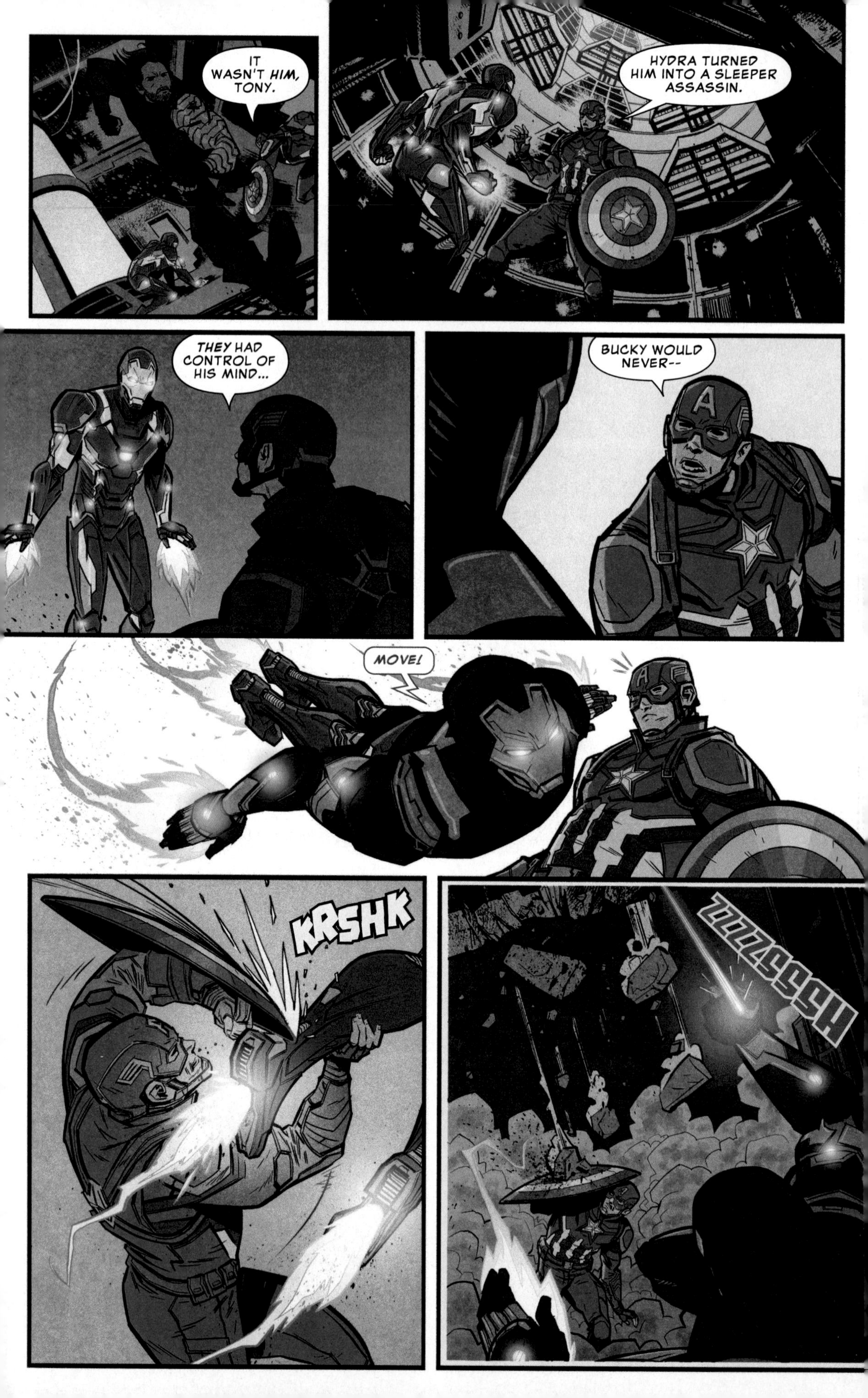
IT WASN'T *HIM*, TONY.
HYDRA TURNED HIM INTO A SLEEPER ASSASSIN.
THEY HAD CONTROL OF HIS MIND...
BUCKY WOULD NEVER--
MOVE!
KRSHK
ZZZZSSSH

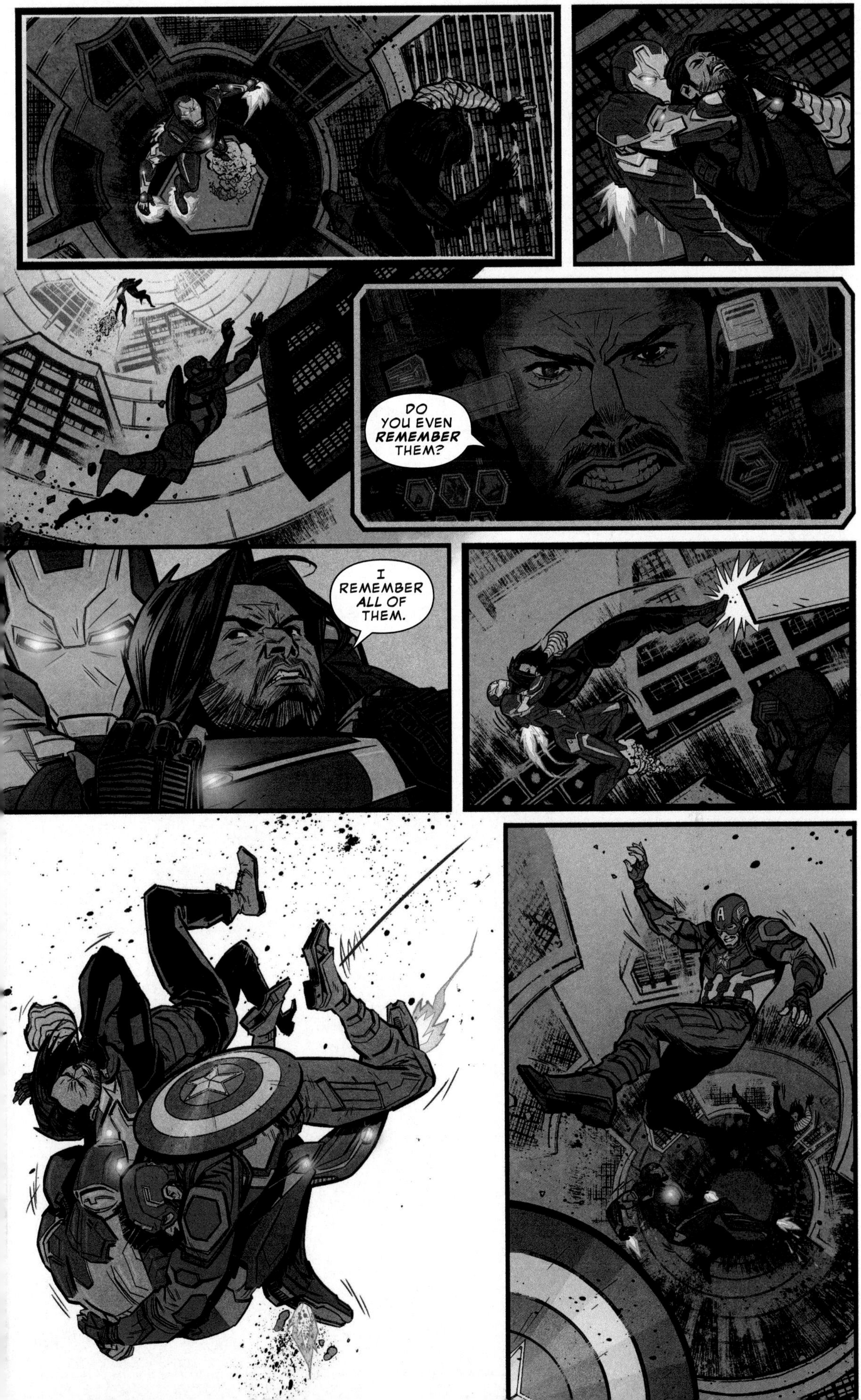
DO YOU EVEN REMEMBER THEM?
I REMEMBER ALL OF THEM.

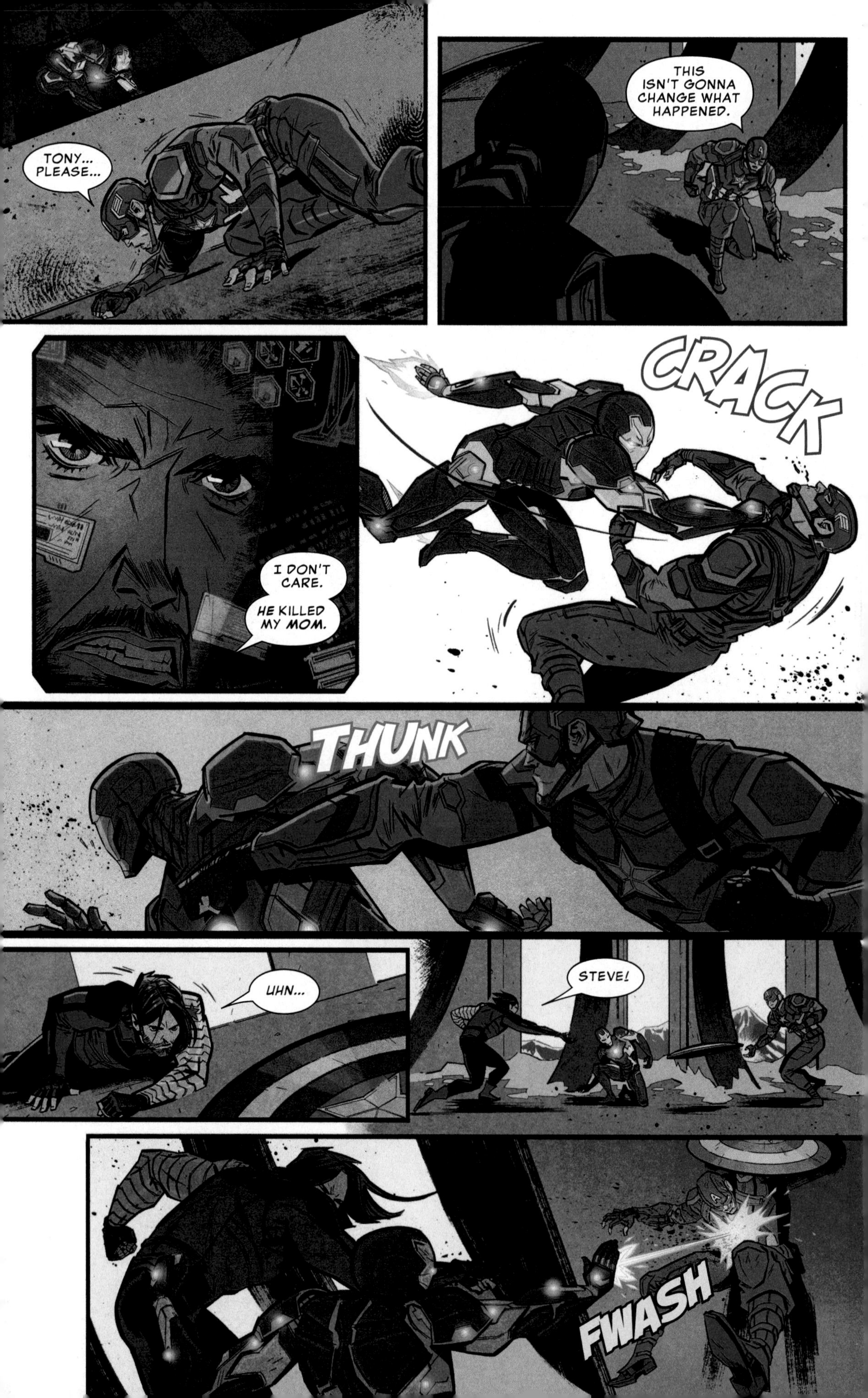
TONY... PLEASE...
THIS ISN'T GONNA CHANGE WHAT HAPPENED.
I DON'T CARE.
HE KILLED MY MOM.
CRACK
THUNK
UHN...
STEVE!
FWASH

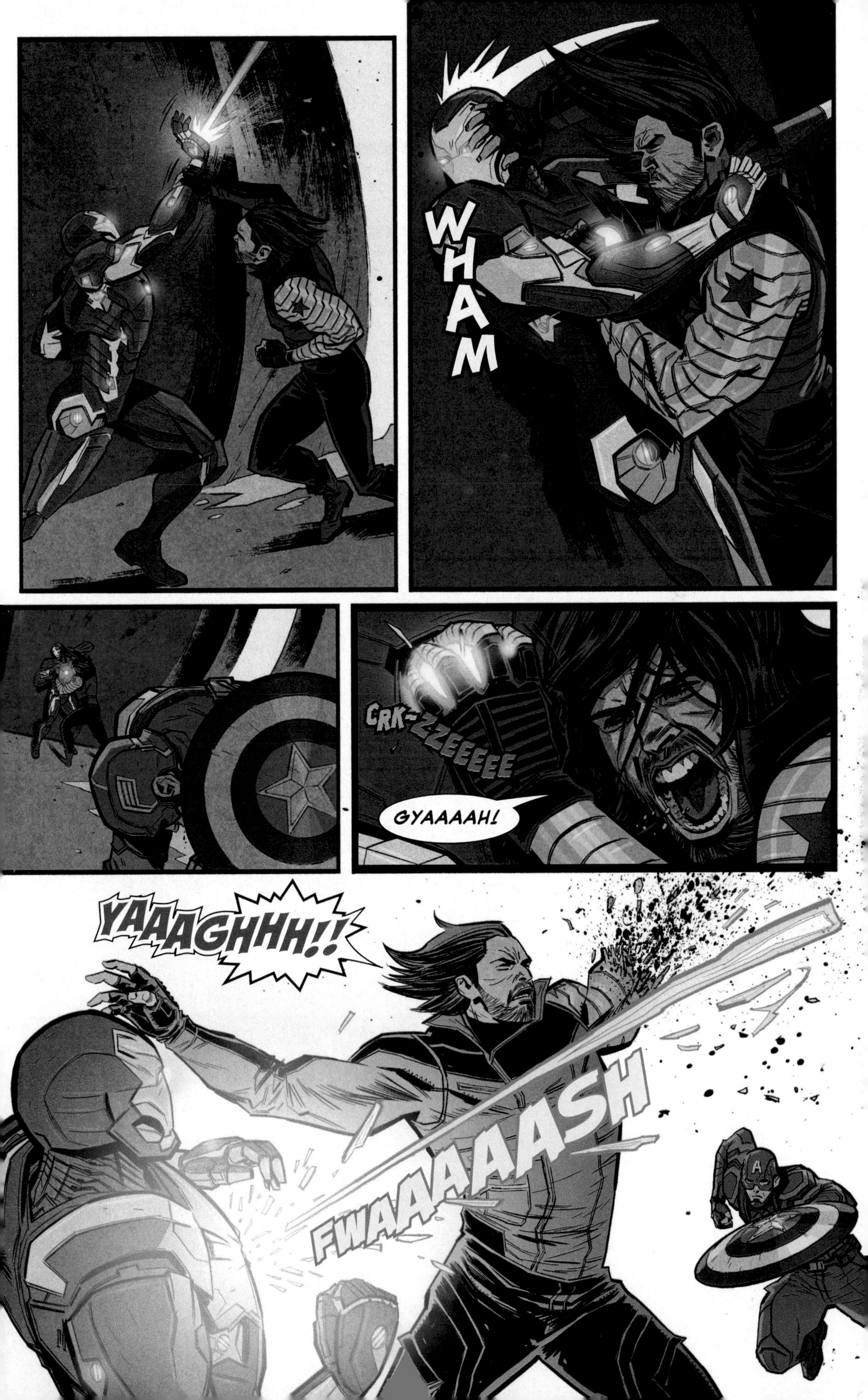
WHAM
CRK-ZZEEEEEE
GYAAAAH!
YAAAGHHH!!
FWAAAAAASH

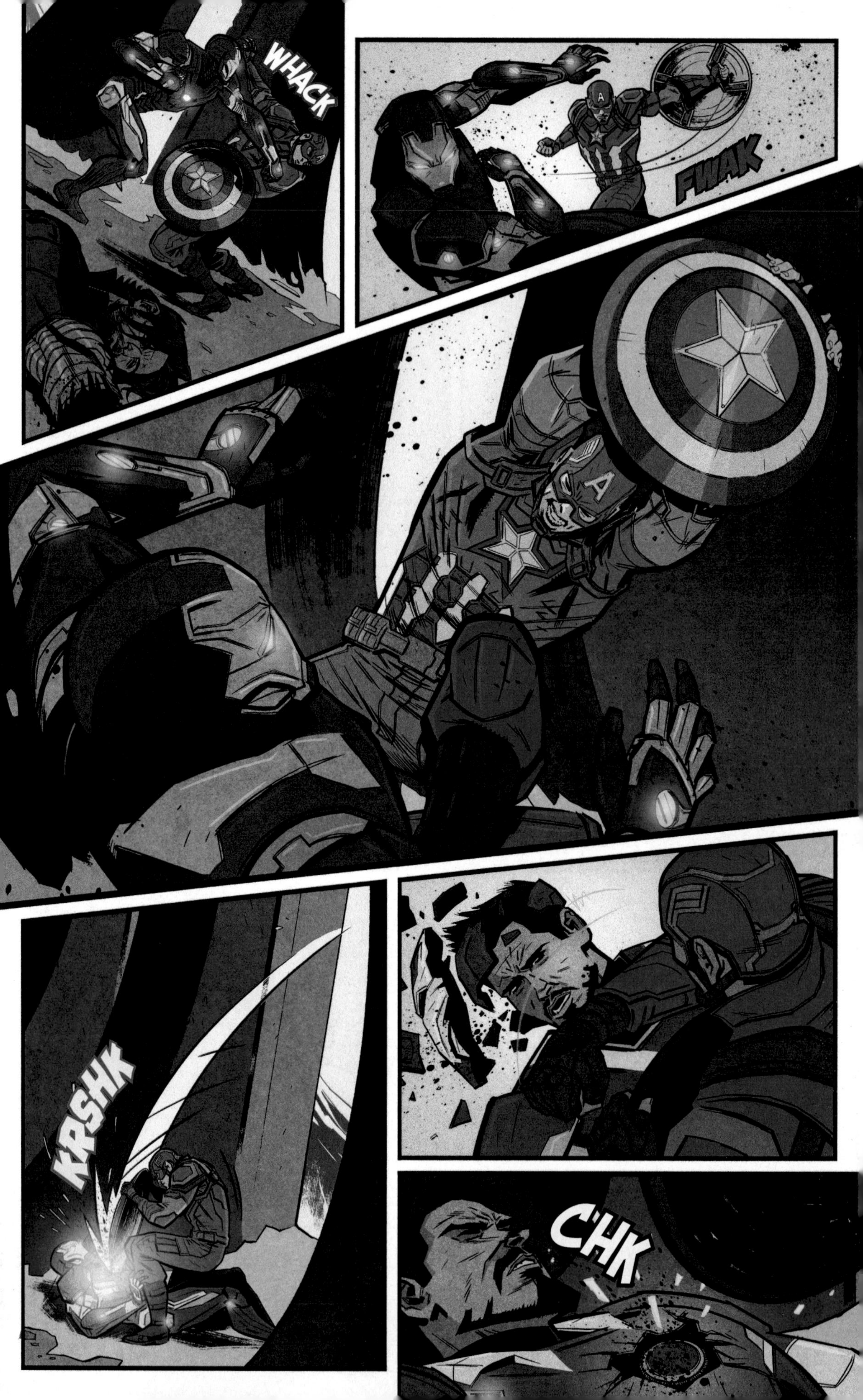
WHACK
FWAK
KRSHK
CHK

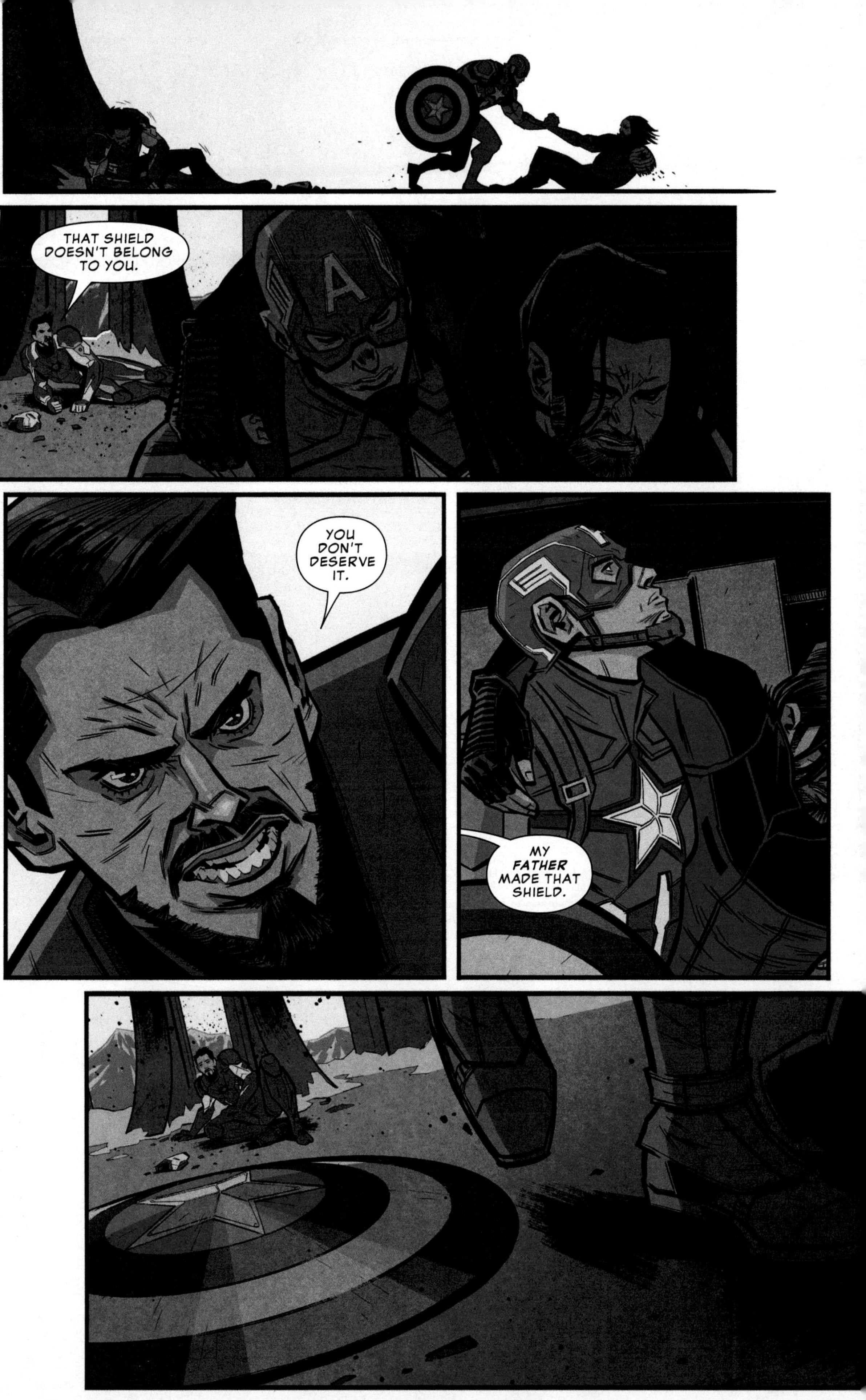
THAT SHIELD DOESN'T BELONG TO YOU.
YOU DON'T DESERVE IT.
MY *FATHER* MADE THAT SHIELD.

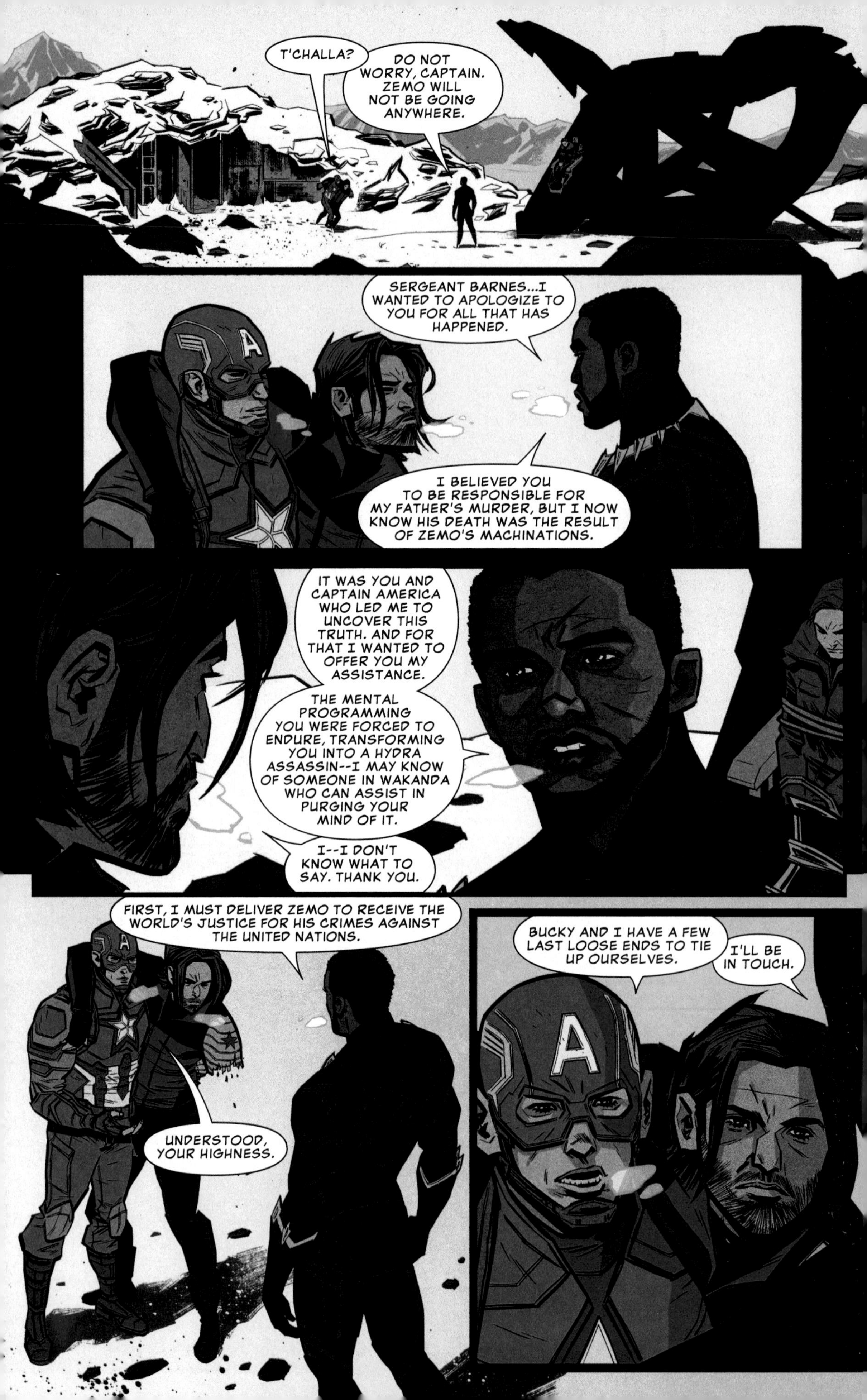
T'CHALLA?
DO NOT WORRY, CAPTAIN. ZEMO WILL NOT BE GOING ANYWHERE.
SERGEANT BARNES...I WANTED TO APOLOGIZE TO YOU FOR ALL THAT HAS HAPPENED.
I BELIEVED YOU TO BE RESPONSIBLE FOR MY FATHER'S MURDER, BUT I NOW KNOW HIS DEATH WAS THE RESULT OF ZEMO'S MACHINATIONS.
IT WAS YOU AND CAPTAIN AMERICA WHO LED ME TO UNCOVER THIS TRUTH. AND FOR THAT I WANTED TO OFFER YOU MY ASSISTANCE.
THE MENTAL PROGRAMMING YOU WERE FORCED TO ENDURE, TRANSFORMING YOU INTO A HYDRA ASSASSIN--I MAY KNOW OF SOMEONE IN WAKANDA WHO CAN ASSIST IN PURGING YOUR MIND OF IT.
I--I DON'T KNOW WHAT TO SAY. THANK YOU.
FIRST, I MUST DELIVER ZEMO TO RECEIVE THE WORLD'S JUSTICE FOR HIS CRIMES AGAINST THE UNITED NATIONS.
UNDERSTOOD, YOUR HIGHNESS.
BUCKY AND I HAVE A FEW LAST LOOSE ENDS TO TIE UP OURSELVES.
I'LL BE IN TOUCH.

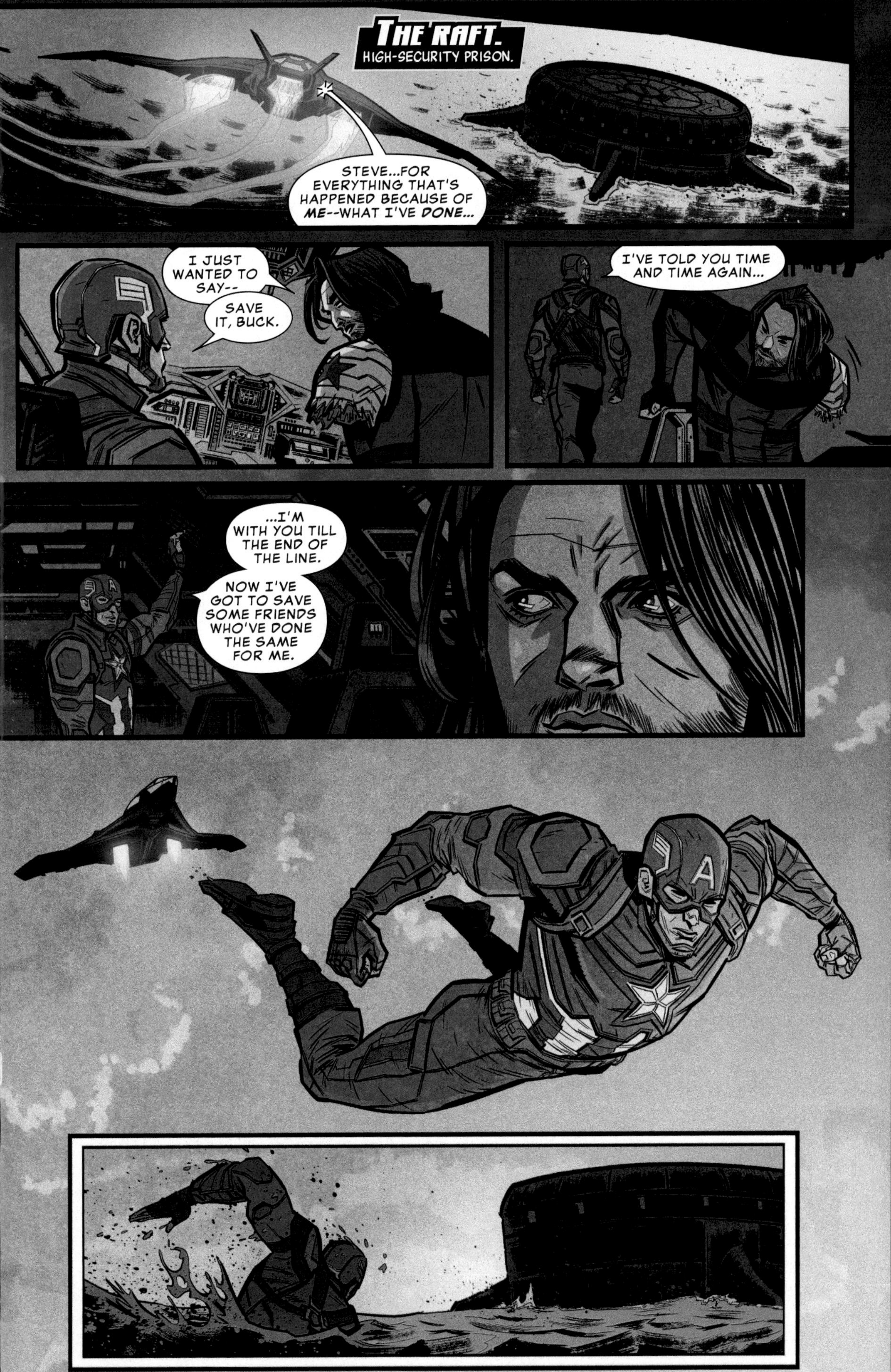
THE RAFT.
HIGH-SECURITY PRISON.
STEVE...FOR EVERYTHING THAT'S HAPPENED BECAUSE OF ME--WHAT I'VE DONE...
I JUST WANTED TO SAY--
SAVE IT, BUCK.
I'VE TOLD YOU TIME AND TIME AGAIN...
...I'M WITH YOU TILL THE END OF THE LINE.
NOW I'VE GOT TO SAVE SOME FRIENDS WHO'VE DONE THE SAME FOR ME.

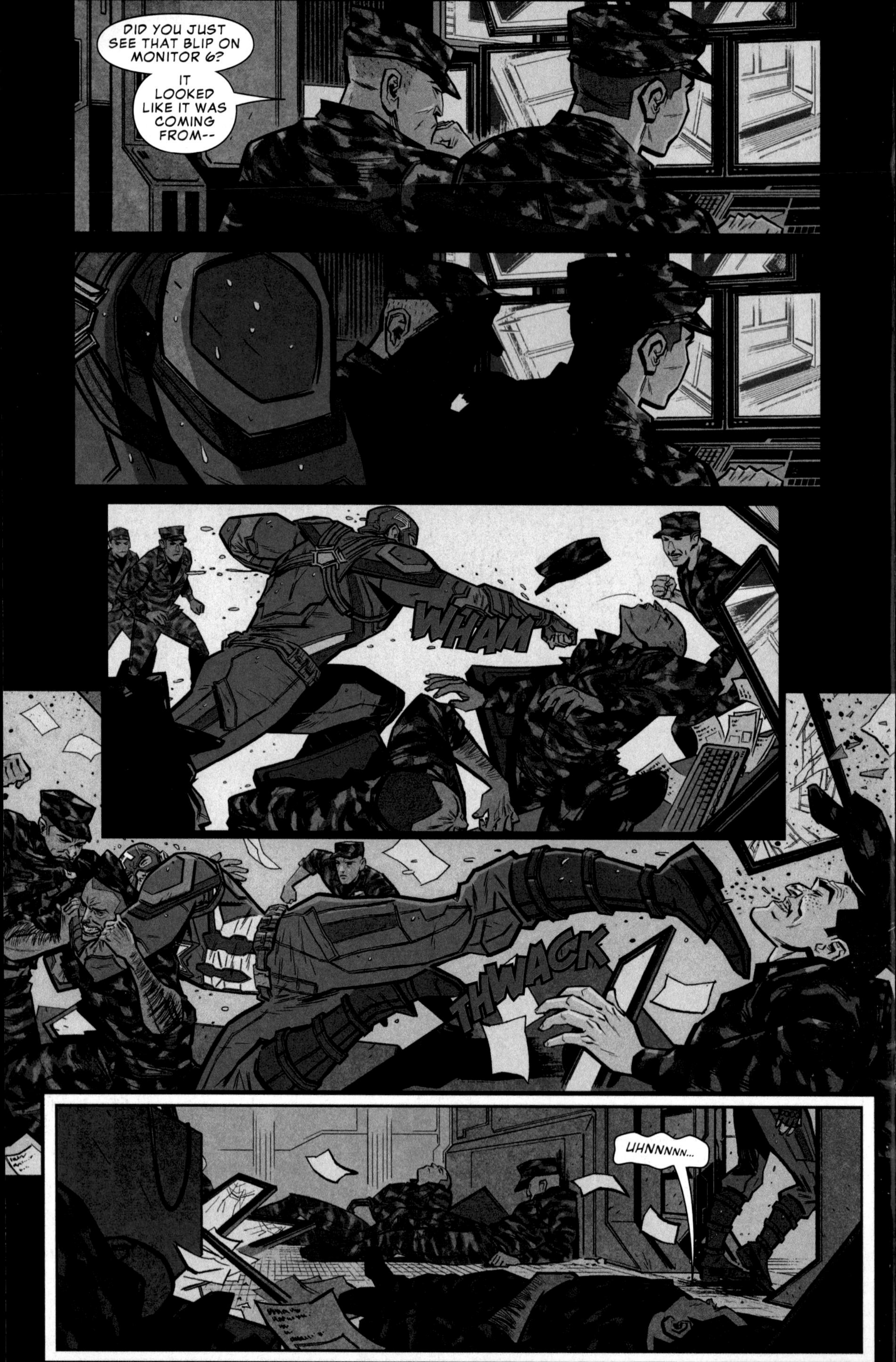
DID YOU JUST SEE THAT BLIP ON MONITOR 6?
IT LOOKED LIKE IT WAS COMING FROM--
WHAM
THWACK
UHNNNNN...

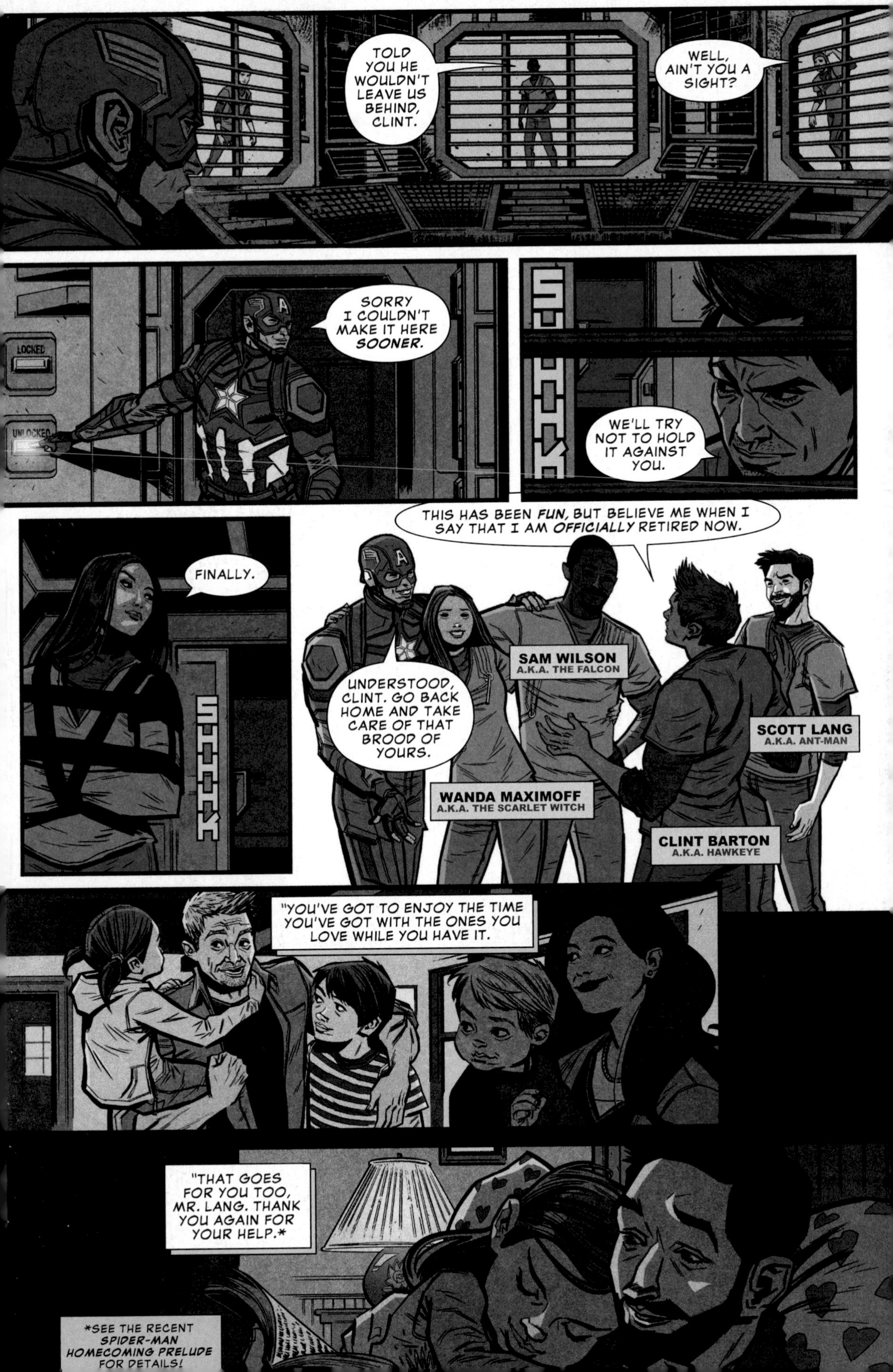
TOLD YOU HE WOULDN'T LEAVE US BEHIND, CLINT.
WELL, AIN'T YOU A SIGHT?
LOCKED
UNLOCKED
SORRY I COULDN'T MAKE IT HERE SOONER.
SHHHK
WE'LL TRY NOT TO HOLD IT AGAINST YOU.
FINALLY.
SHHHK
THIS HAS BEEN FUN, BUT BELIEVE ME WHEN I SAY THAT I AM OFFICIALLY RETIRED NOW.
UNDERSTOOD, CLINT. GO BACK HOME AND TAKE CARE OF THAT BROOD OF YOURS.
SAM WILSON A.K.A. THE FALCON
SCOTT LANG A.K.A. ANT-MAN
WANDA MAXIMOFF A.K.A. THE SCARLET WITCH
CLINT BARTON A.K.A. HAWKEYE
"YOU'VE GOT TO ENJOY THE TIME YOU'VE GOT WITH THE ONES YOU LOVE WHILE YOU HAVE IT.
"THAT GOES FOR YOU TOO, MR. LANG. THANK YOU AGAIN FOR YOUR HELP.*
*SEE THE RECENT SPIDER-MAN HOMECOMING PRELUDE FOR DETAILS!

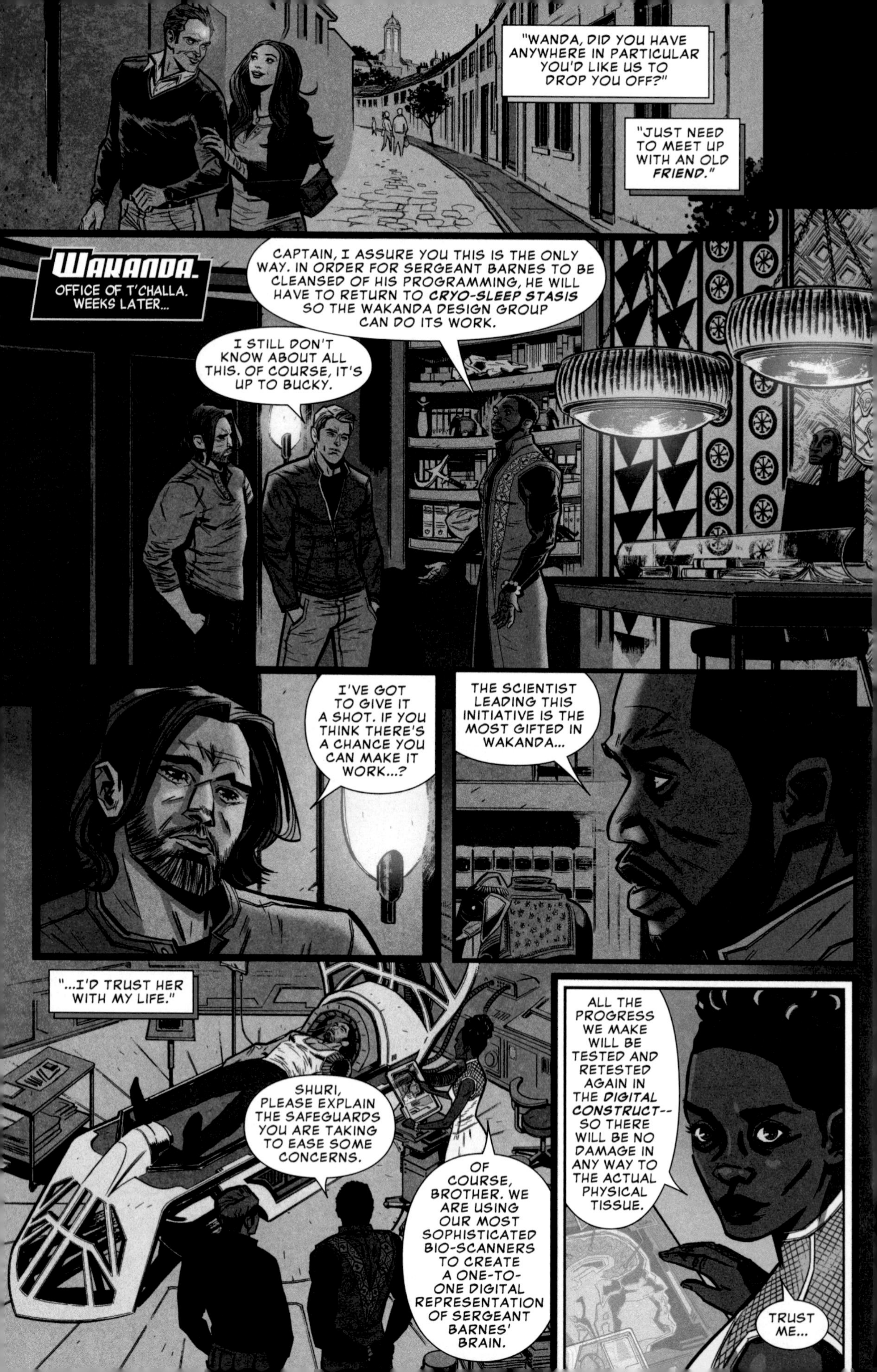

"WANDA, DID YOU HAVE ANYWHERE IN PARTICULAR YOU'D LIKE US TO DROP YOU OFF?"
"JUST NEED TO MEET UP WITH AN OLD FRIEND."
WAKANDA. OFFICE OF T'CHALLA. WEEKS LATER...
CAPTAIN, I ASSURE YOU THIS IS THE ONLY WAY. IN ORDER FOR SERGEANT BARNES TO BE CLEANSED OF HIS PROGRAMMING, HE WILL HAVE TO RETURN TO CRYO-SLEEP STASIS SO THE WAKANDA DESIGN GROUP CAN DO ITS WORK.
I STILL DON'T KNOW ABOUT ALL THIS. OF COURSE, IT'S UP TO BUCKY.
I'VE GOT TO GIVE IT A SHOT. IF YOU THINK THERE'S A CHANCE YOU CAN MAKE IT WORK...?
THE SCIENTIST LEADING THIS INITIATIVE IS THE MOST GIFTED IN WAKANDA...
"...I'D TRUST HER WITH MY LIFE."
SHURI, PLEASE EXPLAIN THE SAFEGUARDS YOU ARE TAKING TO EASE SOME CONCERNS.
OF COURSE, BROTHER. WE ARE USING OUR MOST SOPHISTICATED BIO-SCANNERS TO CREATE A ONE-TO-ONE DIGITAL REPRESENTATION OF SERGEANT BARNES' BRAIN.
ALL THE PROGRESS WE MAKE WILL BE TESTED AND RETESTED AGAIN IN THE DIGITAL CONSTRUCT--SO THERE WILL BE NO DAMAGE IN ANY WAY TO THE ACTUAL PHYSICAL TISSUE.
TRUST ME...

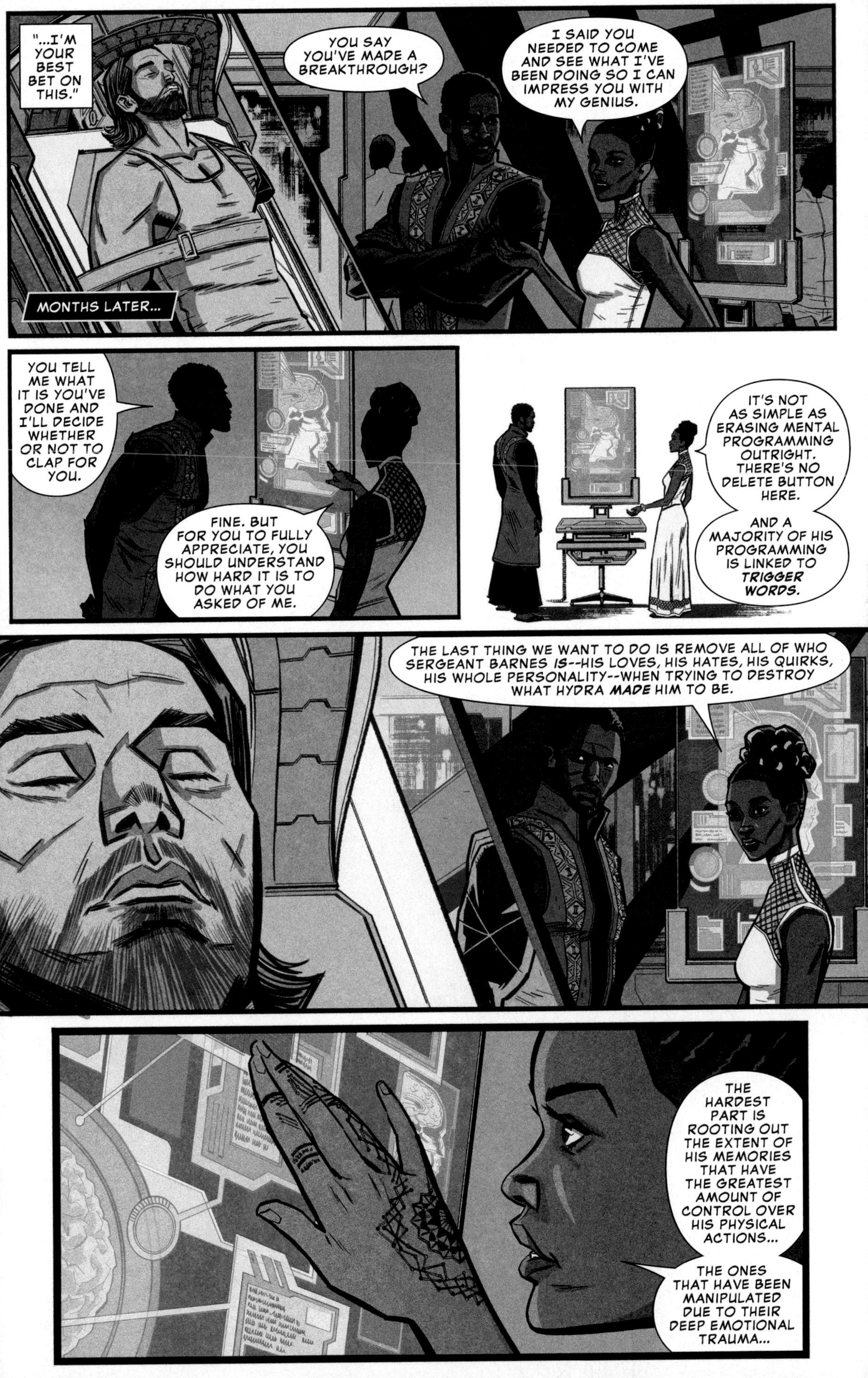
"...I'M YOUR BEST BET ON THIS."
MONTHS LATER...
YOU SAY YOU'VE MADE A BREAKTHROUGH?
I SAID YOU NEEDED TO COME AND SEE WHAT I'VE BEEN DOING SO I CAN IMPRESS YOU WITH MY GENIUS.
YOU TELL ME WHAT IT IS YOU'VE DONE AND I'LL DECIDE WHETHER OR NOT TO CLAP FOR YOU.
FINE. BUT FOR YOU TO FULLY APPRECIATE, YOU SHOULD UNDERSTAND HOW HARD IT IS TO DO WHAT YOU ASKED OF ME.
IT'S NOT AS SIMPLE AS ERASING MENTAL PROGRAMMING OUTRIGHT. THERE'S NO DELETE BUTTON HERE.
AND A MAJORITY OF HIS PROGRAMMING IS LINKED TO TRIGGER WORDS.
THE LAST THING WE WANT TO DO IS REMOVE ALL OF WHO SERGEANT BARNES IS--HIS LOVES, HIS HATES, HIS QUIRKS, HIS WHOLE PERSONALITY--WHEN TRYING TO DESTROY WHAT HYDRA MADE HIM TO BE.
THE HARDEST PART IS ROOTING OUT THE EXTENT OF HIS MEMORIES THAT HAVE THE GREATEST AMOUNT OF CONTROL OVER HIS PHYSICAL ACTIONS...
THE ONES THAT HAVE BEEN MANIPULATED DUE TO THEIR DEEP EMOTIONAL TRAUMA...

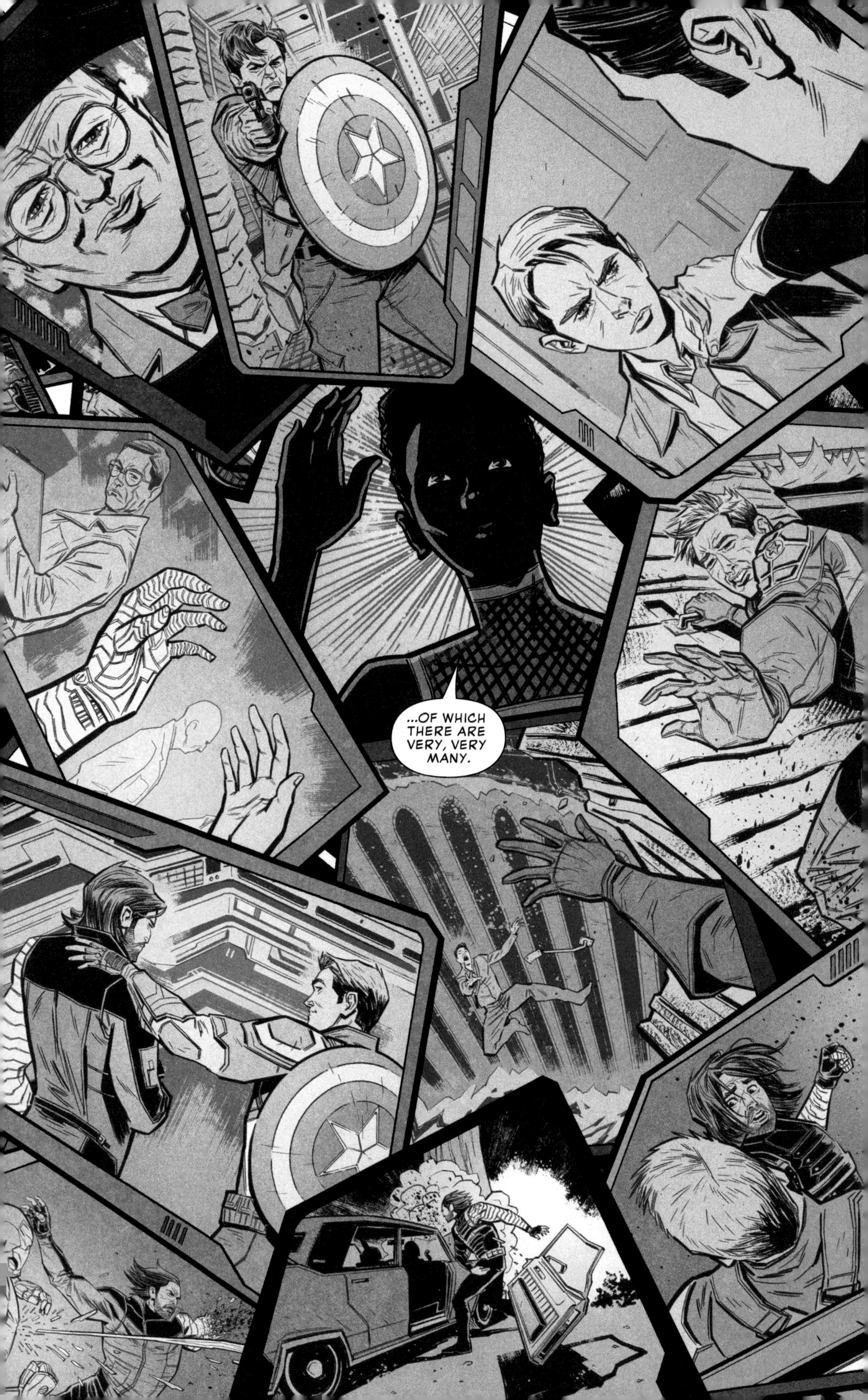
...OF WHICH THERE ARE VERY, VERY MANY.

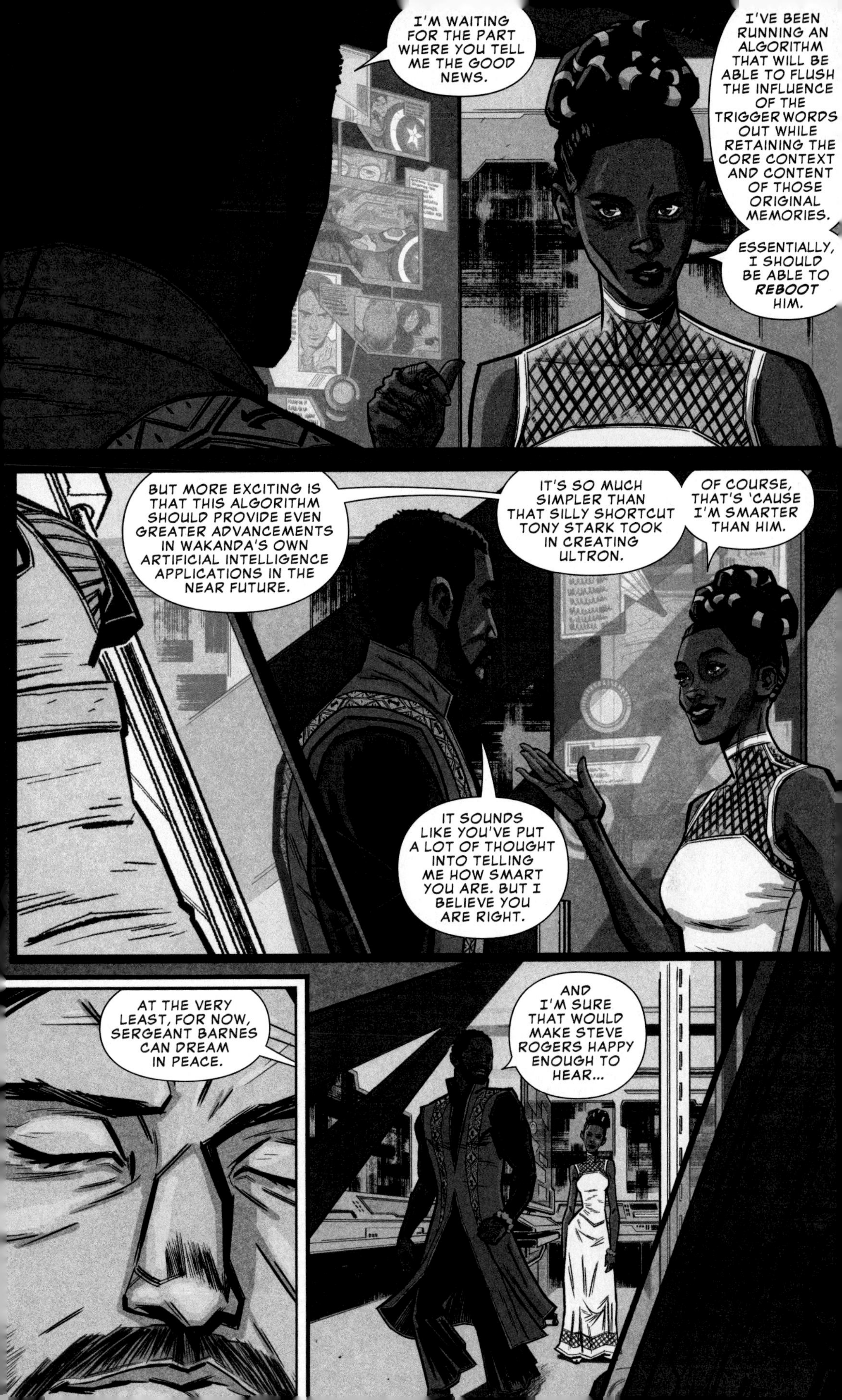
I'M WAITING FOR THE PART WHERE YOU TELL ME THE GOOD NEWS.
I'VE BEEN RUNNING AN ALGORITHM THAT WILL BE ABLE TO FLUSH THE INFLUENCE OF THE TRIGGER WORDS OUT WHILE RETAINING THE CORE CONTEXT AND CONTENT OF THOSE ORIGINAL MEMORIES.
ESSENTIALLY, I SHOULD BE ABLE TO *REBOOT* HIM.
BUT MORE EXCITING IS THAT THIS ALGORITHM SHOULD PROVIDE EVEN GREATER ADVANCEMENTS IN WAKANDA'S OWN ARTIFICIAL INTELLIGENCE APPLICATIONS IN THE NEAR FUTURE.
IT'S SO MUCH SIMPLER THAN THAT SILLY SHORTCUT TONY STARK TOOK IN CREATING ULTRON.
OF COURSE, THAT'S 'CAUSE I'M SMARTER THAN HIM.
IT SOUNDS LIKE YOU'VE PUT A LOT OF THOUGHT INTO TELLING ME HOW SMART YOU ARE. BUT I BELIEVE YOU ARE RIGHT.
AT THE VERY LEAST, FOR NOW, SERGEANT BARNES CAN DREAM IN PEACE.
AND I'M SURE THAT WOULD MAKE STEVE ROGERS HAPPY ENOUGH TO HEAR...

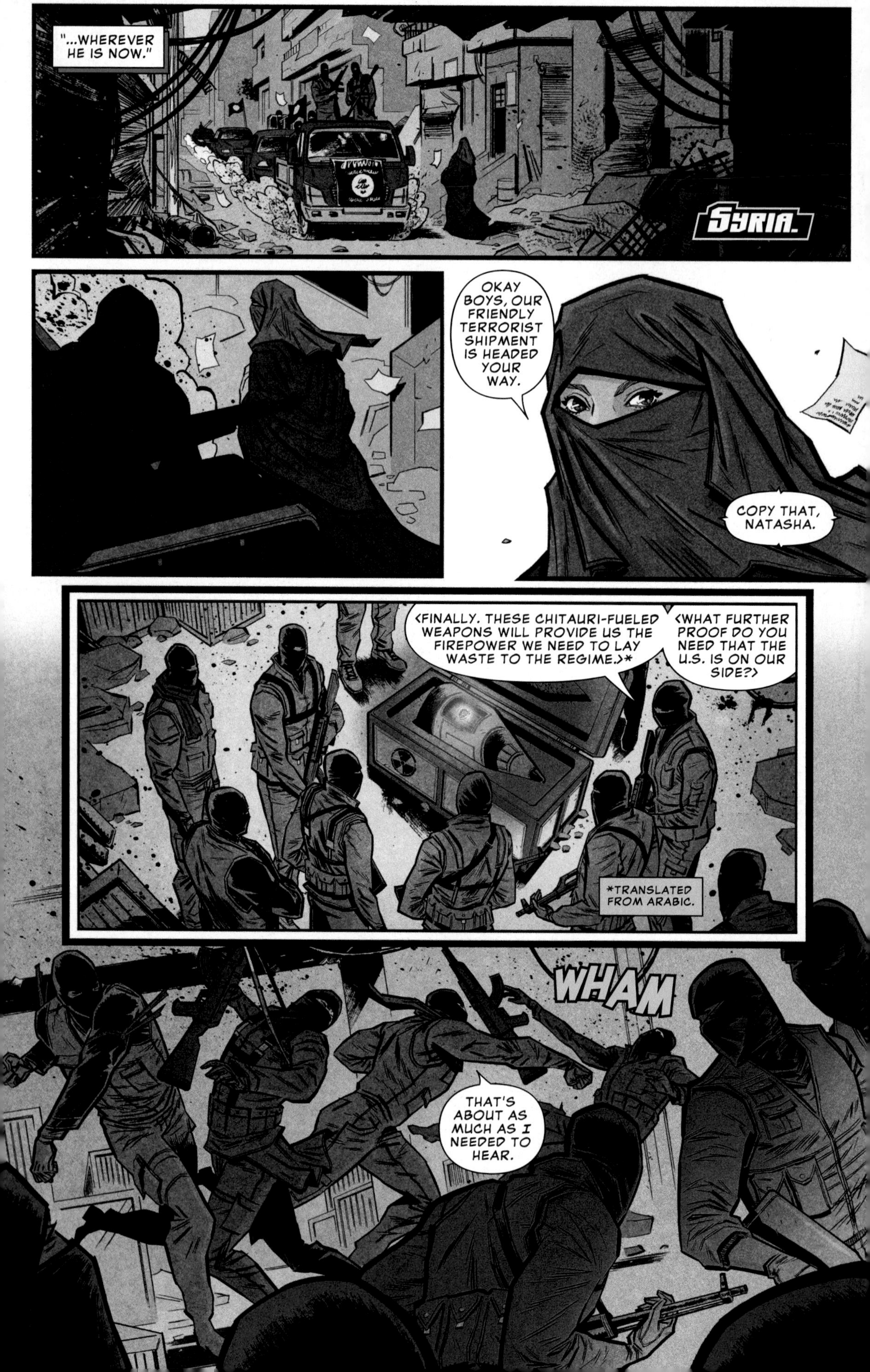
"...WHEREVER HE IS NOW."
SYRIA.
OKAY BOYS, OUR FRIENDLY TERRORIST SHIPMENT IS HEADED YOUR WAY.
COPY THAT, NATASHA.
<FINALLY. THESE CHITAURI-FUELED WEAPONS WILL PROVIDE US THE FIREPOWER WE NEED TO LAY WASTE TO THE REGIME.>*
<WHAT FURTHER PROOF DO YOU NEED THAT THE U.S. IS ON OUR SIDE?>
*TRANSLATED FROM ARABIC.
WHAM
THAT'S ABOUT AS MUCH AS I NEEDED TO HEAR.

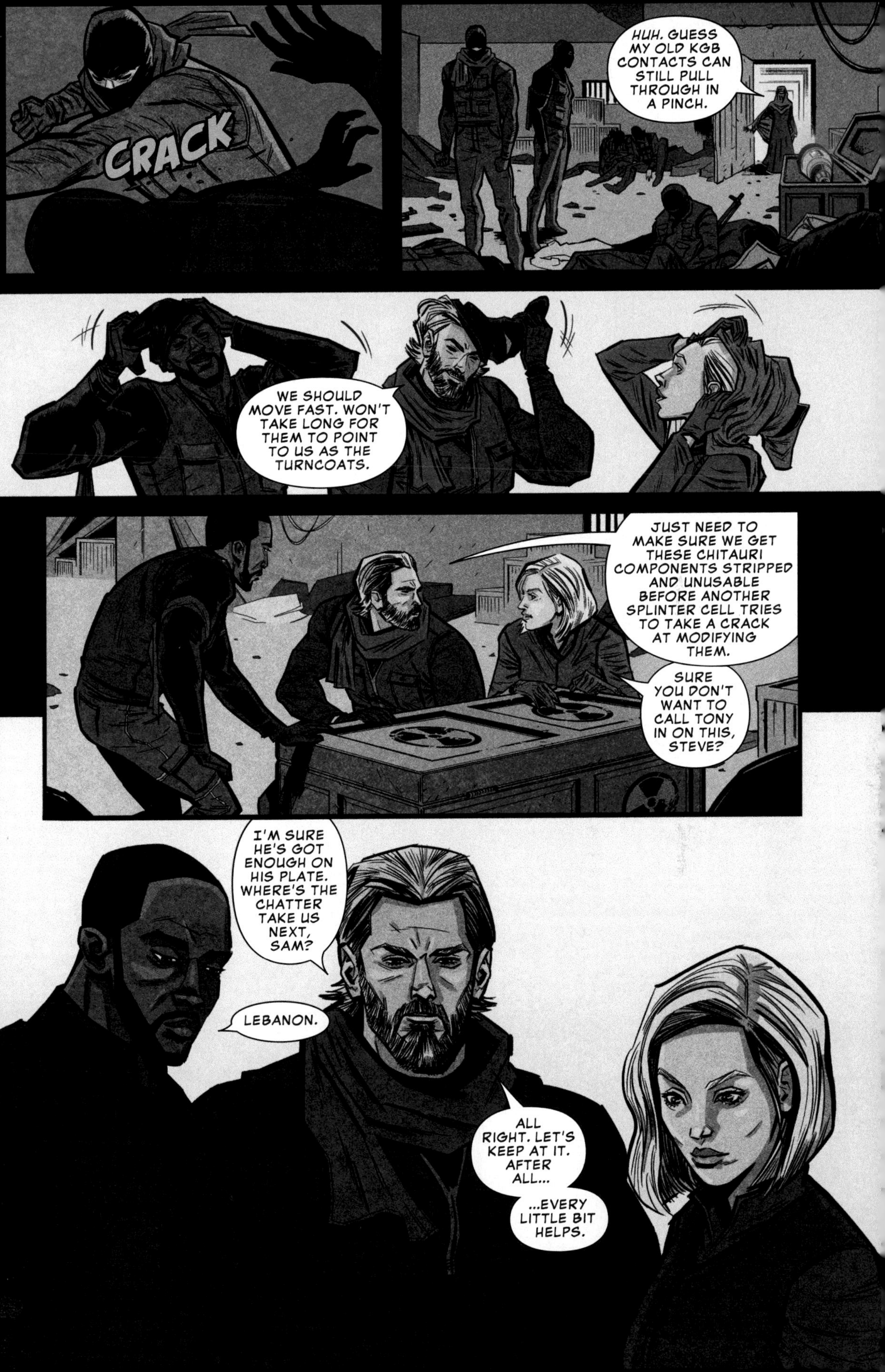
CRACK
HUH. GUESS MY OLD KGB CONTACTS CAN STILL PULL THROUGH IN A PINCH.
WE SHOULD MOVE FAST. WON'T TAKE LONG FOR THEM TO POINT TO US AS THE TURNCOATS.
JUST NEED TO MAKE SURE WE GET THESE CHITAURI COMPONENTS STRIPPED AND UNUSABLE BEFORE ANOTHER SPLINTER CELL TRIES TO TAKE A CRACK AT MODIFYING THEM.
SURE YOU DON'T WANT TO CALL TONY IN ON THIS, STEVE?
I'M SURE HE'S GOT ENOUGH ON HIS PLATE. WHERE'S THE CHATTER TAKE US NEXT, SAM?
LEBANON.
ALL RIGHT. LET'S KEEP AT IT. AFTER ALL...
...EVERY LITTLE BIT HELPS.

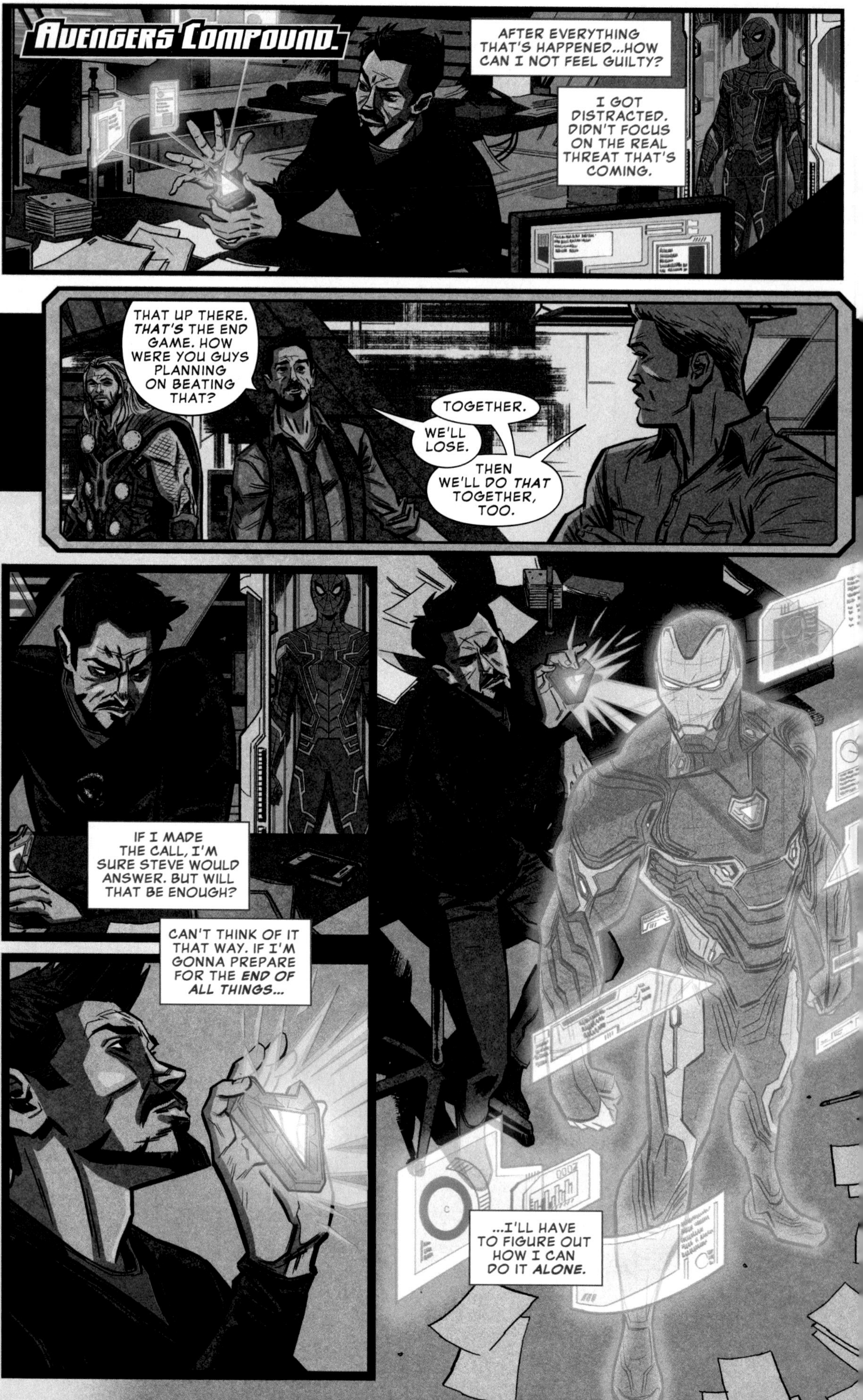
AVENGERS COMPOUND.
AFTER EVERYTHING THAT'S HAPPENED...HOW CAN I NOT FEEL GUILTY?
I GOT DISTRACTED. DIDN'T FOCUS ON THE REAL THREAT THAT'S COMING.
THAT UP THERE. *THAT'S* THE END GAME. HOW WERE YOU GUYS PLANNING ON BEATING THAT?
TOGETHER.
WE'LL LOSE.
THEN WE'LL *DO THAT* TOGETHER, TOO.
IF I MADE THE CALL, I'M SURE STEVE WOULD ANSWER. BUT WILL THAT BE ENOUGH?
CAN'T THINK OF IT THAT WAY. IF I'M GONNA PREPARE FOR THE *END OF ALL THINGS...*
...I'LL HAVE TO FIGURE OUT HOW I CAN DO IT *ALONE.*

MARVEL STUDIOS' AVENGERS:
INFINITY WAR PRELUDE #2

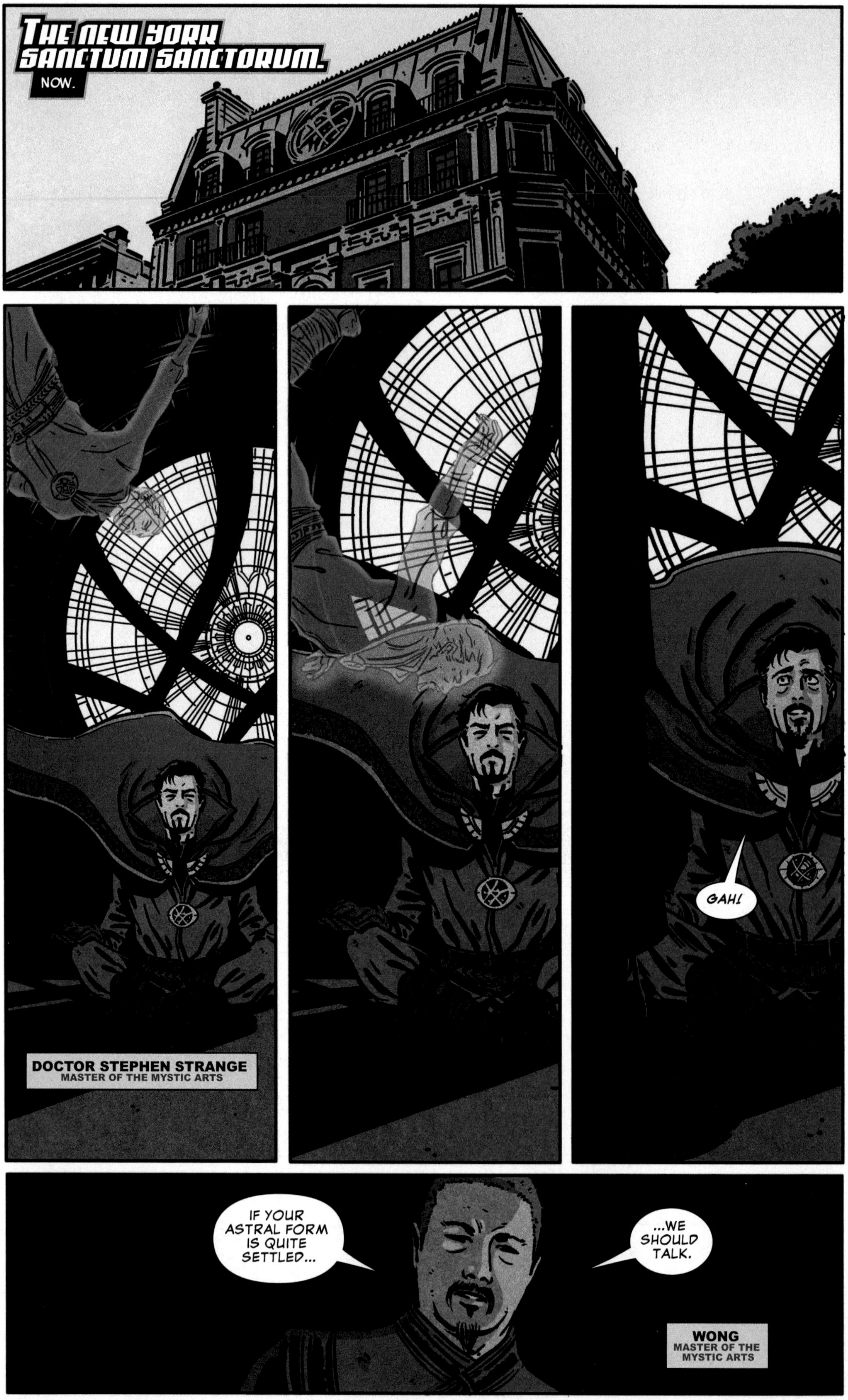
THE NEW YORK SANCTUM SANCTORUM.
NOW.
DOCTOR STEPHEN STRANGE
MASTER OF THE MYSTIC ARTS
GAH!
IF YOUR ASTRAL FORM IS QUITE SETTLED...
...WE SHOULD TALK.
WONG
MASTER OF THE MYSTIC ARTS

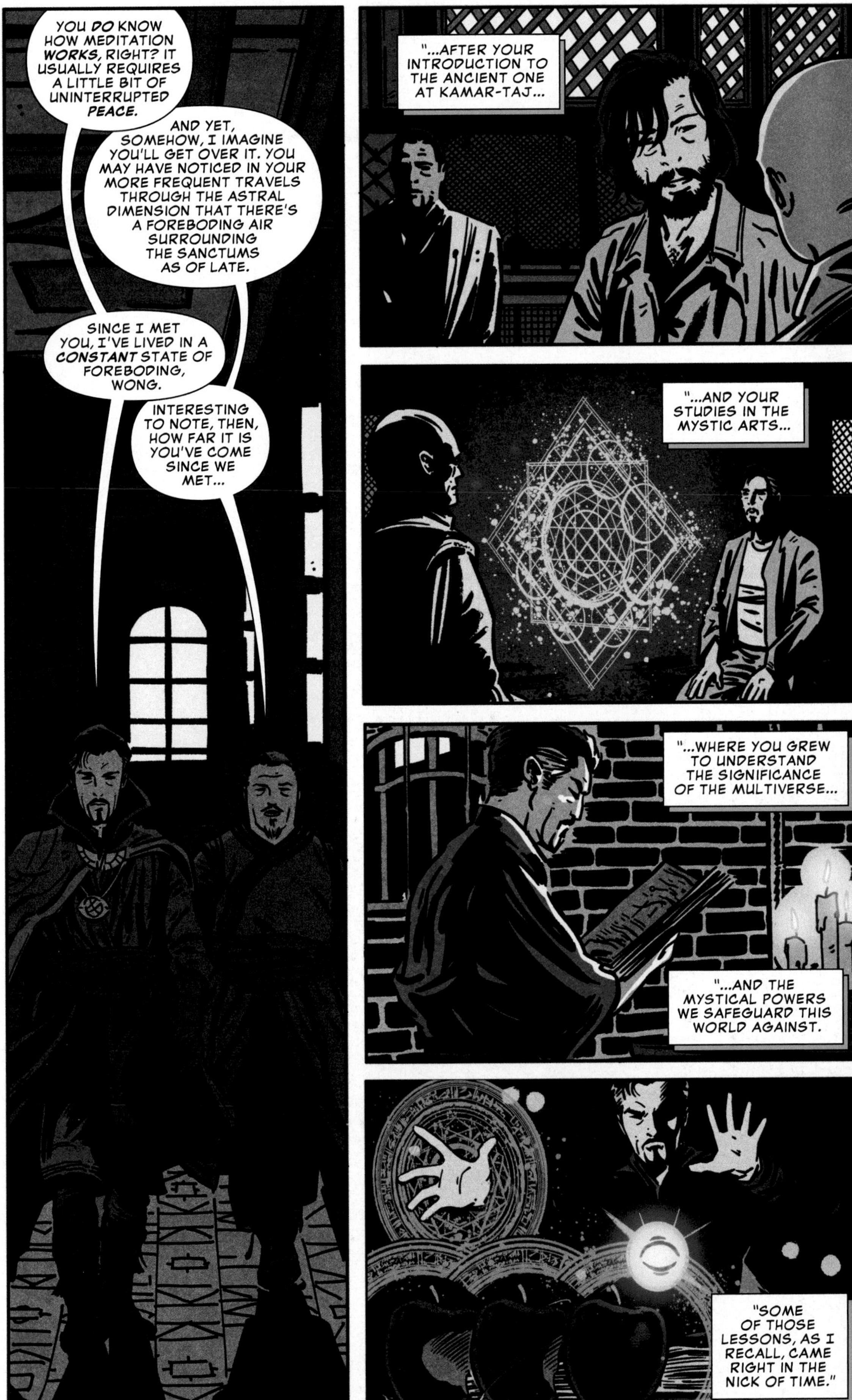

YOU DO KNOW HOW MEDITATION WORKS, RIGHT? IT USUALLY REQUIRES A LITTLE BIT OF UNINTERRUPTED PEACE.
AND YET, SOMEHOW, I IMAGINE YOU'LL GET OVER IT. YOU MAY HAVE NOTICED IN YOUR MORE FREQUENT TRAVELS THROUGH THE ASTRAL DIMENSION THAT THERE'S A FOREBODING AIR SURROUNDING THE SANCTUMS AS OF LATE.
SINCE I MET YOU, I'VE LIVED IN A CONSTANT STATE OF FOREBODING, WONG.
INTERESTING TO NOTE, THEN, HOW FAR IT IS YOU'VE COME SINCE WE MET...
"...AFTER YOUR INTRODUCTION TO THE ANCIENT ONE AT KAMAR-TAJ...
"...AND YOUR STUDIES IN THE MYSTIC ARTS...
"...WHERE YOU GREW TO UNDERSTAND THE SIGNIFICANCE OF THE MULTIVERSE...
"...AND THE MYSTICAL POWERS WE SAFEGUARD THIS WORLD AGAINST.
"SOME OF THOSE LESSONS, AS I RECALL, CAME RIGHT IN THE NICK OF TIME."

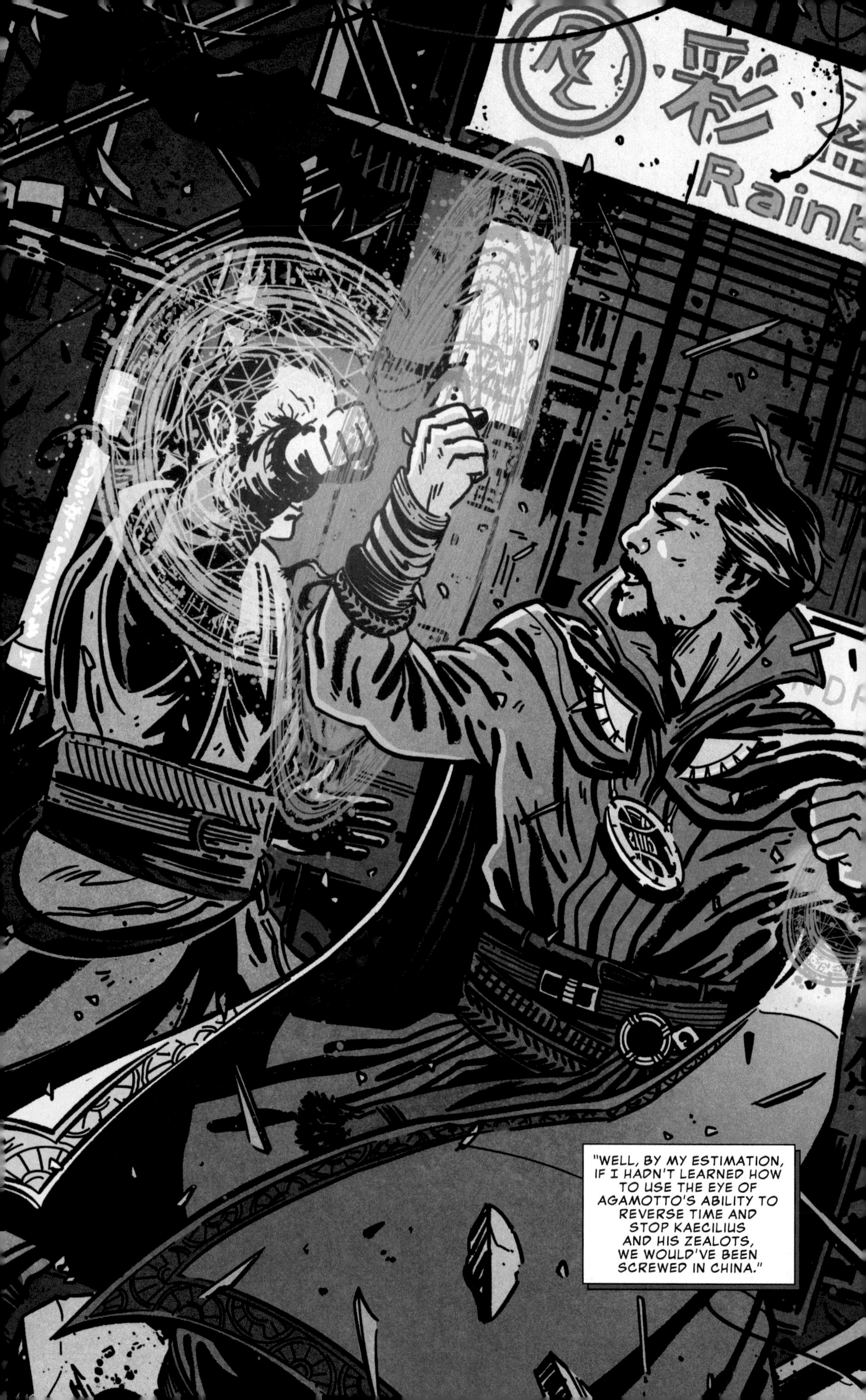

"WELL, BY MY ESTIMATION, IF I HADN'T LEARNED HOW TO USE THE EYE OF AGAMOTTO'S ABILITY TO REVERSE TIME AND STOP KAECILIUS AND HIS ZEALOTS, WE WOULD'VE BEEN SCREWED IN CHINA."

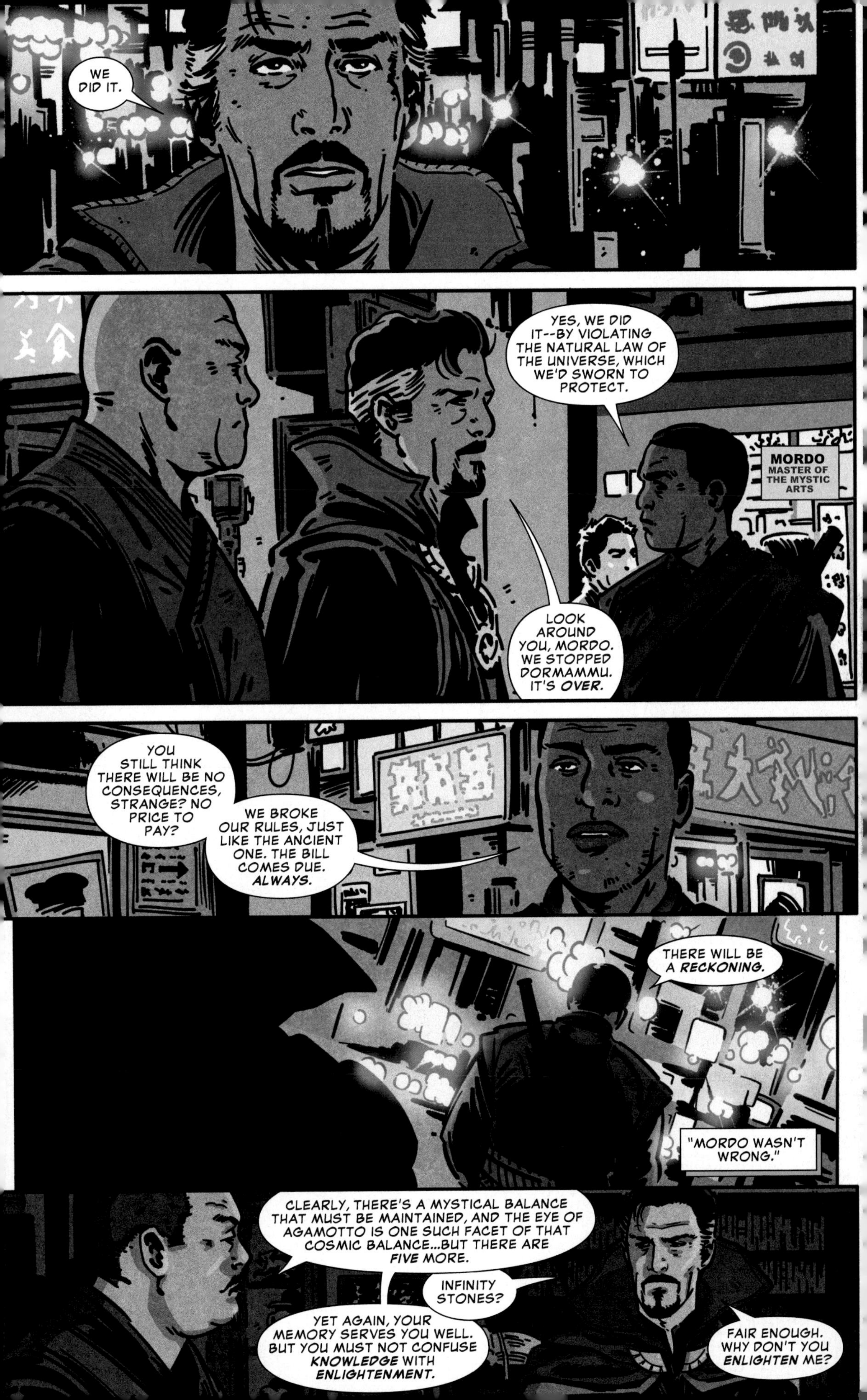
WE DID IT.
YES, WE DID IT--BY VIOLATING THE NATURAL LAW OF THE UNIVERSE, WHICH WE'D SWORN TO PROTECT.
MORDO MASTER OF THE MYSTIC ARTS
LOOK AROUND YOU, MORDO. WE STOPPED DORMAMMU. IT'S OVER.
YOU STILL THINK THERE WILL BE NO CONSEQUENCES, STRANGE? NO PRICE TO PAY?
WE BROKE OUR RULES, JUST LIKE THE ANCIENT ONE. THE BILL COMES DUE. ALWAYS.
THERE WILL BE A RECKONING.
"MORDO WASN'T WRONG."
CLEARLY, THERE'S A MYSTICAL BALANCE THAT MUST BE MAINTAINED, AND THE EYE OF AGAMOTTO IS ONE SUCH FACET OF THAT COSMIC BALANCE...BUT THERE ARE FIVE MORE.
INFINITY STONES?
YET AGAIN, YOUR MEMORY SERVES YOU WELL. BUT YOU MUST NOT CONFUSE KNOWLEDGE WITH ENLIGHTENMENT.
FAIR ENOUGH. WHY DON'T YOU ENLIGHTEN ME?

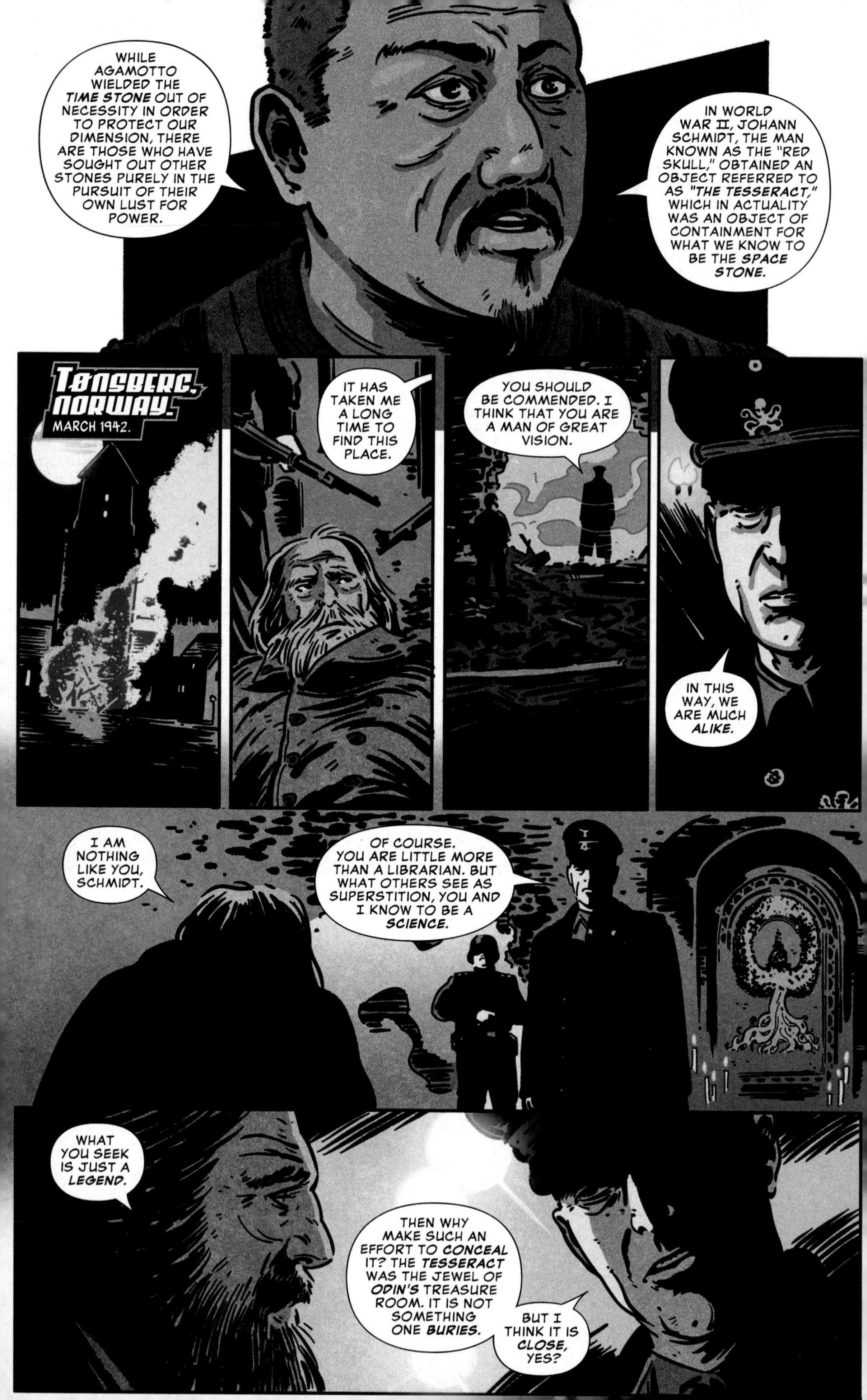
WHILE AGAMOTTO WIELDED THE TIME STONE OUT OF NECESSITY IN ORDER TO PROTECT OUR DIMENSION, THERE ARE THOSE WHO HAVE SOUGHT OUT OTHER STONES PURELY IN THE PURSUIT OF THEIR OWN LUST FOR POWER.
IN WORLD WAR II, JOHANN SCHMIDT, THE MAN KNOWN AS THE "RED SKULL," OBTAINED AN OBJECT REFERRED TO AS "THE TESSERACT," WHICH IN ACTUALITY WAS AN OBJECT OF CONTAINMENT FOR WHAT WE KNOW TO BE THE SPACE STONE.
TØNSBERG, NORWAY.
MARCH 1942.
IT HAS TAKEN ME A LONG TIME TO FIND THIS PLACE.
YOU SHOULD BE COMMENDED. I THINK THAT YOU ARE A MAN OF GREAT VISION.
IN THIS WAY, WE ARE MUCH ALIKE.
I AM NOTHING LIKE YOU, SCHMIDT.
OF COURSE. YOU ARE LITTLE MORE THAN A LIBRARIAN. BUT WHAT OTHERS SEE AS SUPERSTITION, YOU AND I KNOW TO BE A SCIENCE.
WHAT YOU SEEK IS JUST A LEGEND.
THEN WHY MAKE SUCH AN EFFORT TO CONCEAL IT? THE TESSERACT WAS THE JEWEL OF ODIN'S TREASURE ROOM. IT IS NOT SOMETHING ONE BURIES.
BUT I THINK IT IS CLOSE, YES?

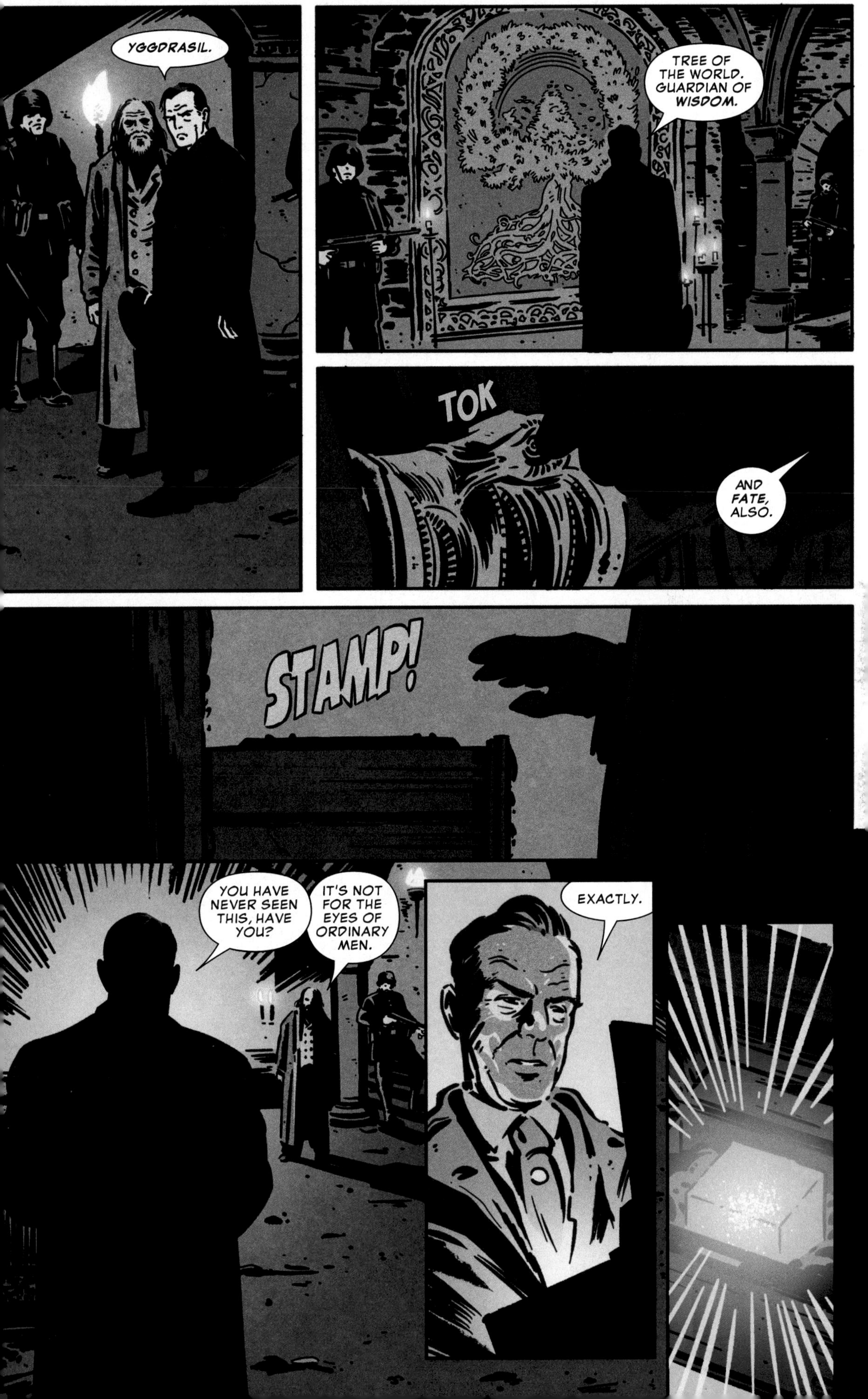
YGGDRASIL.
TREE OF THE WORLD. GUARDIAN OF WISDOM.
TOK
AND FATE, ALSO.
STAMP!
YOU HAVE NEVER SEEN THIS, HAVE YOU?
IT'S NOT FOR THE EYES OF ORDINARY MEN.
EXACTLY.

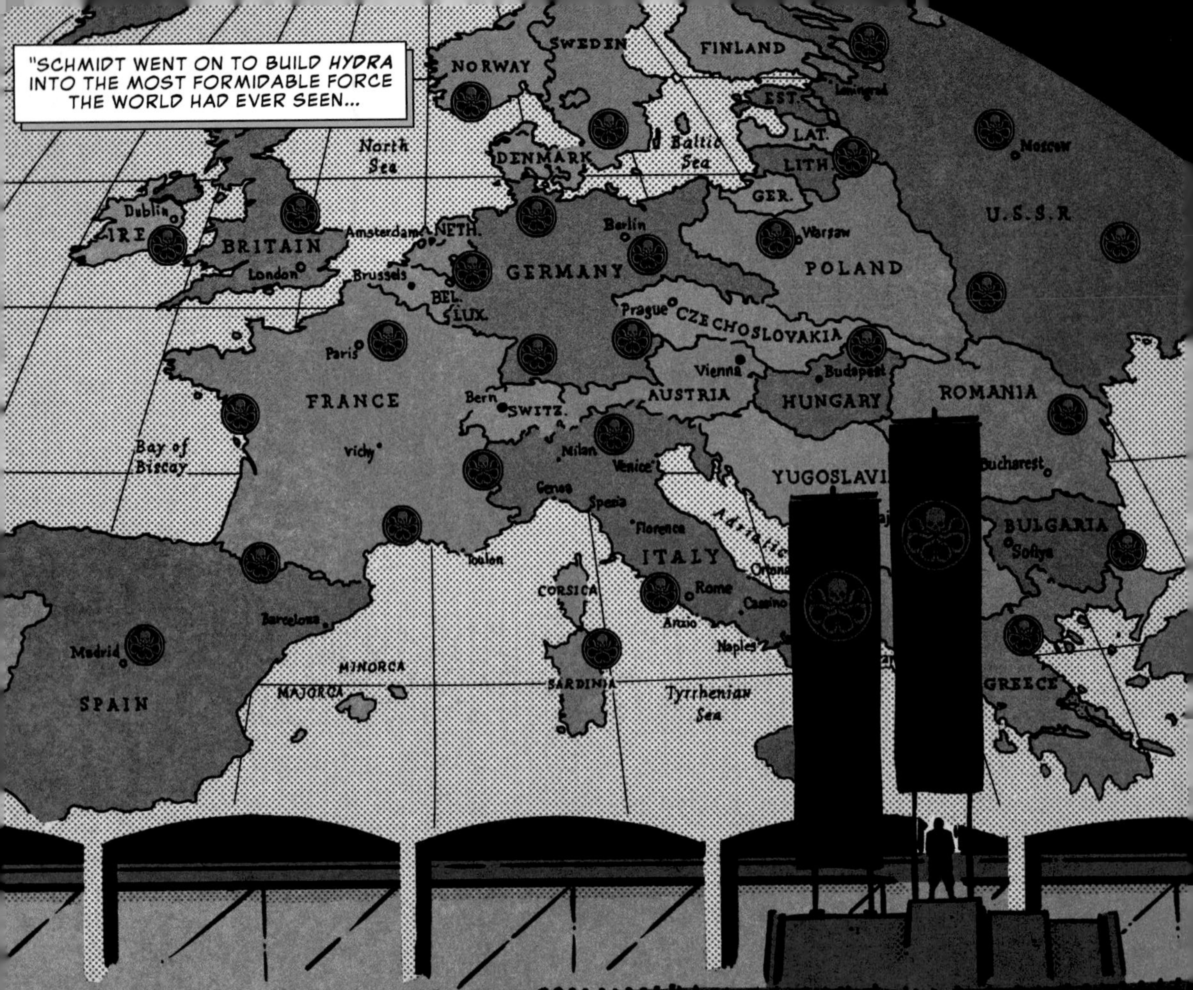
"SCHMIDT WENT ON TO BUILD *HYDRA* INTO THE MOST FORMIDABLE FORCE THE WORLD HAD EVER SEEN...
NORWAY
SWEDEN
FINLAND
EST.
LAT.
LITH.
Moscow
North Sea
DENMARK
Baltic Sea
GER.
U.S.S.R.
Dublin
IRE
BRITAIN
London
Amsterdam
NETH.
Berlin
Warsaw
POLAND
Brussels
GERMANY
BEL.
LUX.
Prague
CZECHOSLOVAKIA
Paris
Vienna
Budapest
FRANCE
Bern
SWITZ.
AUSTRIA
HUNGARY
ROMANIA
Bay of Biscay
Vichy
Milan
Venice
YUGOSLAVI
Bucharest
Genoa
Spezia
Florence
BULGARIA
Sofiya
Toulon
ITALY
CORSICA
Rome
Barcelona
Anzio
Madrid
Naples
MINORCA
MAJORCA
SARDINIA
Tyrrhenian Sea
GREECE
SPAIN

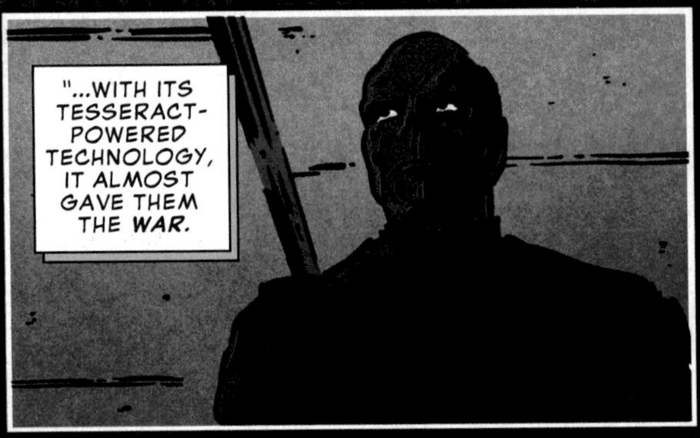
"...WITH ITS TESSERACT-POWERED TECHNOLOGY, IT ALMOST GAVE THEM THE *WAR*.

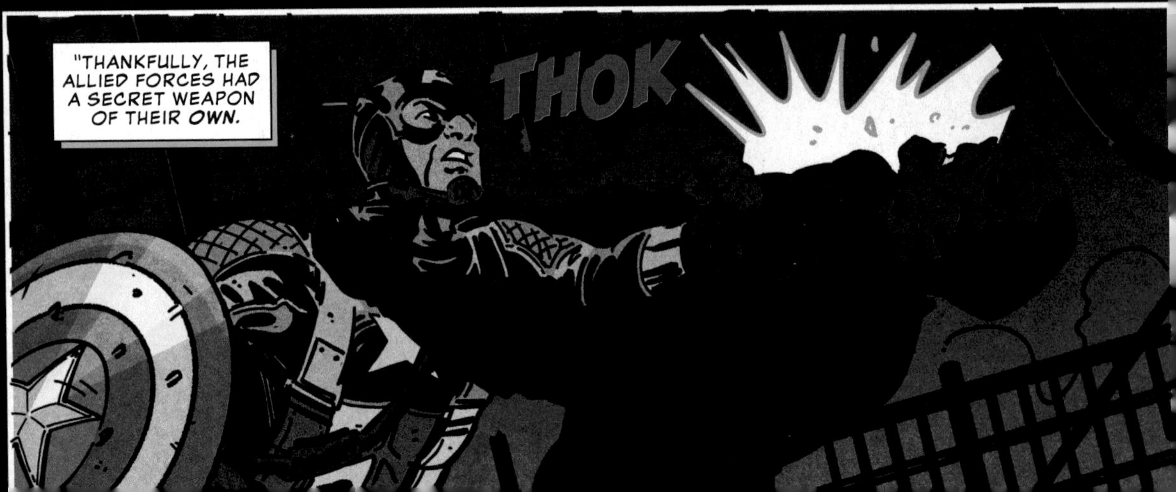
"THANKFULLY, THE ALLIED FORCES HAD A SECRET WEAPON OF THEIR *OWN*.
THOK

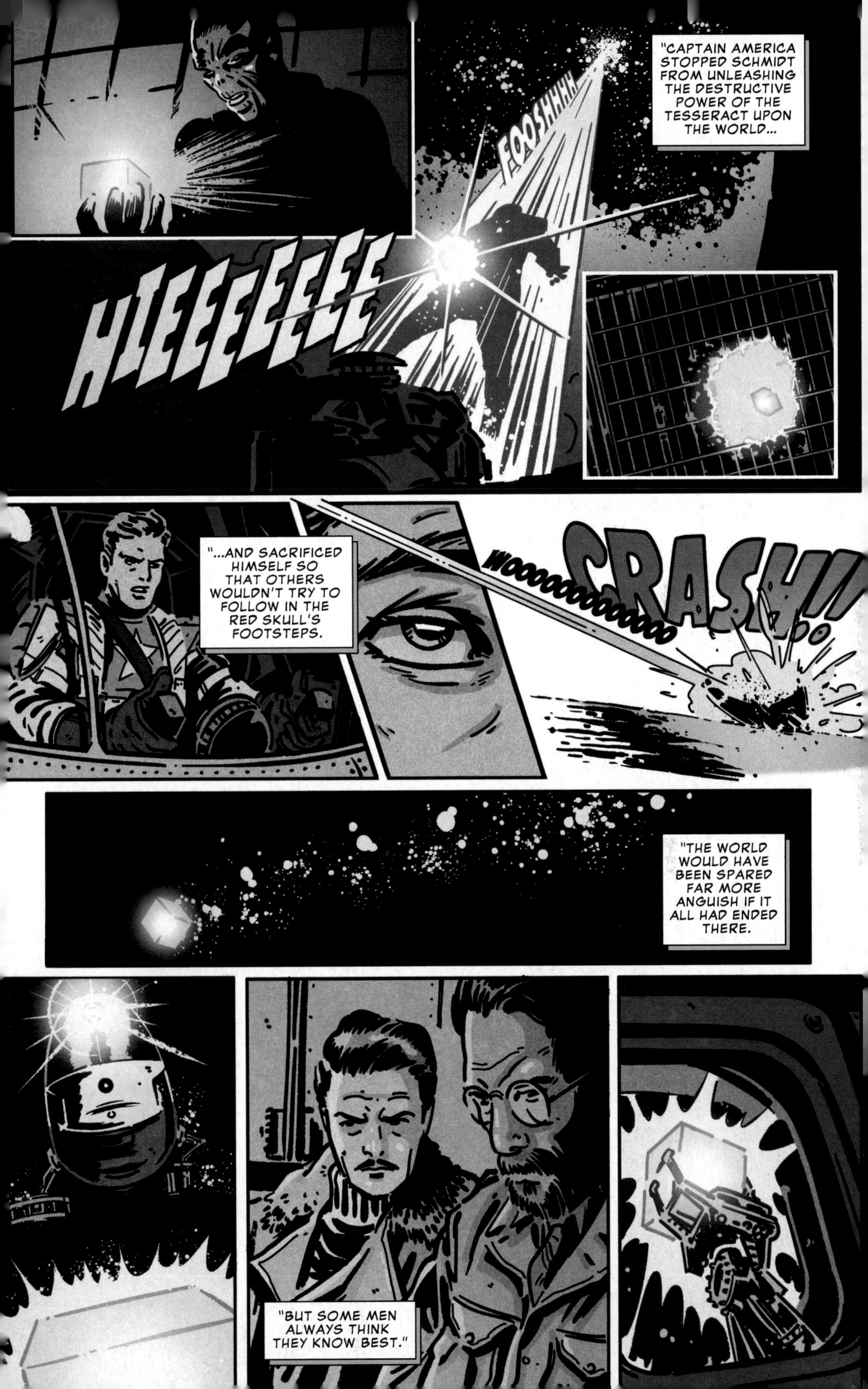
"CAPTAIN AMERICA STOPPED SCHMIDT FROM UNLEASHING THE DESTRUCTIVE POWER OF THE TESSERACT UPON THE WORLD...
FOOSHHHH
HIEEEEEEEE
"...AND SACRIFICED HIMSELF SO THAT OTHERS WOULDN'T TRY TO FOLLOW IN THE RED SKULL'S FOOTSTEPS.
WOOOOOOOOOOOOO
CRASH!!
"THE WORLD WOULD HAVE BEEN SPARED FAR MORE ANGUISH IF IT ALL HAD ENDED THERE.
"BUT SOME MEN ALWAYS THINK THEY KNOW BEST."

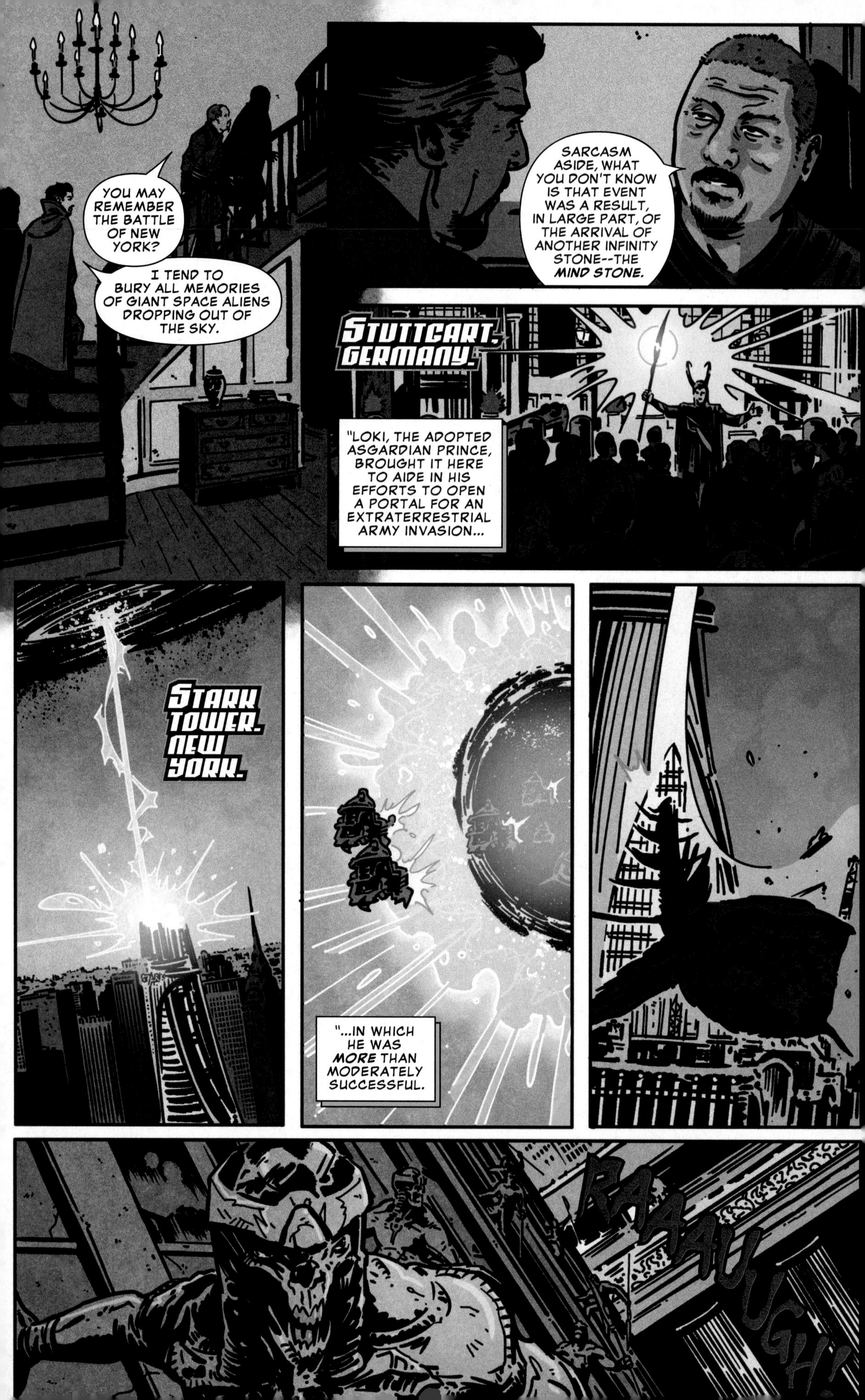
YOU MAY REMEMBER THE BATTLE OF NEW YORK?
I TEND TO BURY ALL MEMORIES OF GIANT SPACE ALIENS DROPPING OUT OF THE SKY.
SARCASM ASIDE, WHAT YOU DON'T KNOW IS THAT EVENT WAS A RESULT, IN LARGE PART, OF THE ARRIVAL OF ANOTHER INFINITY STONE--THE *MIND STONE.*
STUTTGART, GERMANY.
"LOKI, THE ADOPTED ASGARDIAN PRINCE, BROUGHT IT HERE TO AIDE IN HIS EFFORTS TO OPEN A PORTAL FOR AN EXTRATERRESTRIAL ARMY INVASION...
STARK TOWER. NEW YORK.
"...IN WHICH HE WAS *MORE* THAN MODERATELY SUCCESSFUL.
RAAAUGH!

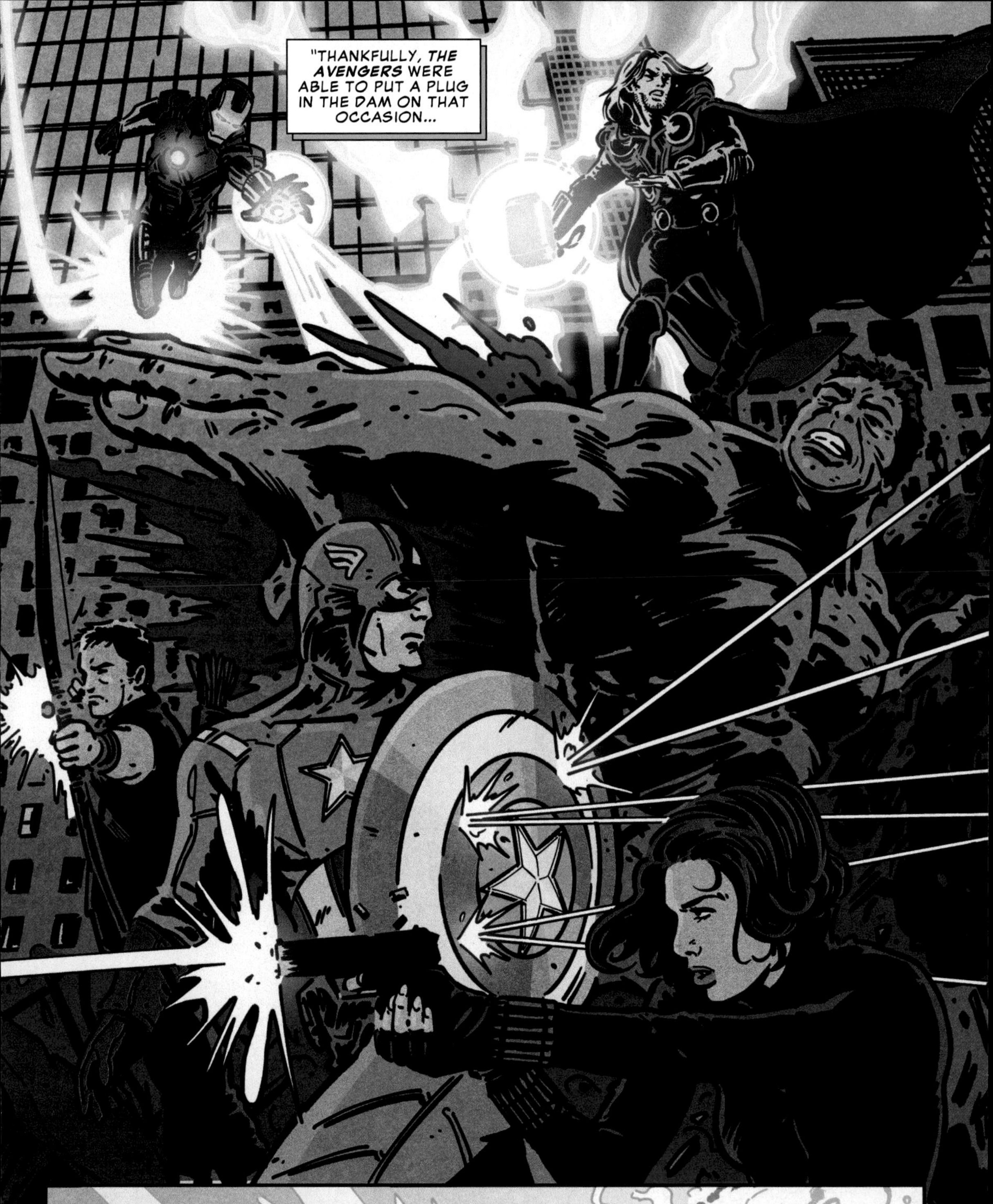
"THANKFULLY, THE AVENGERS WERE ABLE TO PUT A PLUG IN THE DAM ON THAT OCCASION...

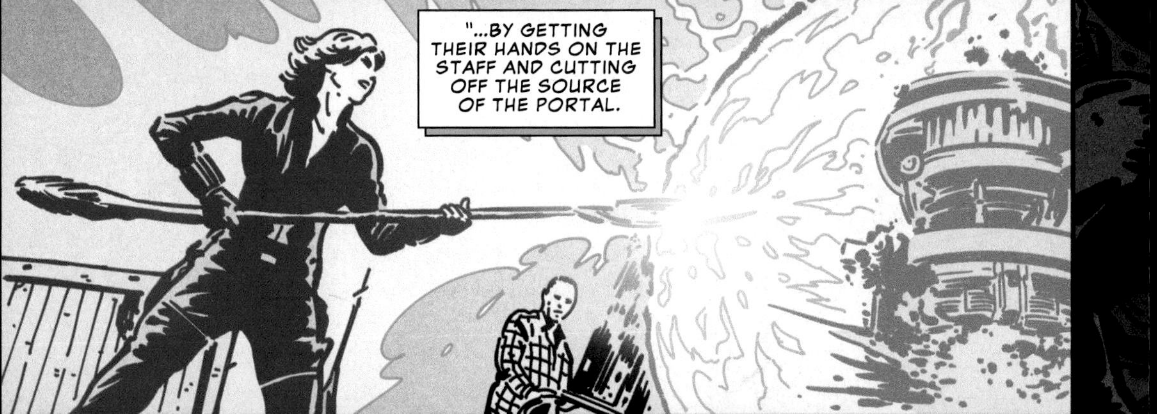
"...BY GETTING THEIR HANDS ON THE STAFF AND CUTTING OFF THE SOURCE OF THE PORTAL.

"LATER ON, THOR ODINSON TOOK HIS BROTHER LOKI INTO CUSTODY...

"...AND RETURNED TO ASGARD WITH THE *TESSERACT*.

"UNFORTUNATELY, THOR RETURNED A SHORT TIME LATER IN ANOTHER EARTH-BOUND BATTLE OVER THE INFINITY STONES...

"...WHEREIN *MALEKITH*, LEADER OF THE DARK ELVES, WIELDED THE AETHER, KNOWN AS THE *REALITY STONE*, IN GREENWICH, ENGLAND.

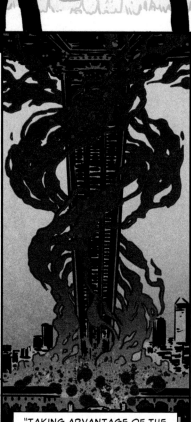

"TAKING ADVANTAGE OF THE COSMIC PHENOMENON KNOWN AS THE CONVERGENCE, HE ATTEMPTED TO BRING THE NINE WORLDS--INCLUDING EARTH--INTO A PERMANENT STATE OF DARKNESS.

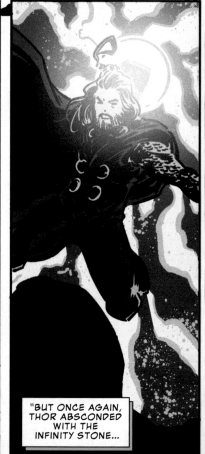

"BUT ONCE AGAIN, THOR ABSCONDED WITH THE INFINITY STONE...

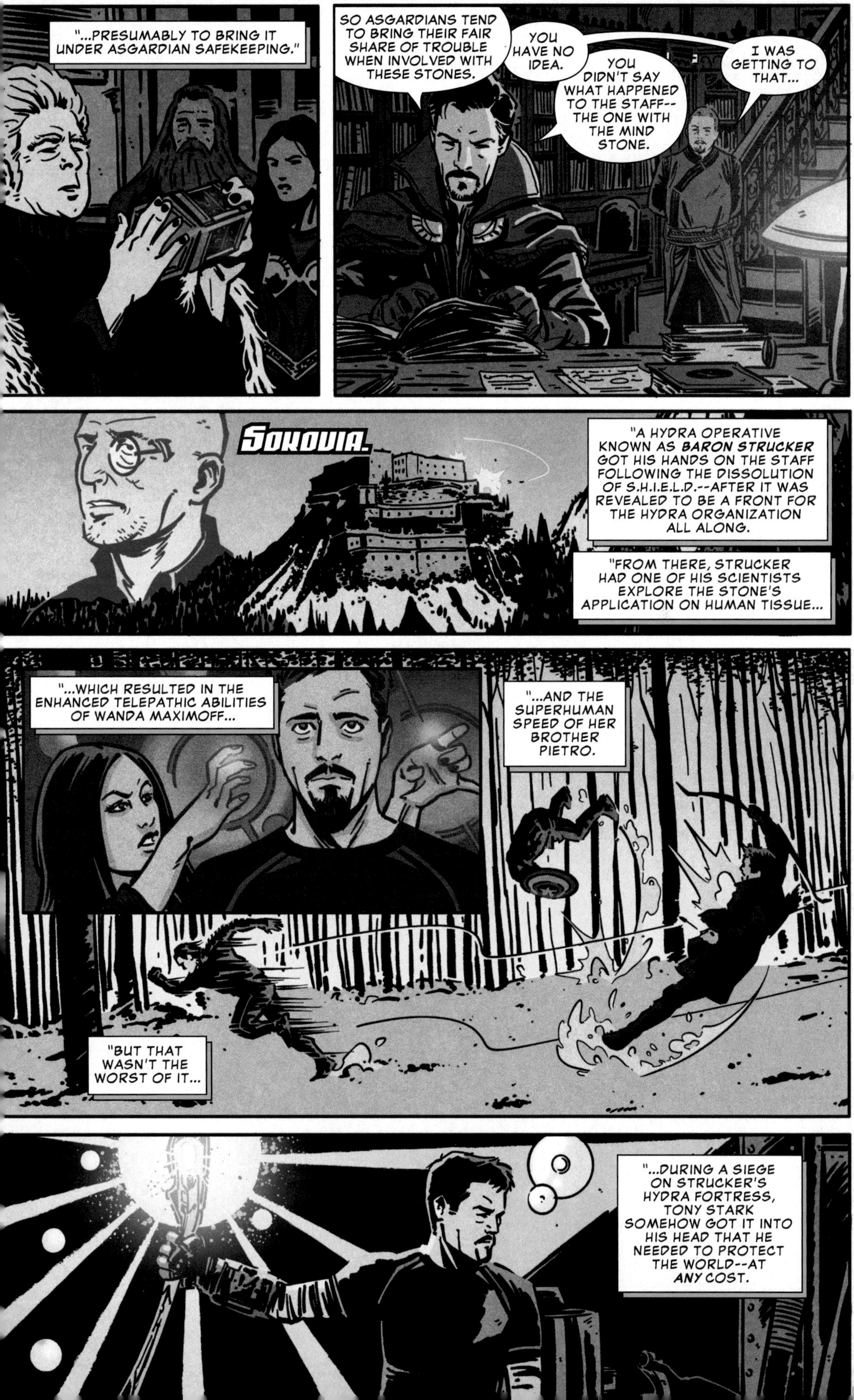
"...PRESUMABLY TO BRING IT UNDER ASGARDIAN SAFEKEEPING."
SO ASGARDIANS TEND TO BRING THEIR FAIR SHARE OF TROUBLE WHEN INVOLVED WITH THESE STONES.
YOU HAVE NO IDEA.
YOU DIDN'T SAY WHAT HAPPENED TO THE STAFF-- THE ONE WITH THE MIND STONE.
I WAS GETTING TO THAT...
SOKOVIA.
"A HYDRA OPERATIVE KNOWN AS BARON STRUCKER GOT HIS HANDS ON THE STAFF FOLLOWING THE DISSOLUTION OF S.H.I.E.L.D.--AFTER IT WAS REVEALED TO BE A FRONT FOR THE HYDRA ORGANIZATION ALL ALONG.
"FROM THERE, STRUCKER HAD ONE OF HIS SCIENTISTS EXPLORE THE STONE'S APPLICATION ON HUMAN TISSUE...
"...WHICH RESULTED IN THE ENHANCED TELEPATHIC ABILITIES OF WANDA MAXIMOFF...
"...AND THE SUPERHUMAN SPEED OF HER BROTHER PIETRO.
"BUT THAT WASN'T THE WORST OF IT...
"...DURING A SIEGE ON STRUCKER'S HYDRA FORTRESS, TONY STARK SOMEHOW GOT IT INTO HIS HEAD THAT HE NEEDED TO PROTECT THE WORLD--AT ANY COST.

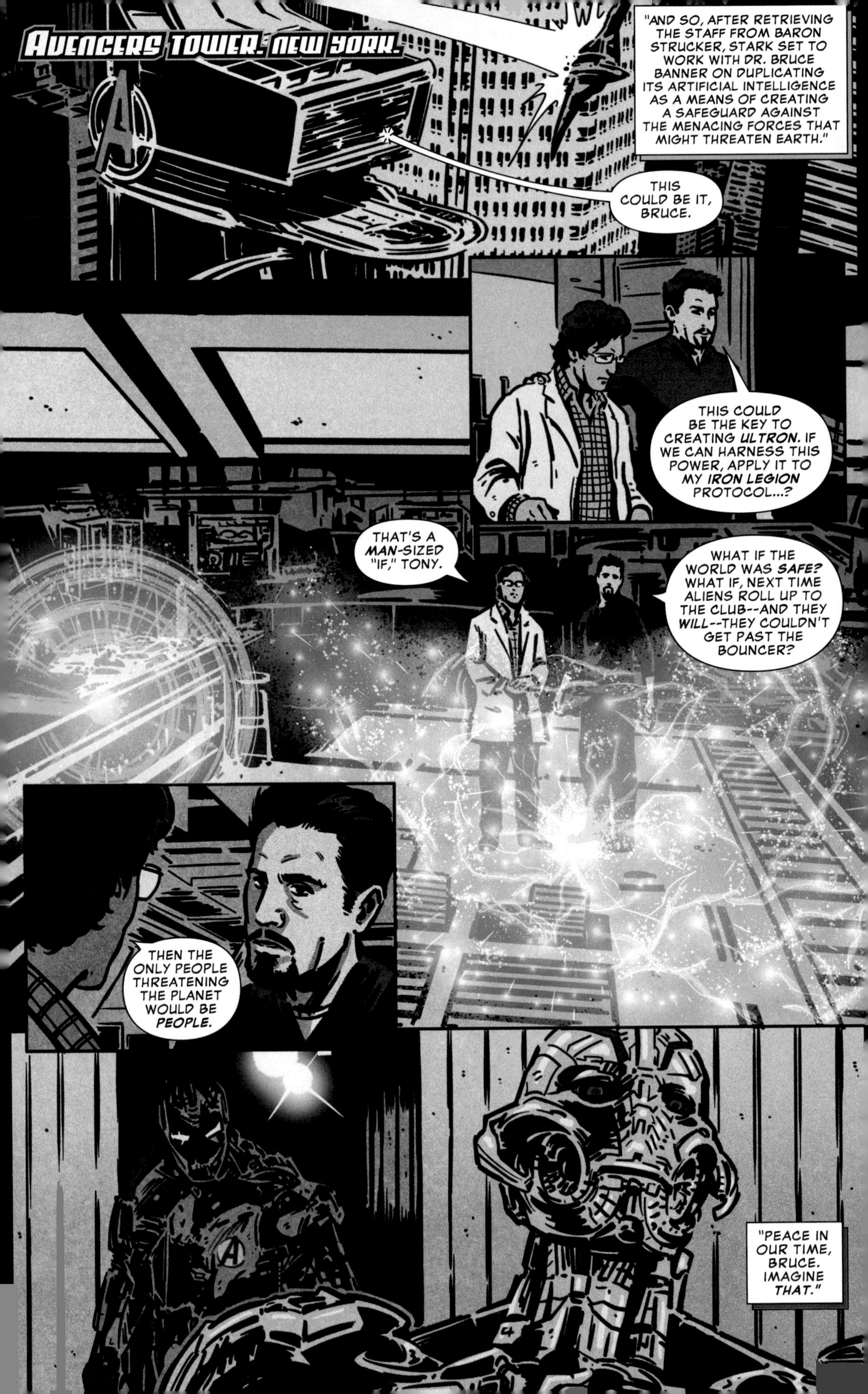
AVENGERS TOWER. NEW YORK.
"AND SO, AFTER RETRIEVING THE STAFF FROM BARON STRUCKER, STARK SET TO WORK WITH DR. BRUCE BANNER ON DUPLICATING ITS ARTIFICIAL INTELLIGENCE AS A MEANS OF CREATING A SAFEGUARD AGAINST THE MENACING FORCES THAT MIGHT THREATEN EARTH."
THIS COULD BE IT, BRUCE.
THIS COULD BE THE KEY TO CREATING ULTRON. IF WE CAN HARNESS THIS POWER, APPLY IT TO MY IRON LEGION PROTOCOL...?
THAT'S A MAN-SIZED "IF," TONY.
WHAT IF THE WORLD WAS SAFE? WHAT IF, NEXT TIME ALIENS ROLL UP TO THE CLUB--AND THEY WILL--THEY COULDN'T GET PAST THE BOUNCER?
THEN THE ONLY PEOPLE THREATENING THE PLANET WOULD BE PEOPLE.
"PEACE IN OUR TIME, BRUCE. IMAGINE THAT."

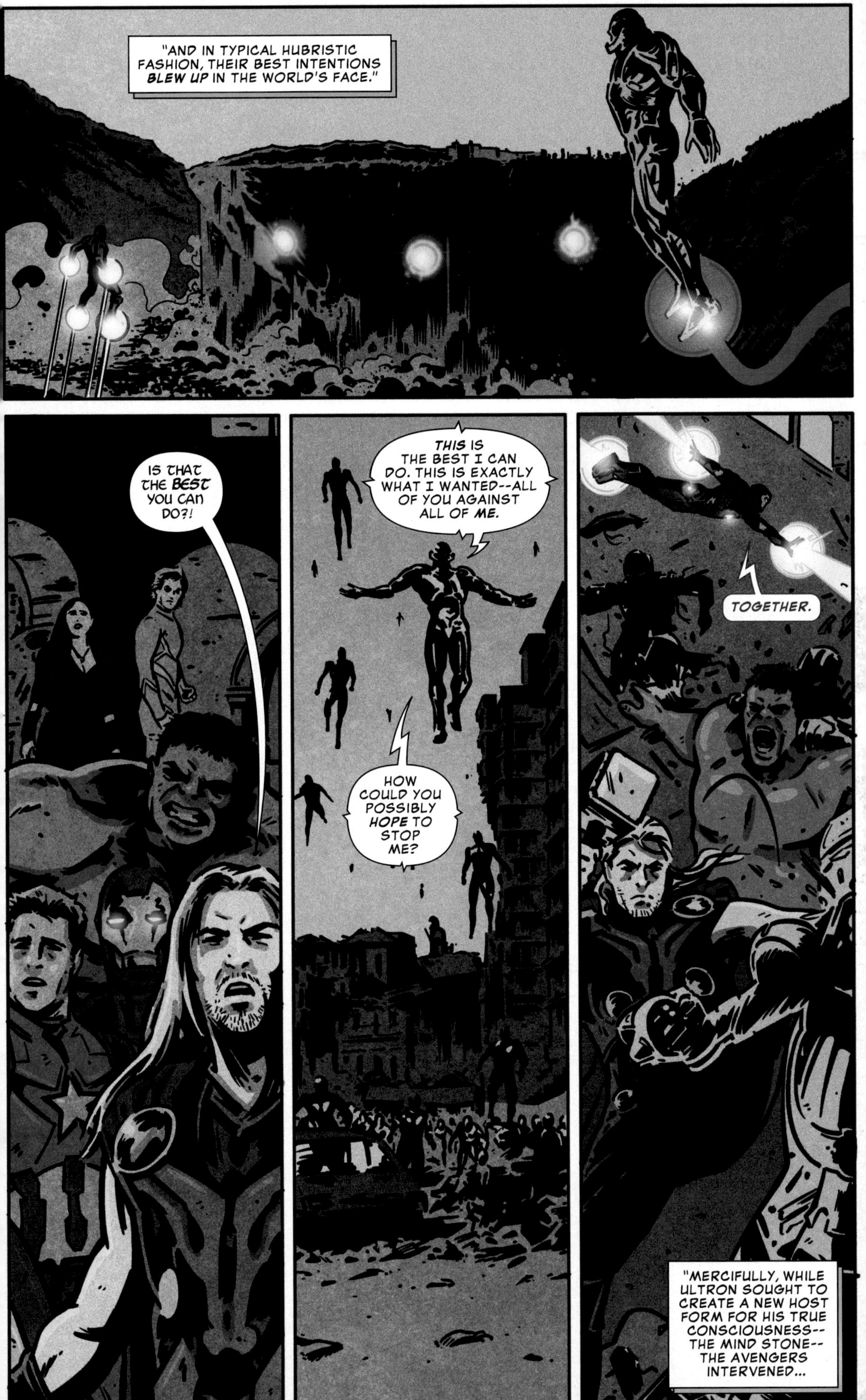
"AND IN TYPICAL HUBRISTIC FASHION, THEIR BEST INTENTIONS BLEW UP IN THE WORLD'S FACE."
IS THAT THE BEST YOU CAN DO?!
THIS IS THE BEST I CAN DO. THIS IS EXACTLY WHAT I WANTED--ALL OF YOU AGAINST ALL OF ME.
HOW COULD YOU POSSIBLY HOPE TO STOP ME?
TOGETHER.
"MERCIFULLY, WHILE ULTRON SOUGHT TO CREATE A NEW HOST FORM FOR HIS TRUE CONSCIOUSNESS-- THE MIND STONE-- THE AVENGERS INTERVENED...

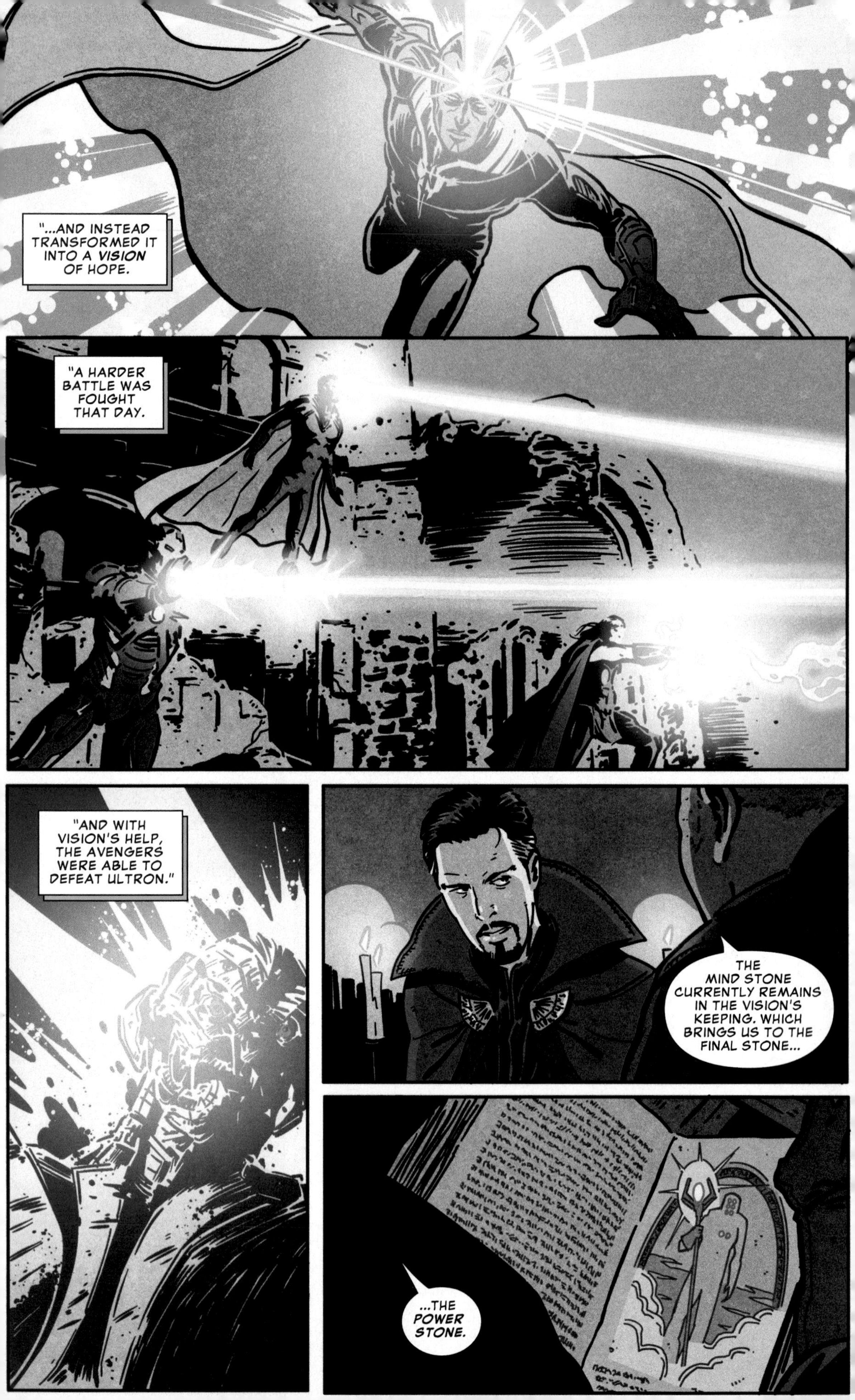
"...AND INSTEAD TRANSFORMED IT INTO A *VISION* OF HOPE.
"A HARDER BATTLE WAS FOUGHT THAT DAY.
"AND WITH VISION'S HELP, THE AVENGERS WERE ABLE TO DEFEAT ULTRON."
THE MIND STONE CURRENTLY REMAINS IN THE VISION'S KEEPING. WHICH BRINGS US TO THE FINAL STONE...
...THE *POWER* STONE.

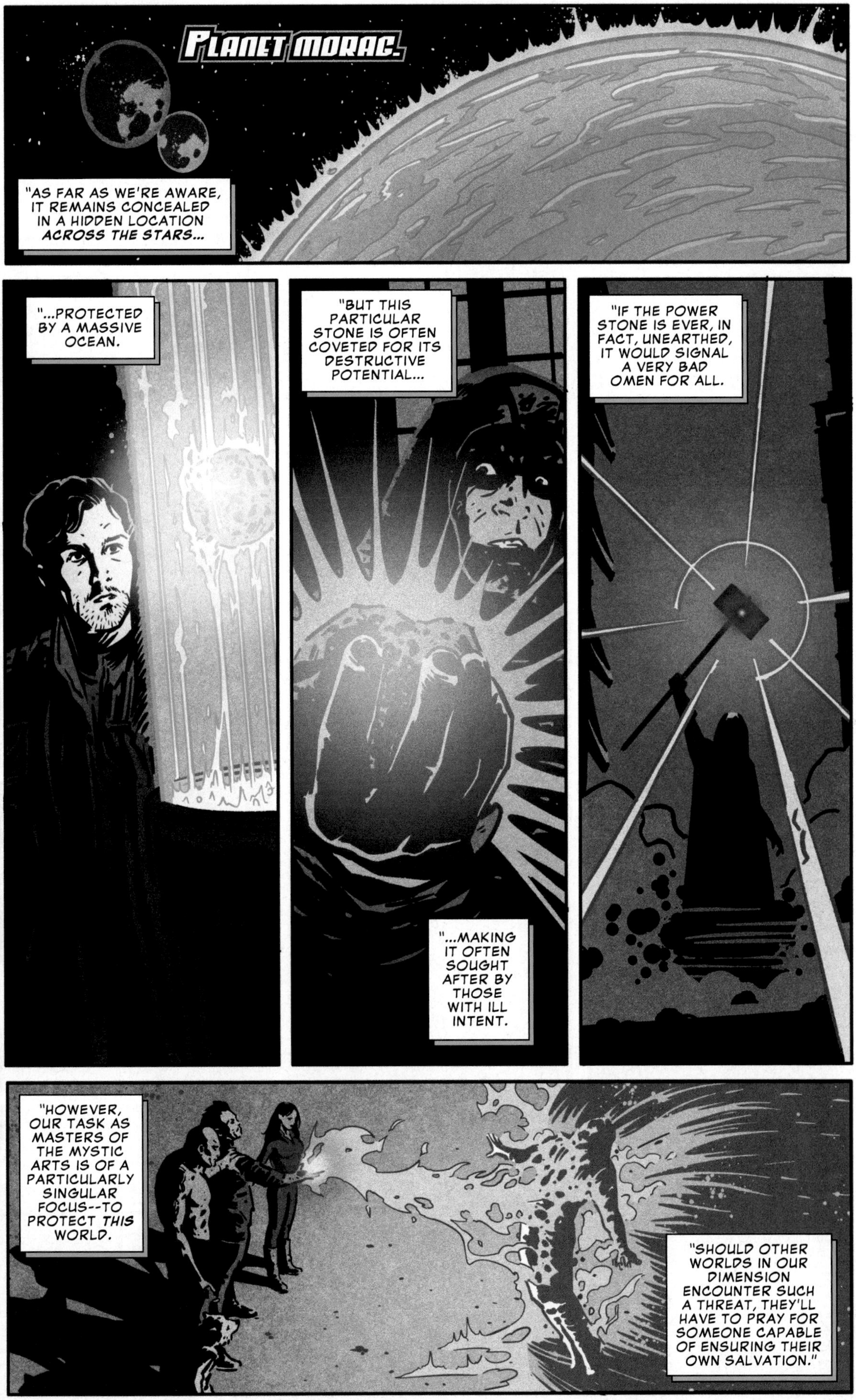
PLANET MORAG.
"AS FAR AS WE'RE AWARE, IT REMAINS CONCEALED IN A HIDDEN LOCATION ACROSS THE STARS...
"...PROTECTED BY A MASSIVE OCEAN.
"BUT THIS PARTICULAR STONE IS OFTEN COVETED FOR ITS DESTRUCTIVE POTENTIAL...
"...MAKING IT OFTEN SOUGHT AFTER BY THOSE WITH ILL INTENT.
"IF THE POWER STONE IS EVER, IN FACT, UNEARTHED, IT WOULD SIGNAL A VERY BAD OMEN FOR ALL.
"HOWEVER, OUR TASK AS MASTERS OF THE MYSTIC ARTS IS OF A PARTICULARLY SINGULAR FOCUS--TO PROTECT THIS WORLD.
"SHOULD OTHER WORLDS IN OUR DIMENSION ENCOUNTER SUCH A THREAT, THEY'LL HAVE TO PRAY FOR SOMEONE CAPABLE OF ENSURING THEIR OWN SALVATION."

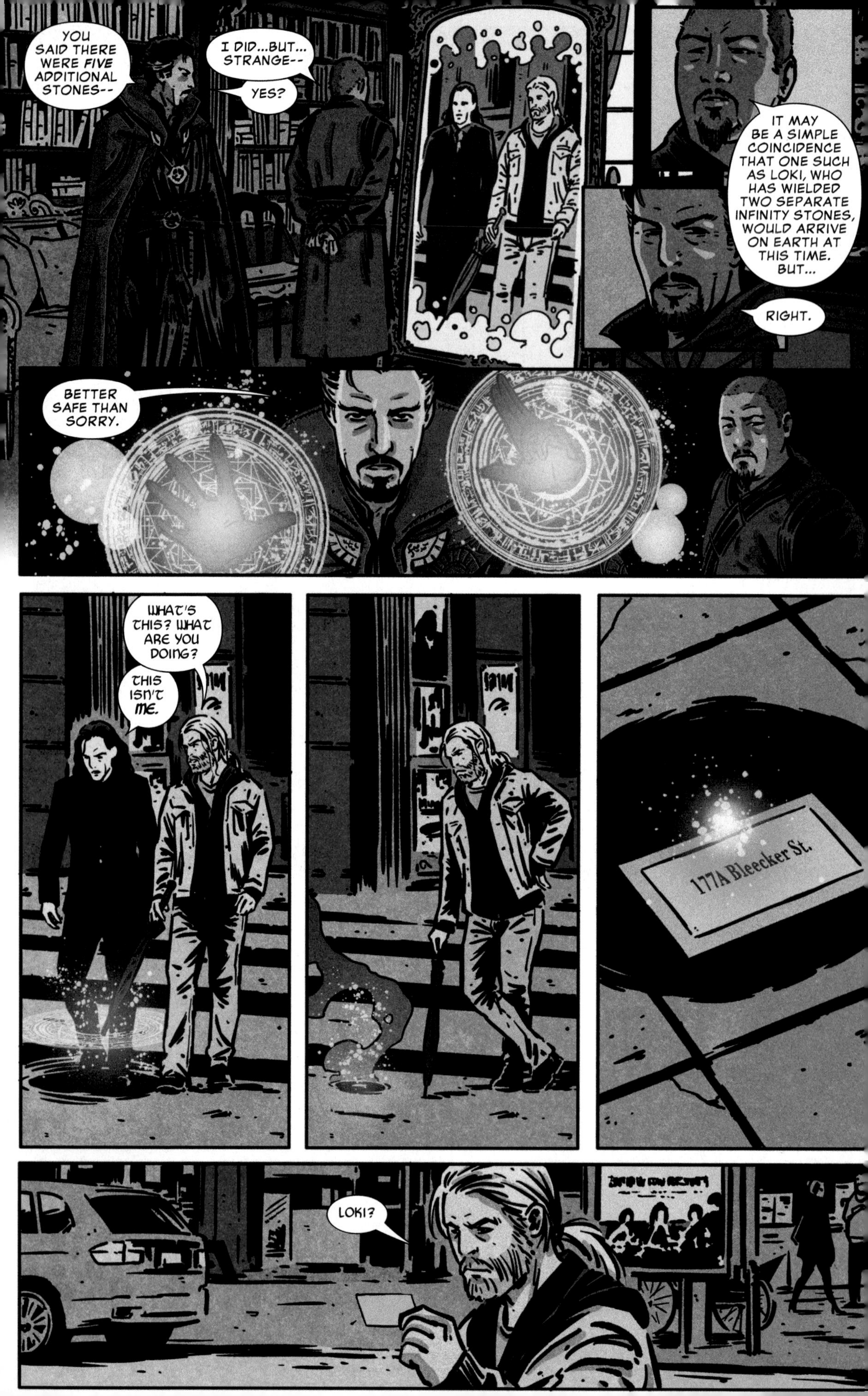
YOU SAID THERE WERE FIVE ADDITIONAL STONES--
I DID...BUT... STRANGE--
YES?
IT MAY BE A SIMPLE COINCIDENCE THAT ONE SUCH AS LOKI, WHO HAS WIELDED TWO SEPARATE INFINITY STONES, WOULD ARRIVE ON EARTH AT THIS TIME. BUT...
RIGHT.
BETTER SAFE THAN SORRY.
WHAT'S THIS? WHAT ARE YOU DOING?
THIS ISN'T ME.
177A Bleecker St.
LOKI?

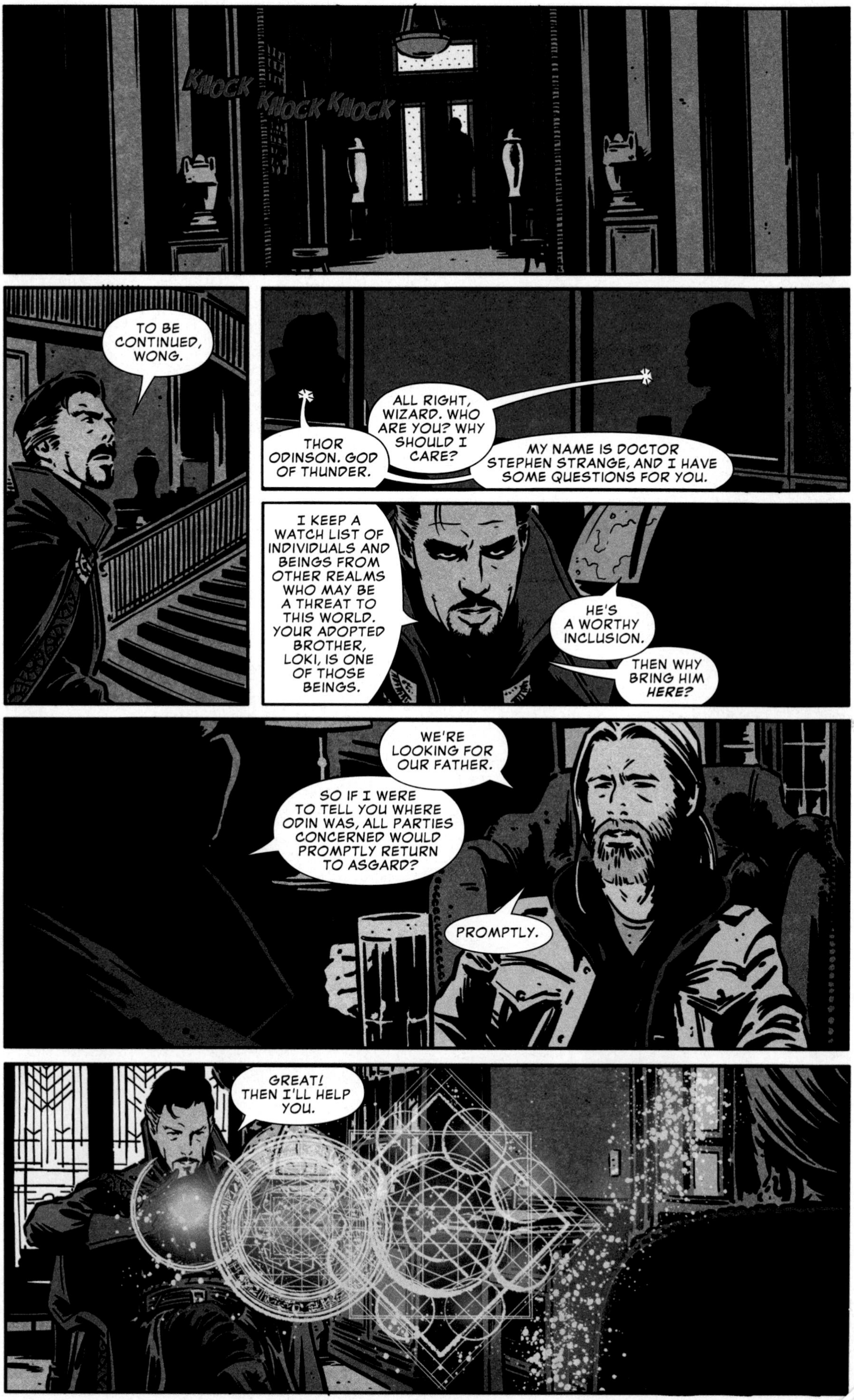
KNOCK KNOCK KNOCK
TO BE CONTINUED, WONG.
ALL RIGHT, WIZARD. WHO ARE YOU? WHY SHOULD I CARE?
THOR ODINSON. GOD OF THUNDER.
MY NAME IS DOCTOR STEPHEN STRANGE, AND I HAVE SOME QUESTIONS FOR YOU.
I KEEP A WATCH LIST OF INDIVIDUALS AND BEINGS FROM OTHER REALMS WHO MAY BE A THREAT TO THIS WORLD. YOUR ADOPTED BROTHER, LOKI, IS ONE OF THOSE BEINGS.
HE'S A WORTHY INCLUSION.
THEN WHY BRING HIM *HERE?*
WE'RE LOOKING FOR OUR FATHER.
SO IF I WERE TO TELL YOU WHERE ODIN WAS, ALL PARTIES CONCERNED WOULD PROMPTLY RETURN TO ASGARD?
PROMPTLY.
GREAT! THEN I'LL HELP YOU.

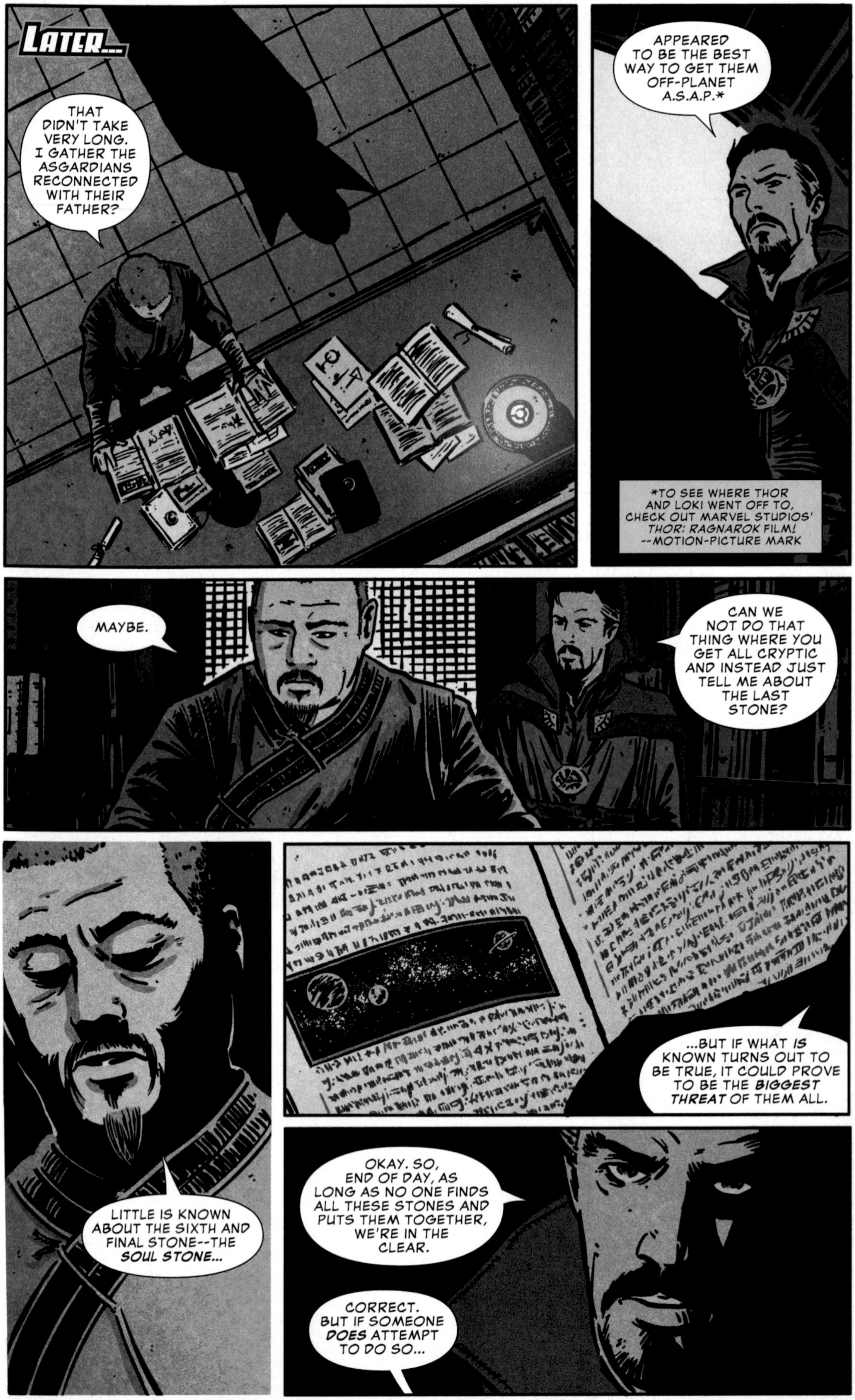
LATER...
THAT DIDN'T TAKE VERY LONG. I GATHER THE ASGARDIANS RECONNECTED WITH THEIR FATHER?
APPEARED TO BE THE BEST WAY TO GET THEM OFF-PLANET A.S.A.P.*
*TO SEE WHERE THOR AND LOKI WENT OFF TO, CHECK OUT MARVEL STUDIOS' THOR: RAGNAROK FILM! --MOTION-PICTURE MARK
MAYBE.
CAN WE NOT DO THAT THING WHERE YOU GET ALL CRYPTIC AND INSTEAD JUST TELL ME ABOUT THE LAST STONE?
LITTLE IS KNOWN ABOUT THE SIXTH AND FINAL STONE--THE SOUL STONE...
...BUT IF WHAT IS KNOWN TURNS OUT TO BE TRUE, IT COULD PROVE TO BE THE BIGGEST THREAT OF THEM ALL.
OKAY. SO, END OF DAY, AS LONG AS NO ONE FINDS ALL THESE STONES AND PUTS THEM TOGETHER, WE'RE IN THE CLEAR.
CORRECT. BUT IF SOMEONE DOES ATTEMPT TO DO SO...

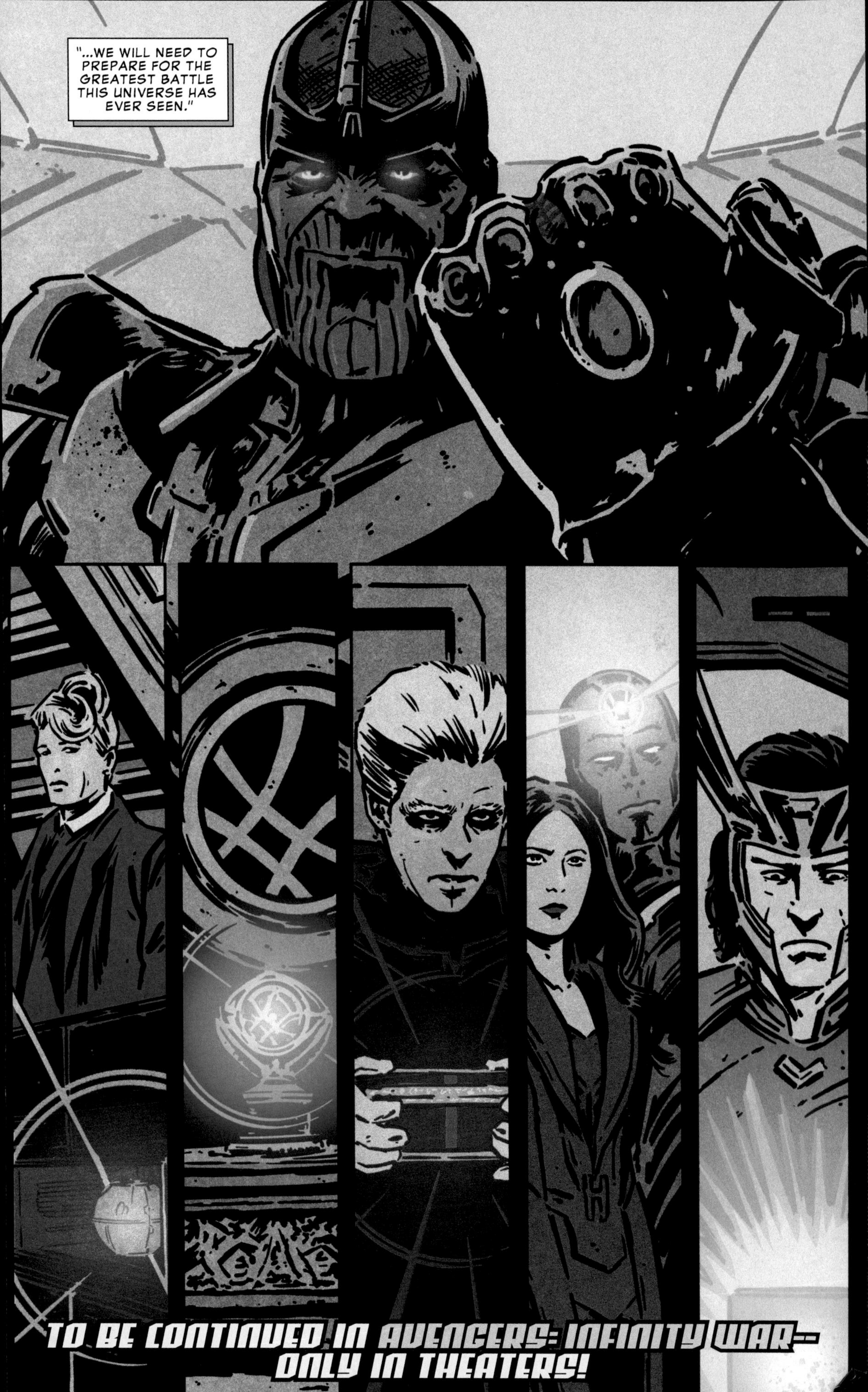
"...WE WILL NEED TO PREPARE FOR THE GREATEST BATTLE THIS UNIVERSE HAS EVER SEEN."
TO BE CONTINUED IN AVENGERS: INFINITY WAR--
ONLY IN THEATERS!

WITH THE AVENGERS DISTRACTED, THANOS SEIZES THE OPPORTUNITY TO STRIKE AT EARTH IN THE FIRST CHAPTER OF JONATHAN HICKMAN'S EPIC *INFINITY*!

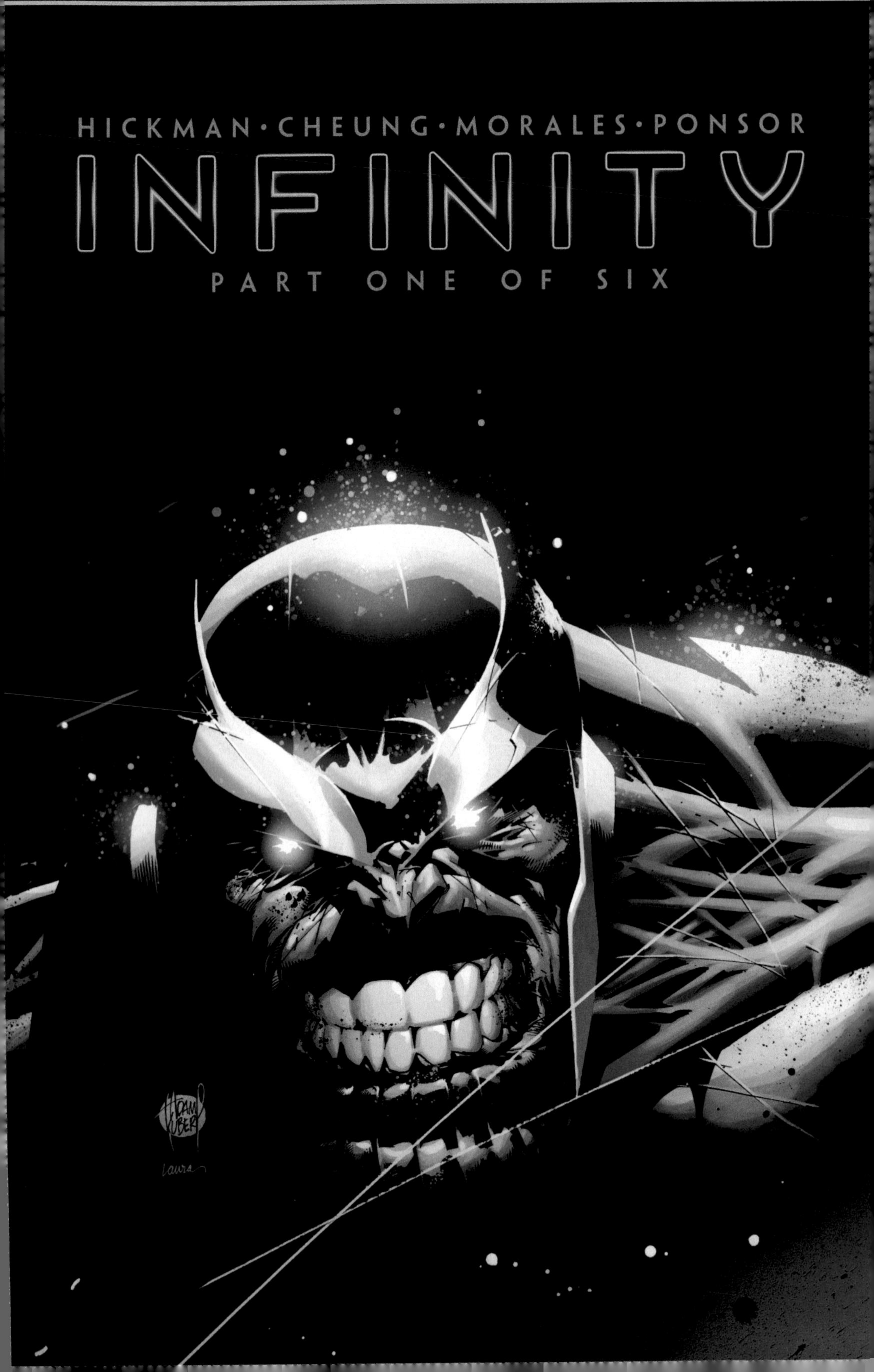
HICKMAN·CHEUNG·MORALES·PONSOR
INFINITY
PART ONE OF SIX

A MARVEL COMICS EVENT

◆

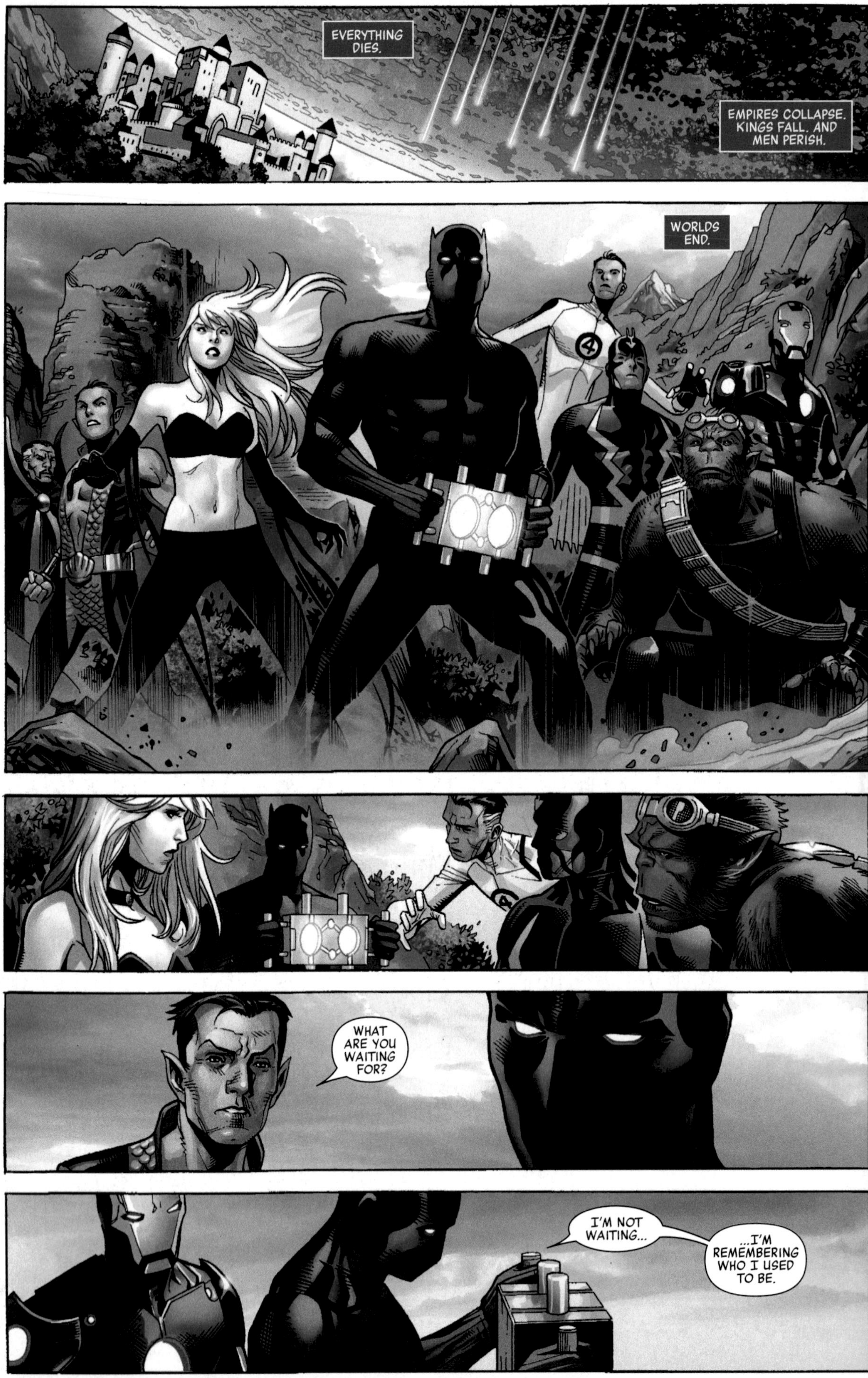
EVERYTHING DIES.
EMPIRES COLLAPSE. KINGS FALL. AND MEN PERISH.
WORLDS END.
WHAT ARE YOU WAITING FOR?
I'M NOT WAITING...
...I'M REMEMBERING WHO I USED TO BE.

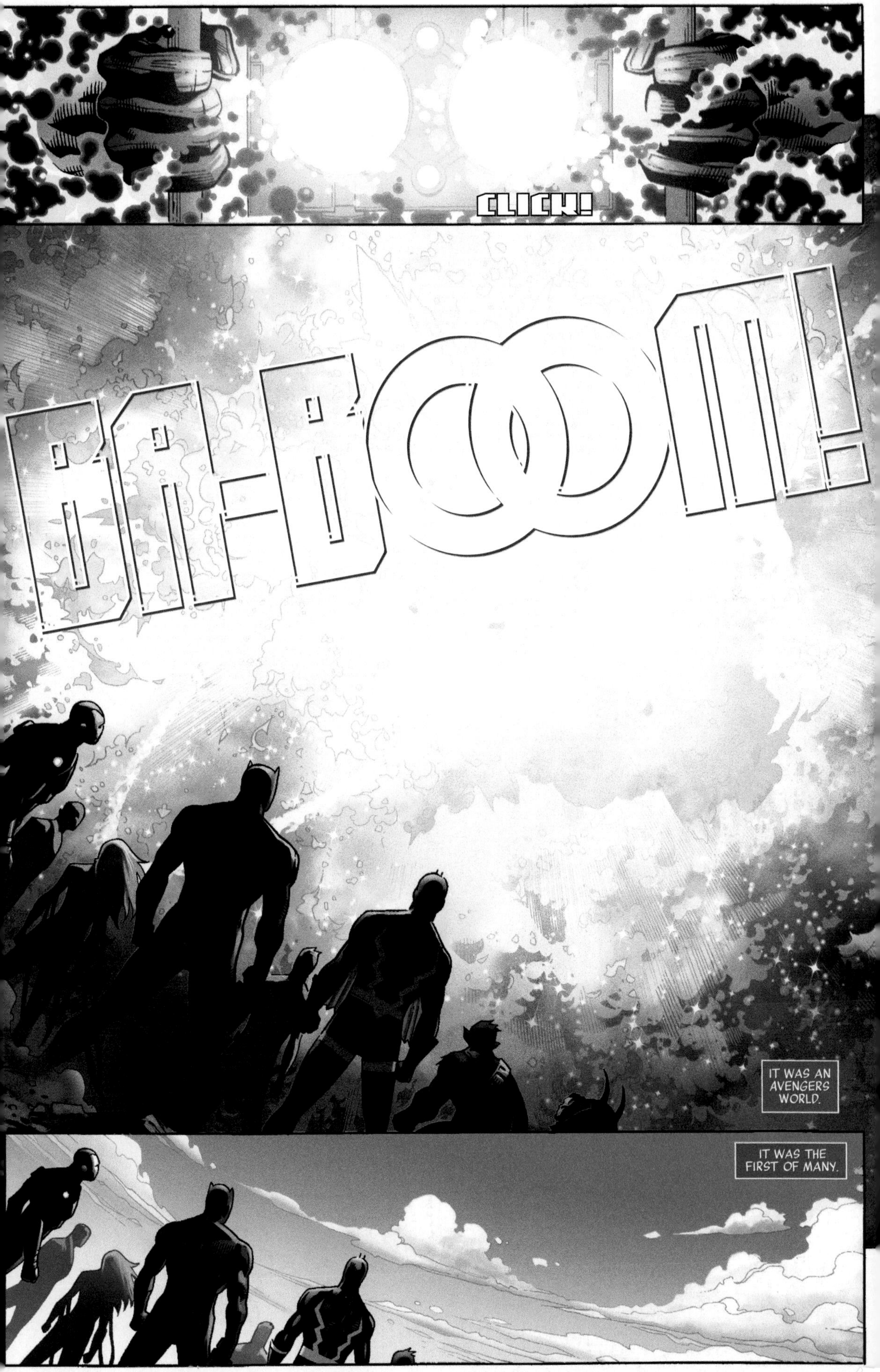
CLICK!
KA-BOOM!
IT WAS AN AVENGERS WORLD.
IT WAS THE FIRST OF MANY.

THE TRIBUTE

TITAN.

OUTRIDERS ARE NOT BORN, THEY ARE MADE. A GENETICALLY ENGINEERED PARASITE-ASSASSIN SOLELY DEVOTED TO THE WHIMS OF ITS MAKER.

THESE CREATURES HAVE NO NAMES, JUST A BINARY EXISTENCE DEFINED BY WHETHER THEY COMPLETE THE TASK GIVEN TO THEM, OR WHETHER THEY FAIL.

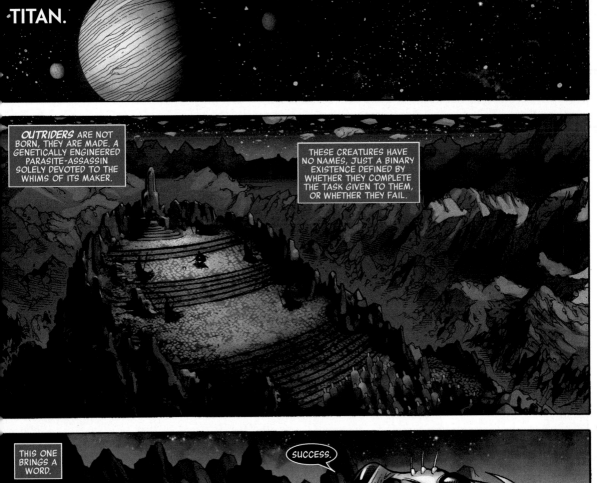

THIS ONE BRINGS A WORD.

SUCCESS.

WHERE?

AHL-AGULLO.

IN THE SHADOW OF THE SPIRAL ABYSS.

AHL-AGULLO.

THAT WAS TWO FULL CYCLES AGO, MASTER.

THE GAUNTLET OF THE TRIBUTE?

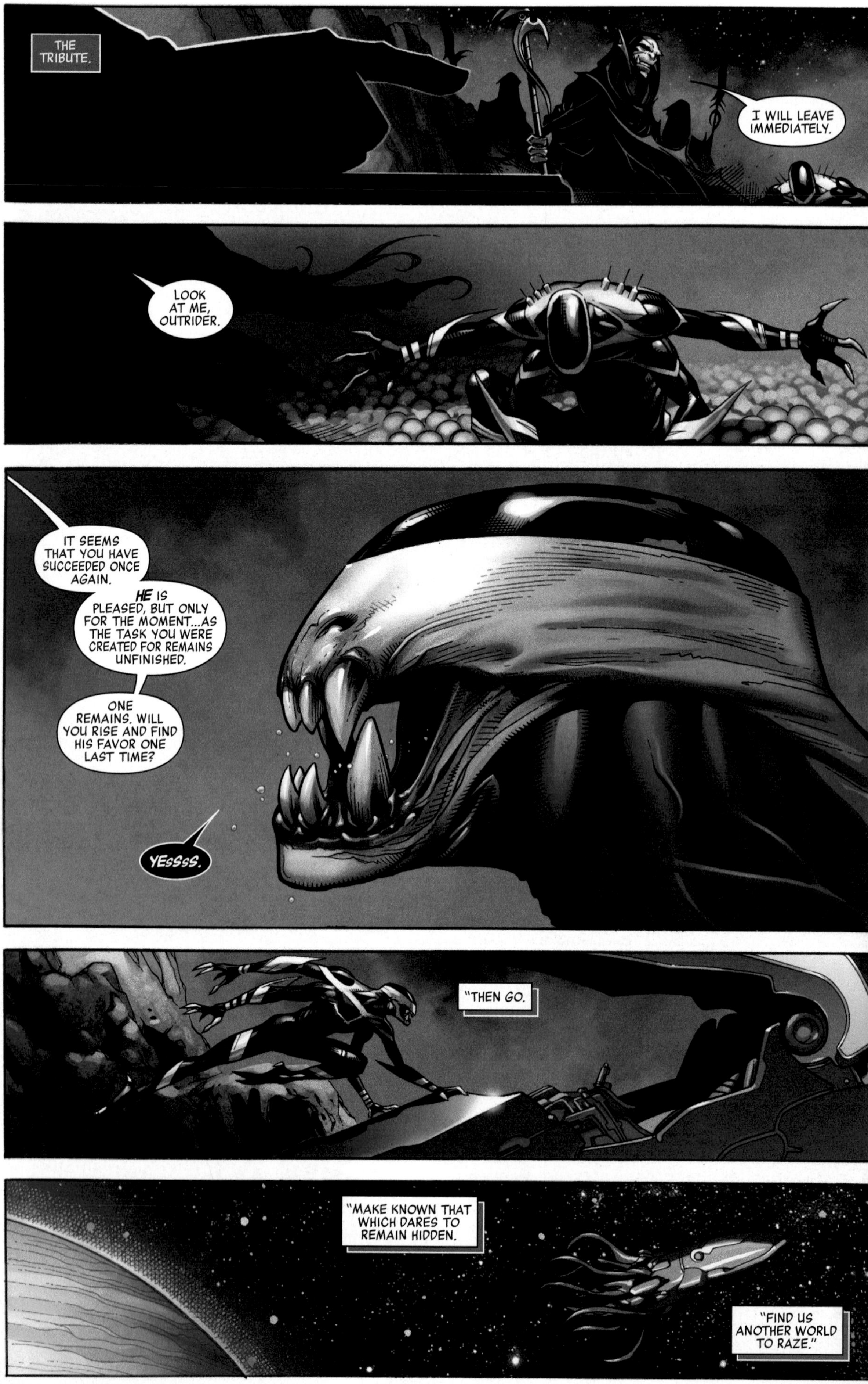
THE TRIBUTE.
I WILL LEAVE IMMEDIATELY.
LOOK AT ME, OUTRIDER.
IT SEEMS THAT YOU HAVE SUCCEEDED ONCE AGAIN.
HE IS PLEASED, BUT ONLY FOR THE MOMENT...AS THE TASK YOU WERE CREATED FOR REMAINS UNFINISHED.
ONE REMAINS. WILL YOU RISE AND FIND HIS FAVOR ONE LAST TIME?
YESSSS.
"THEN GO.
"MAKE KNOWN THAT WHICH DARES TO REMAIN HIDDEN.
"FIND US ANOTHER WORLD TO RAZE."

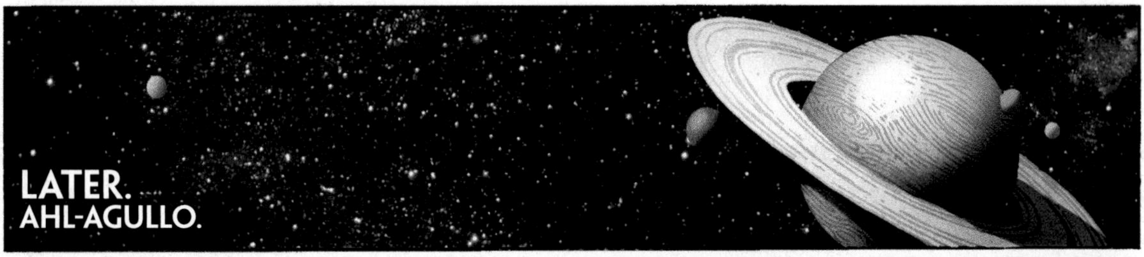
LATER.
AHL-AGULLO.

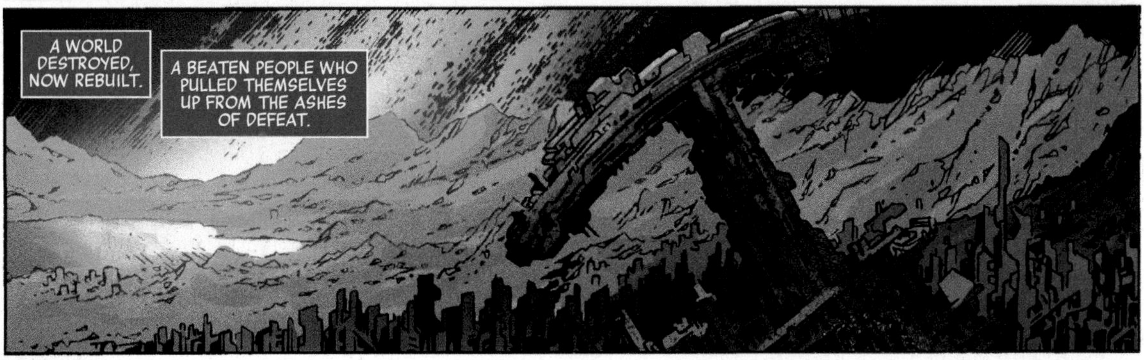
A WORLD DESTROYED, NOW REBUILT.
A BEATEN PEOPLE WHO PULLED THEMSELVES UP FROM THE ASHES OF DEFEAT.

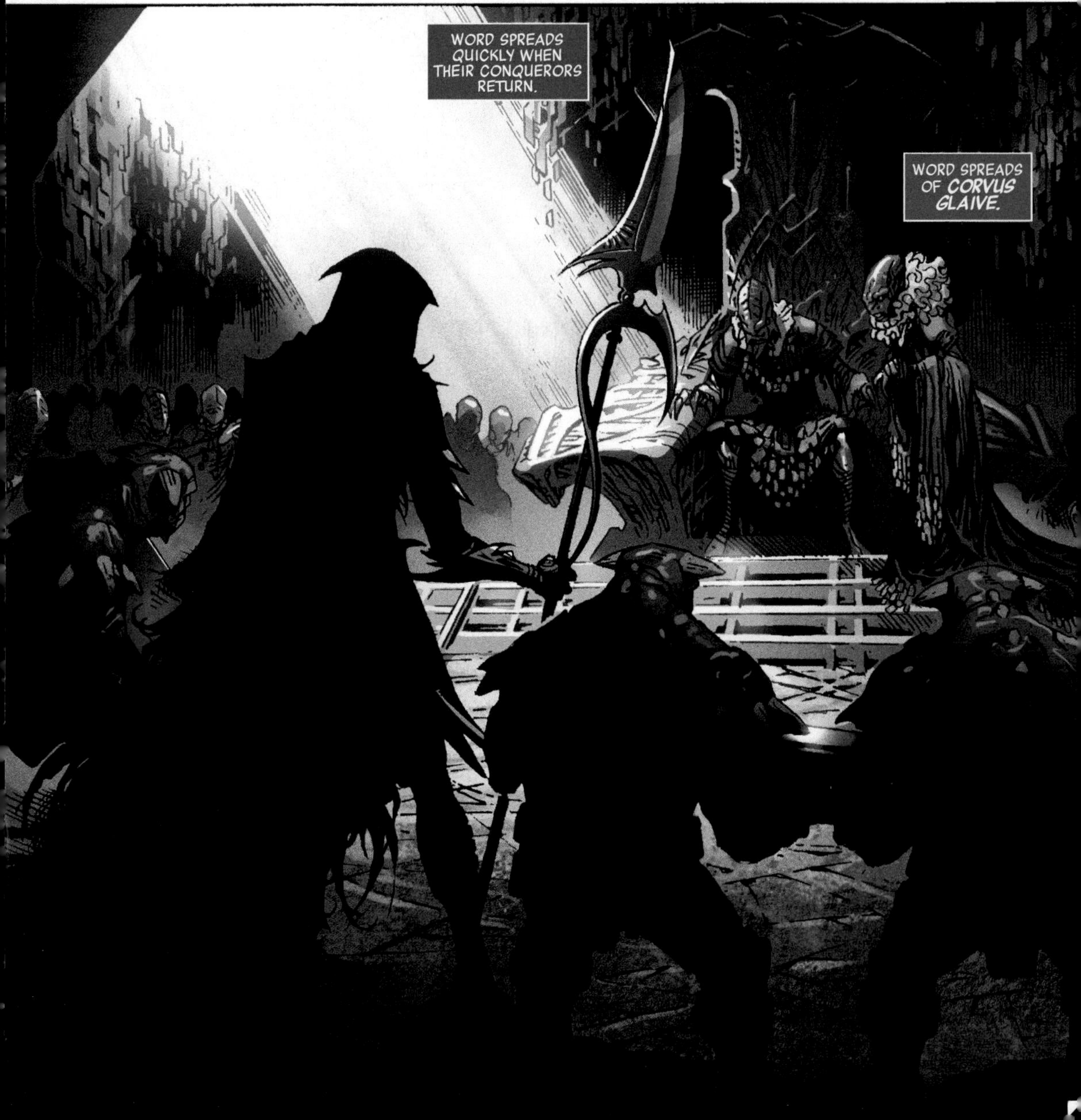
WORD SPREADS QUICKLY WHEN THEIR CONQUERORS RETURN.
WORD SPREADS OF *CORVUS GLAIVE.*

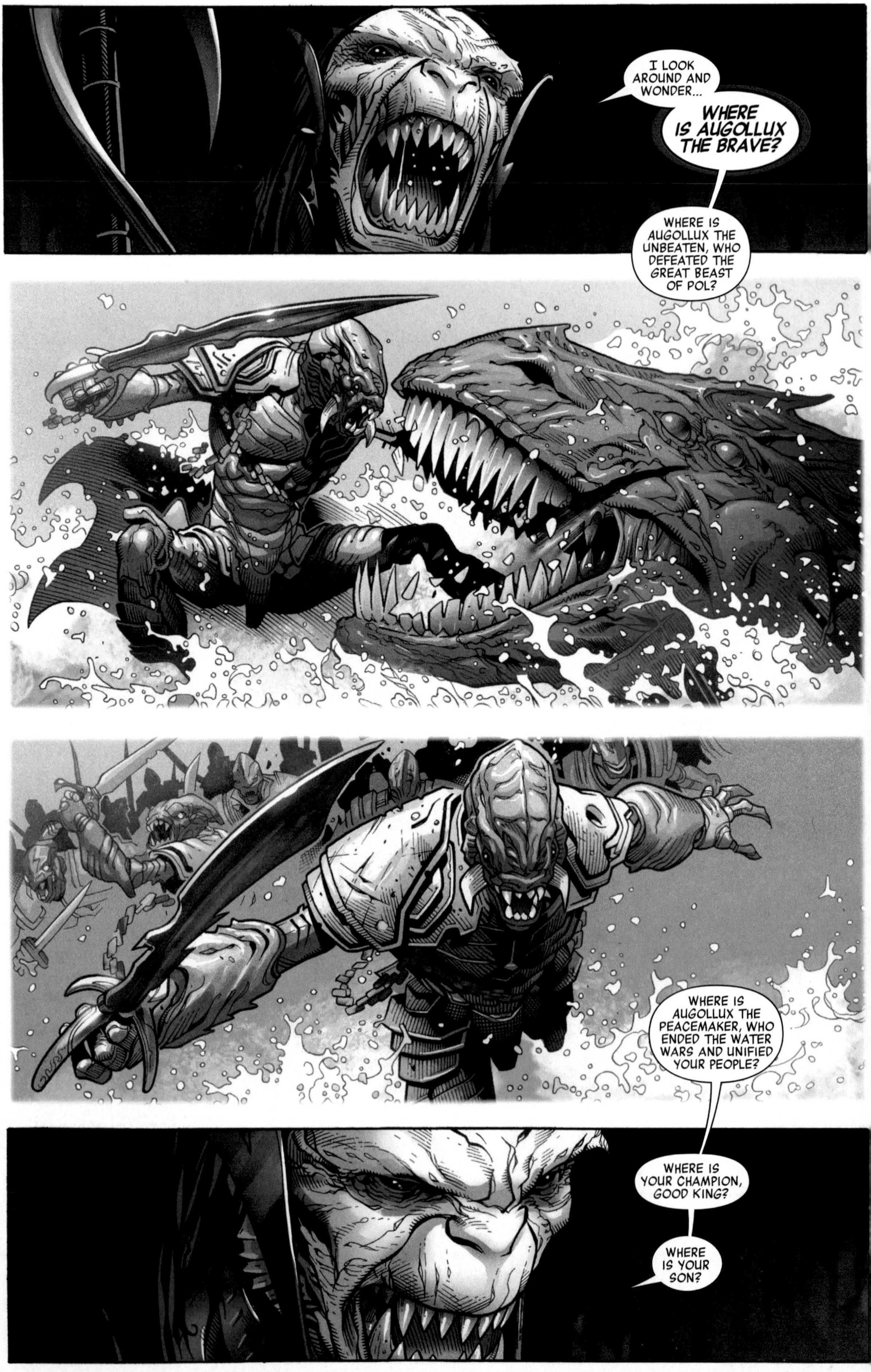
I LOOK AROUND AND WONDER...
WHERE IS AUGOLLUX THE BRAVE?
WHERE IS AUGOLLUX THE UNBEATEN, WHO DEFEATED THE GREAT BEAST OF POL?
WHERE IS AUGOLLUX THE PEACEMAKER, WHO ENDED THE WATER WARS AND UNIFIED YOUR PEOPLE?
WHERE IS YOUR CHAMPION, GOOD KING?
WHERE IS YOUR SON?

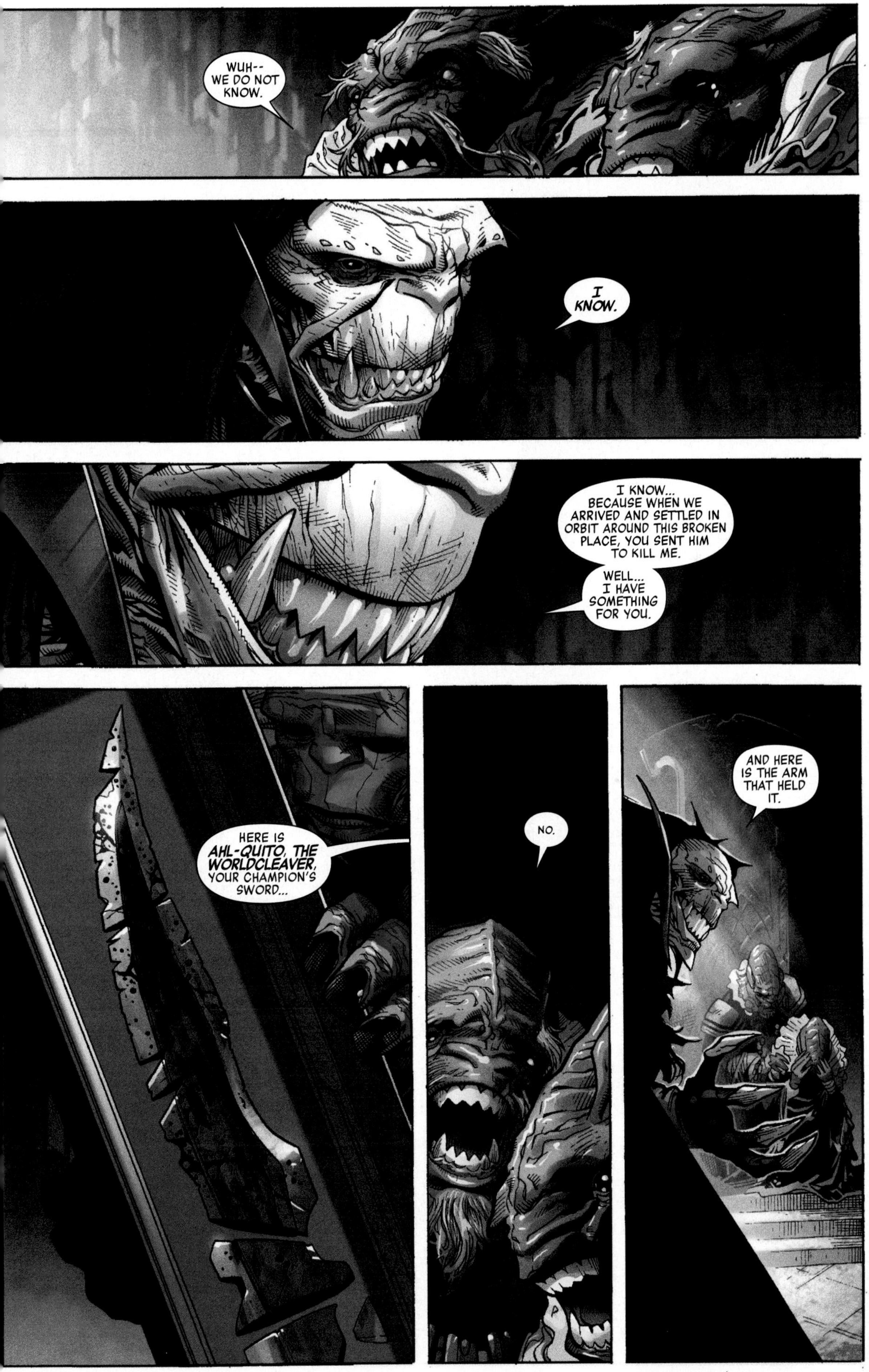
WUH-- WE DO NOT KNOW.
I KNOW.
I KNOW... BECAUSE WHEN WE ARRIVED AND SETTLED IN ORBIT AROUND THIS BROKEN PLACE, YOU SENT HIM TO KILL ME.
WELL... I HAVE SOMETHING FOR YOU.
HERE IS AHL-QUITO, THE WORLDCLEAVER, YOUR CHAMPION'S SWORD...
NO.
AND HERE IS THE ARM THAT HELD IT.

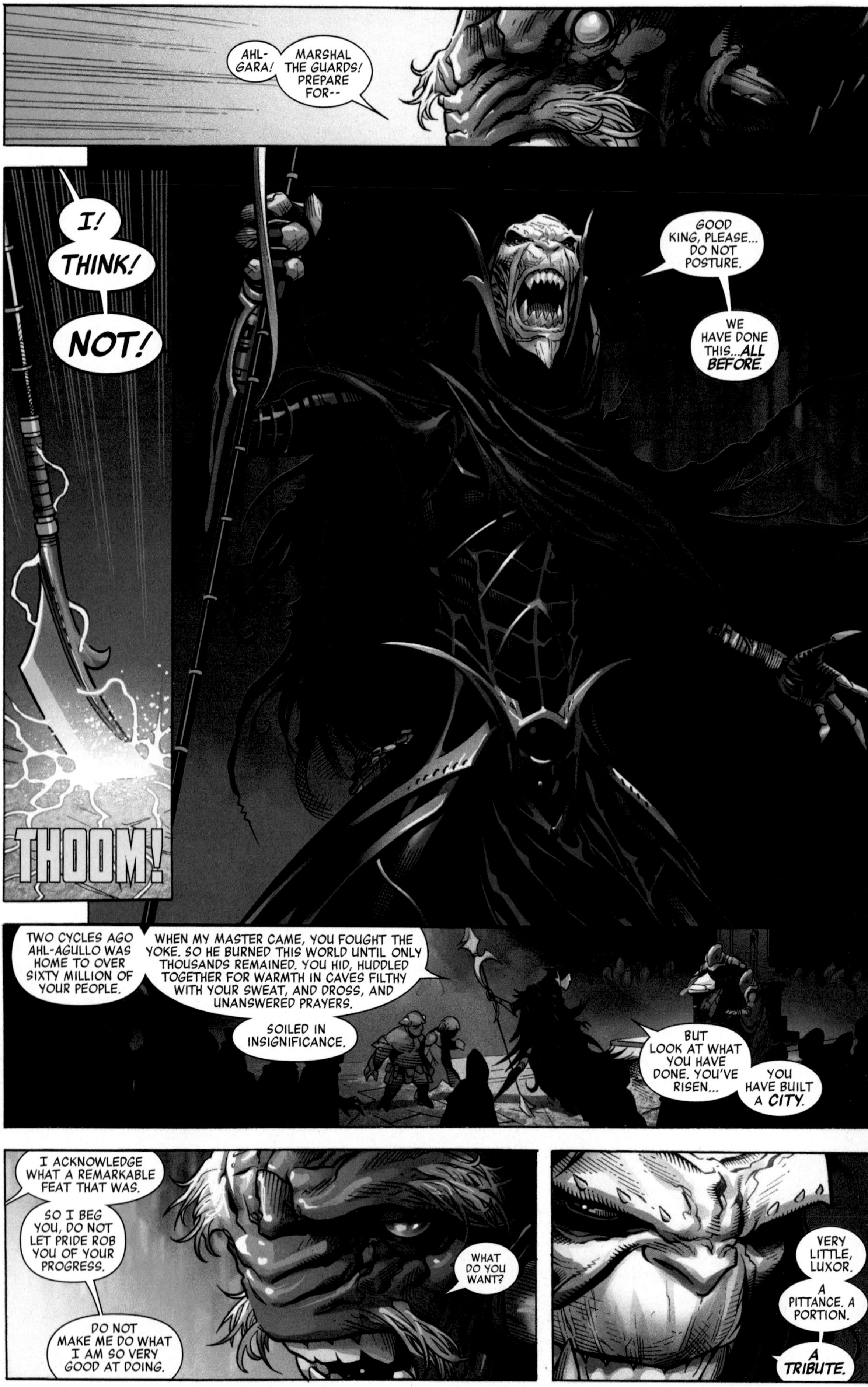
AHL-GARA!
MARSHAL THE GUARDS! PREPARE FOR--
I! THINK! NOT!
THOOM!
GOOD KING, PLEASE... DO NOT POSTURE.
WE HAVE DONE THIS...ALL BEFORE.
TWO CYCLES AGO AHL-AGULLO WAS HOME TO OVER SIXTY MILLION OF YOUR PEOPLE.
WHEN MY MASTER CAME, YOU FOUGHT THE YOKE. SO HE BURNED THIS WORLD UNTIL ONLY THOUSANDS REMAINED. YOU HID, HUDDLED TOGETHER FOR WARMTH IN CAVES FILTHY WITH YOUR SWEAT, AND DROSS, AND UNANSWERED PRAYERS.
SOILED IN INSIGNIFICANCE.
BUT LOOK AT WHAT YOU HAVE DONE. YOU'VE RISEN...
YOU HAVE BUILT A CITY.
I ACKNOWLEDGE WHAT A REMARKABLE FEAT THAT WAS.
SO I BEG YOU, DO NOT LET PRIDE ROB YOU OF YOUR PROGRESS.
DO NOT MAKE ME DO WHAT I AM SO VERY GOOD AT DOING.
WHAT DO YOU WANT?
VERY LITTLE, LUXOR.
A PITTANCE. A PORTION.
A TRIBUTE.

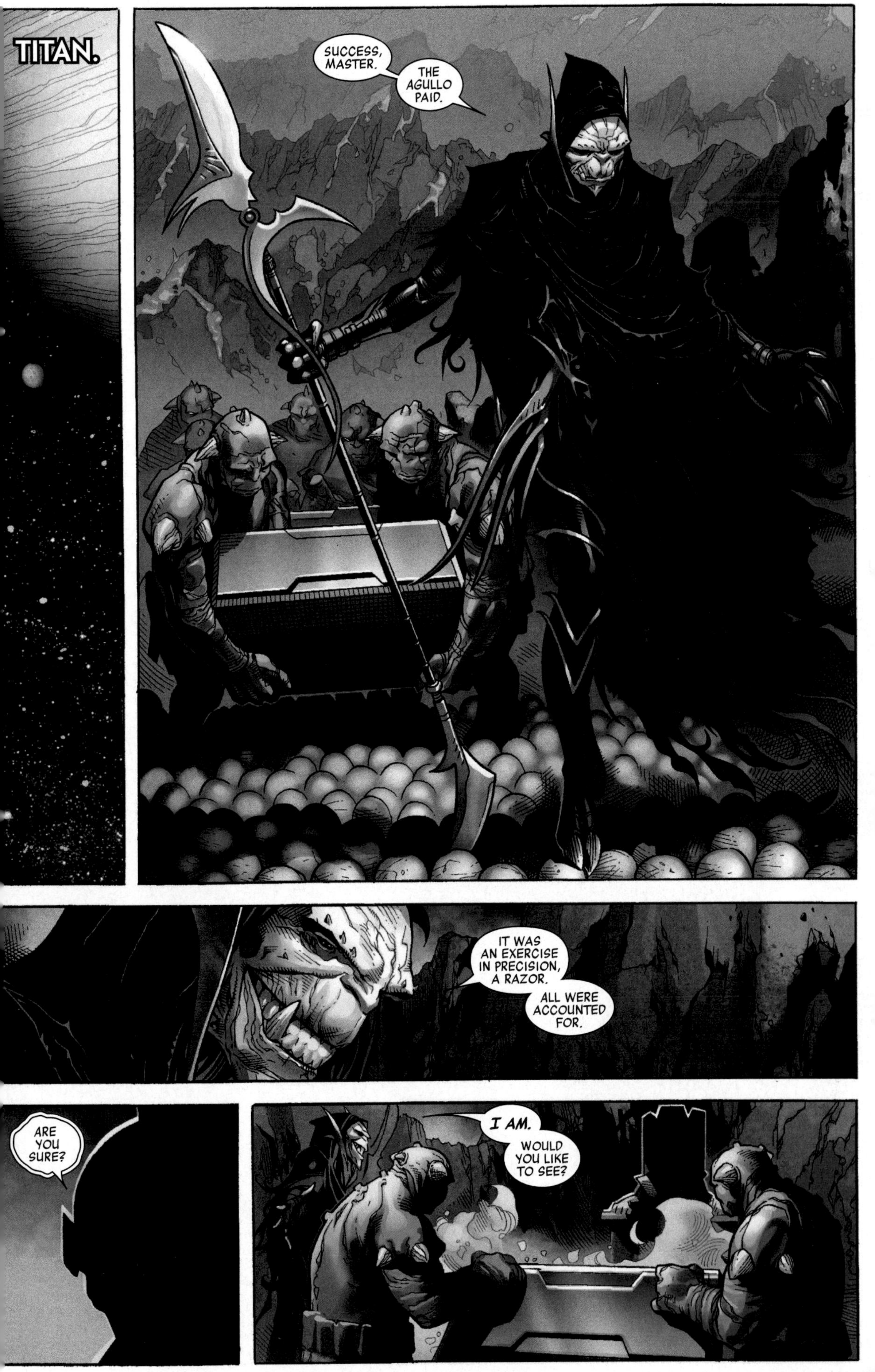
TITAN.
SUCCESS, MASTER.
THE AGULLO PAID.
IT WAS AN EXERCISE IN PRECISION, A RAZOR.
ALL WERE ACCOUNTED FOR.
ARE YOU SURE?
I AM.
WOULD YOU LIKE TO SEE?

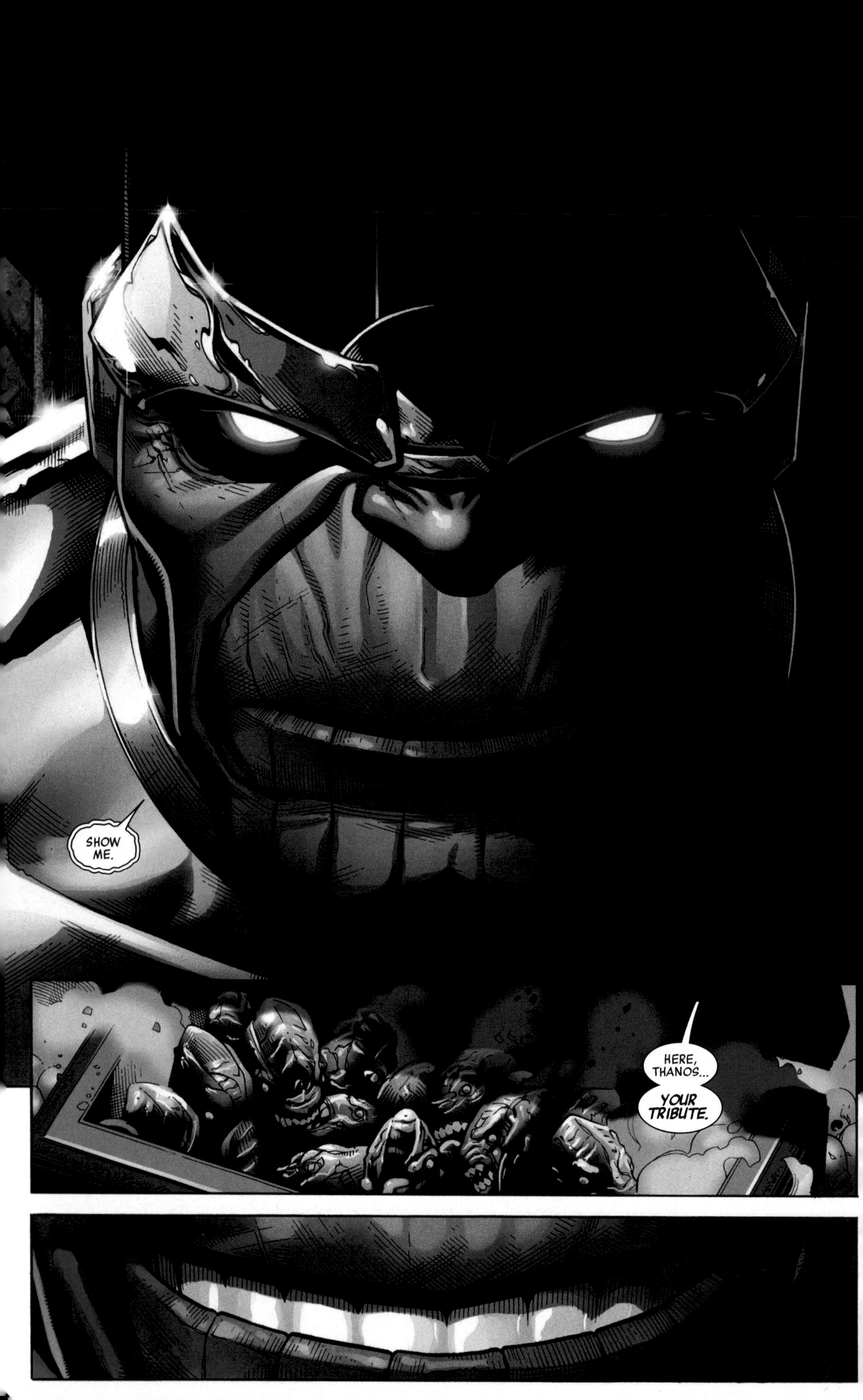
SHOW ME.
HERE, THANOS...
YOUR TRIBUTE.

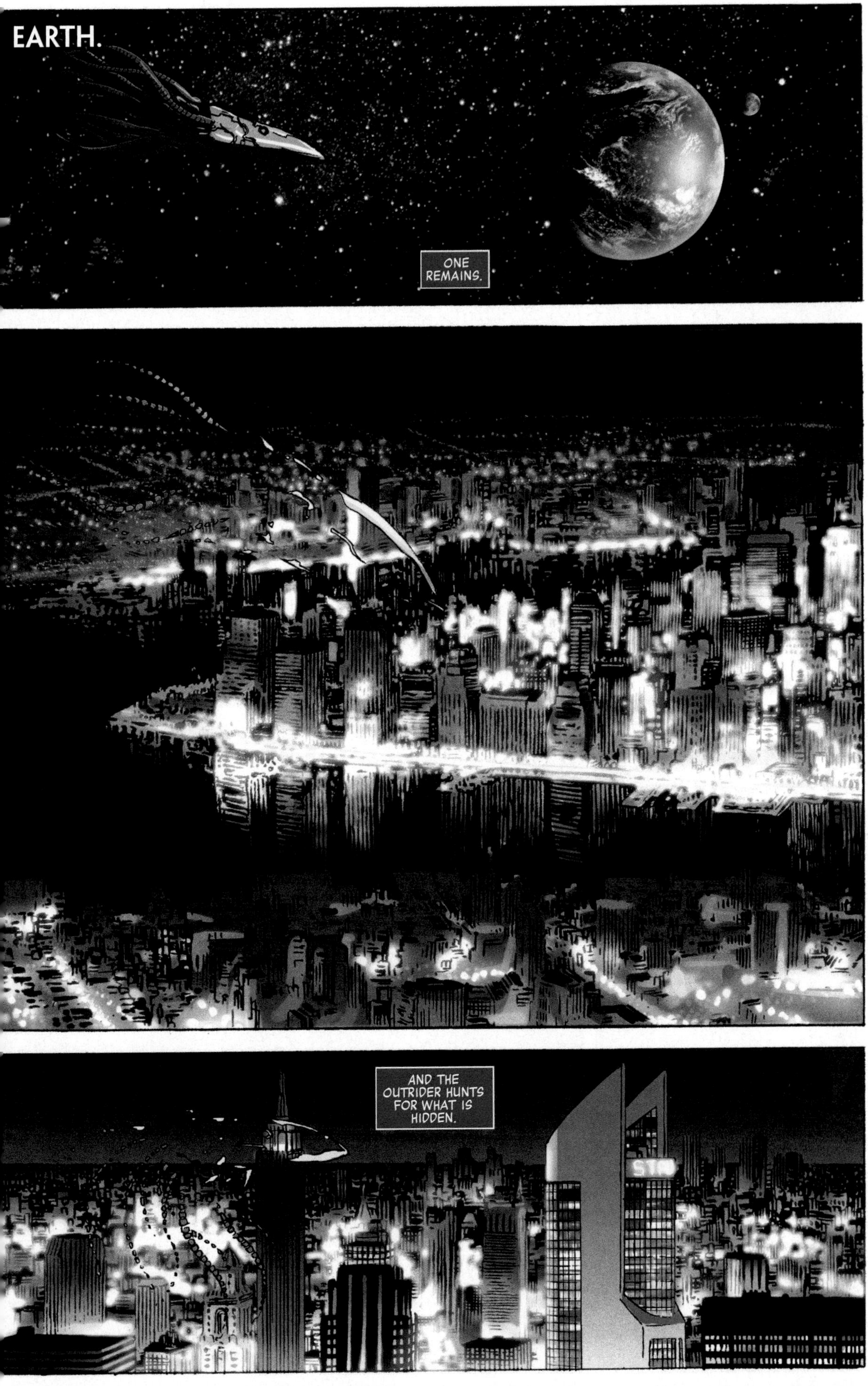
EARTH.
ONE REMAINS.
AND THE OUTRIDER HUNTS FOR WHAT IS HIDDEN.

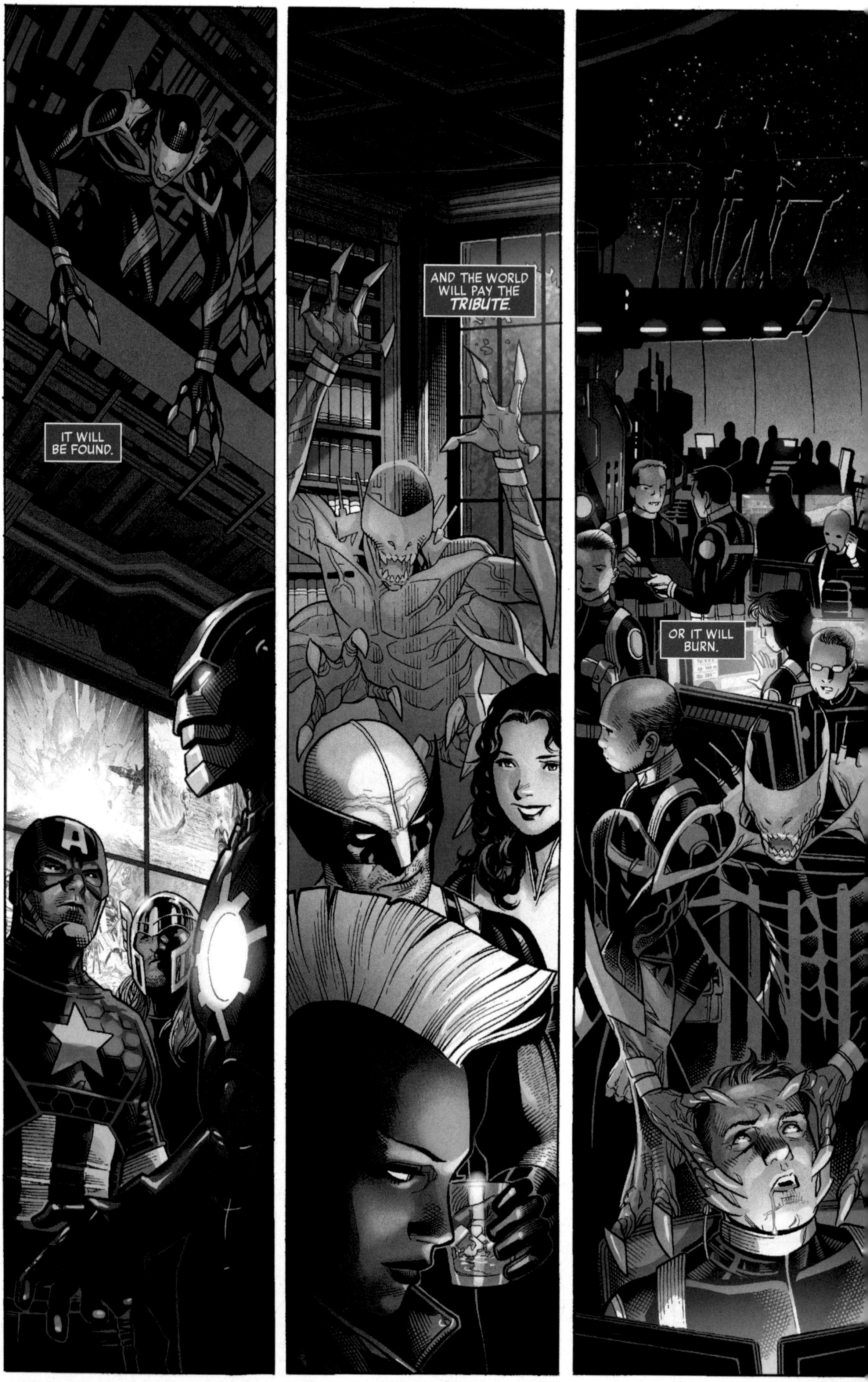
IT WILL BE FOUND.
AND THE WORLD WILL PAY THE TRIBUTE.
OR IT WILL BURN.

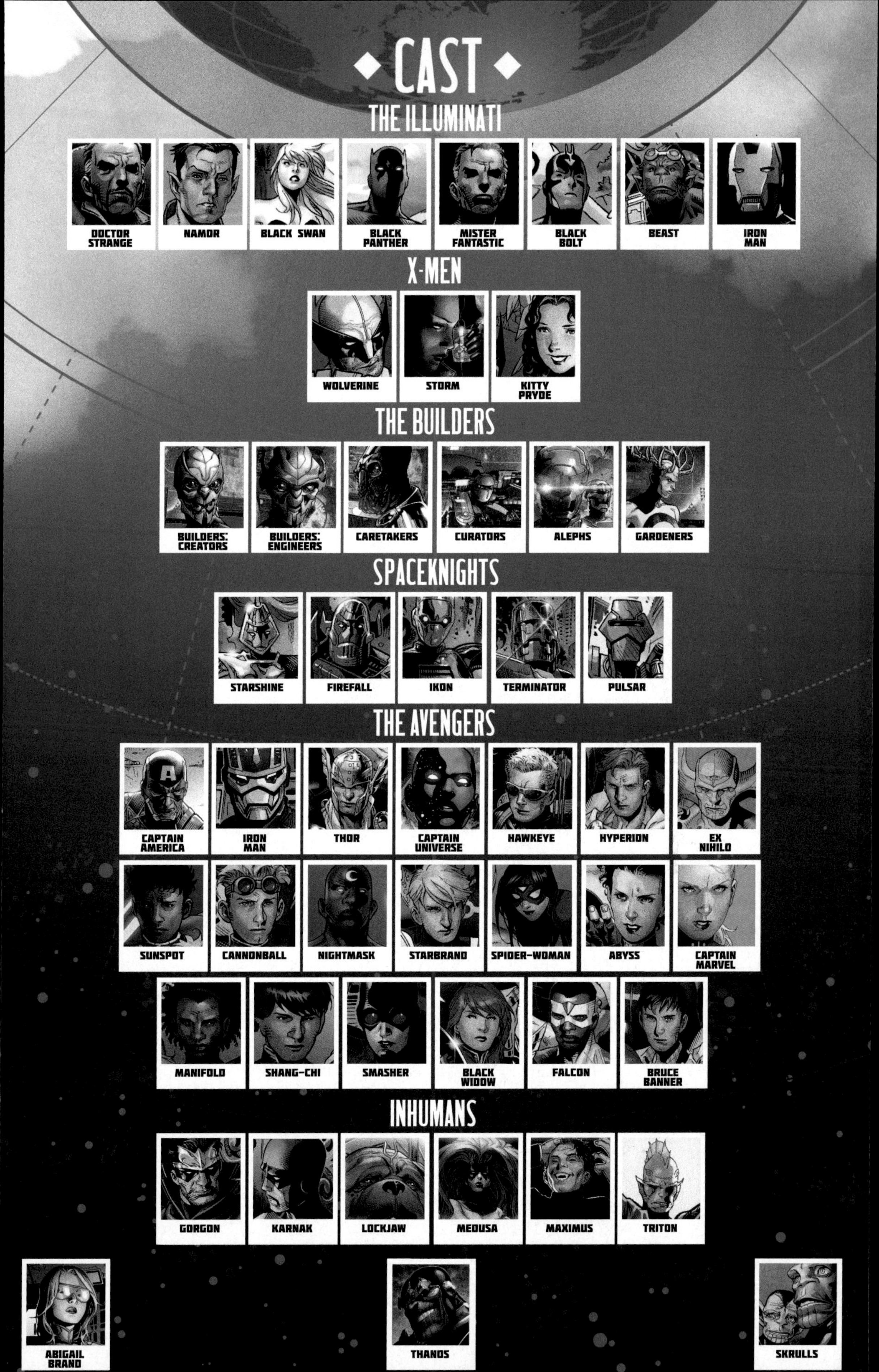
CAST
THE ILLUMINATI
DOCTOR STRANGE
NAMOR
BLACK SWAN
BLACK PANTHER
MISTER FANTASTIC
BLACK BOLT
BEAST
IRON MAN
X-MEN
WOLVERINE
STORM
KITTY PRYDE
THE BUILDERS
BUILDERS: CREATORS
BUILDERS: ENGINEERS
CARETAKERS
CURATORS
ALEPHS
GARDENERS
SPACEKNIGHTS
STARSHINE
FIREFALL
IKON
TERMINATOR
PULSAR
THE AVENGERS
CAPTAIN AMERICA
IRON MAN
THOR
CAPTAIN UNIVERSE
HAWKEYE
HYPERION
EX NIHILO
SUNSPOT
CANNONBALL
NIGHTMASK
STARBRAND
SPIDER-WOMAN
ABYSS
CAPTAIN MARVEL
MANIFOLD
SHANG-CHI
SMASHER
BLACK WIDOW
FALCON
BRUCE BANNER
INHUMANS
GORGON
KARNAK
LOCKJAW
MEDUSA
MAXIMUS
TRITON
ABIGAIL BRAND
THANOS
SKRULLS

MARVEL COMICS PRESENTS:

INFI

WRITER : JONATHAN HICKMAN
PENCILER : JIM CHEUNG
INKERS : MARK MORALES
WITH JOHN LIVESAY, DAVID MEIKIS AND JIM CHEUNG
COLORIST : JUSTIN PONSOR
LETTERERS : CHRIS ELIOPOULOS
WITH JOE CARAMAGNA

COVER : ADAM KUBERT & LAURA MARTIN
VARIANT COVERS : ARTHUR ADAMS & PETE STEIGERWALD;
IN-HYUK LEE; MARKO DJURDJEVIC;
SKOTTIE YOUNG; MARK BROOKS;
JEROME OPENA

NITY

ASSISTANT EDITOR: JAKE THOMAS
EDITORS: TOM BREVOORT
WITH LAUREN SANKOVITCH

EDITOR IN CHIEF: AXEL ALONSO
CHIEF CREATIVE OFFICER: JOE QUESADA
PUBLISHER: DAN BUCKLEY
EXECUTIVE PRODUCER: ALAN FINE

CONSTRUCTING
APOCALYPSE

◆

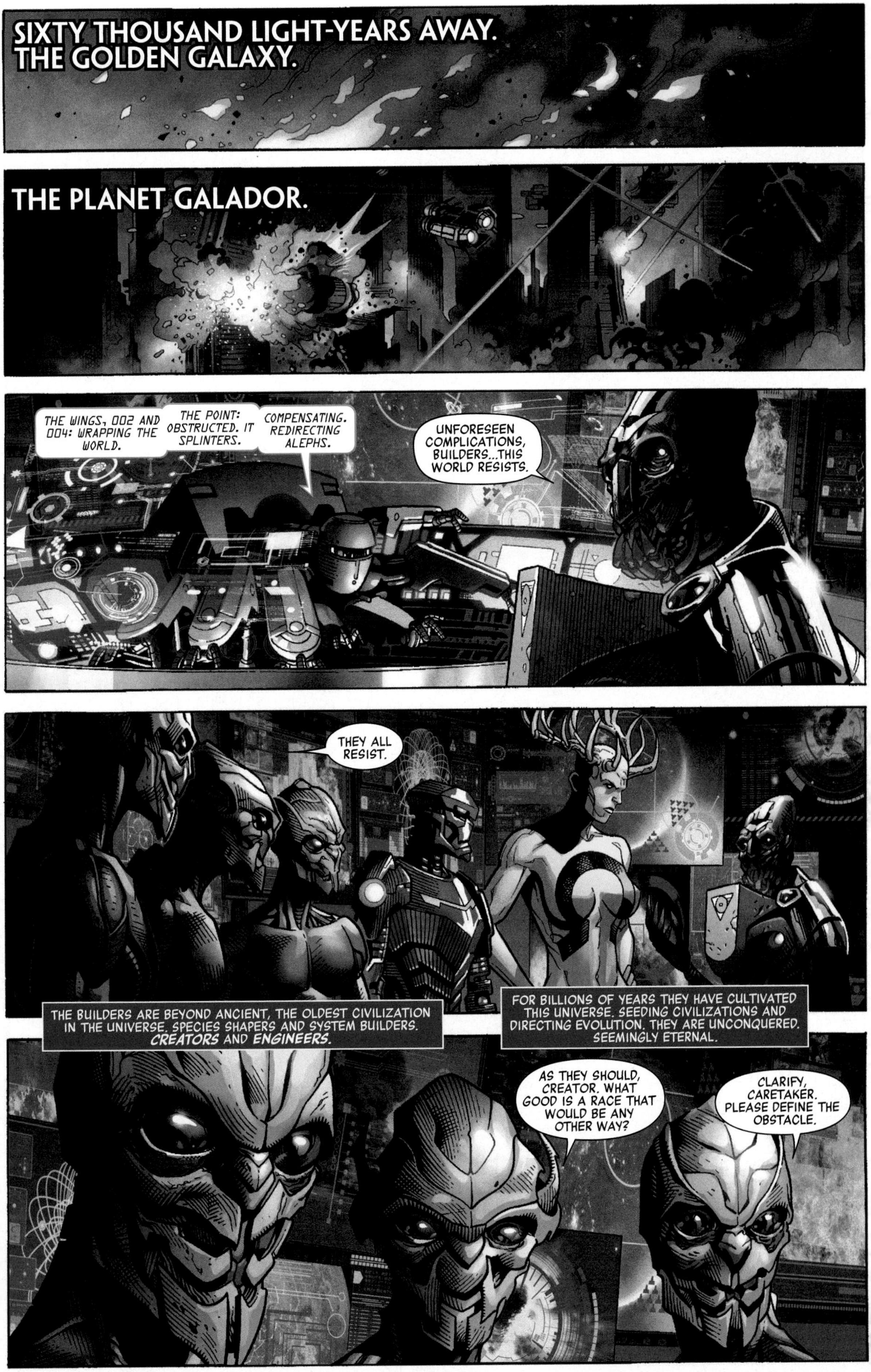
SIXTY THOUSAND LIGHT-YEARS AWAY. THE GOLDEN GALAXY.
THE PLANET GALADOR.
THE WINGS, 002 AND 004: WRAPPING THE WORLD.
THE POINT: OBSTRUCTED. IT SPLINTERS.
COMPENSATING. REDIRECTING ALEPHS.
UNFORESEEN COMPLICATIONS, BUILDERS...THIS WORLD RESISTS.
THEY ALL RESIST.
THE BUILDERS ARE BEYOND ANCIENT, THE OLDEST CIVILIZATION IN THE UNIVERSE. SPECIES SHAPERS AND SYSTEM BUILDERS. CREATORS AND ENGINEERS.
FOR BILLIONS OF YEARS THEY HAVE CULTIVATED THIS UNIVERSE. SEEDING CIVILIZATIONS AND DIRECTING EVOLUTION. THEY ARE UNCONQUERED. SEEMINGLY ETERNAL.
AS THEY SHOULD, CREATOR. WHAT GOOD IS A RACE THAT WOULD BE ANY OTHER WAY?
CLARIFY, CARETAKER. PLEASE DEFINE THE OBSTACLE.

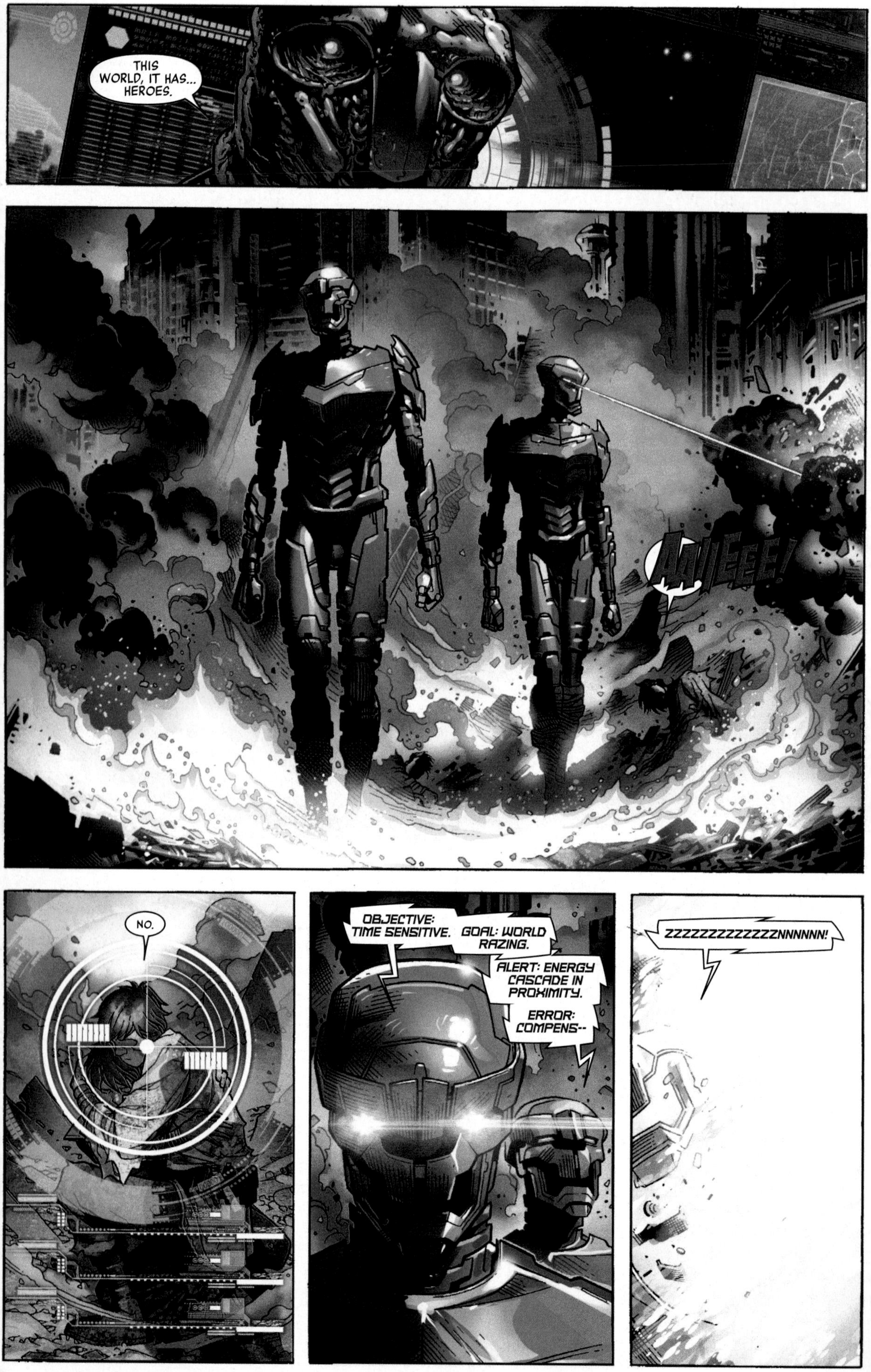
THIS WORLD, IT HAS... HEROES.
AAIIEEE!
NO.
OBJECTIVE: TIME SENSITIVE.
GOAL: WORLD RAZING.
ALERT: ENERGY CASCADE IN PROXIMITY.
ERROR: COMPENS--
ZZZZZZZZZZZZZZNNNNNN!

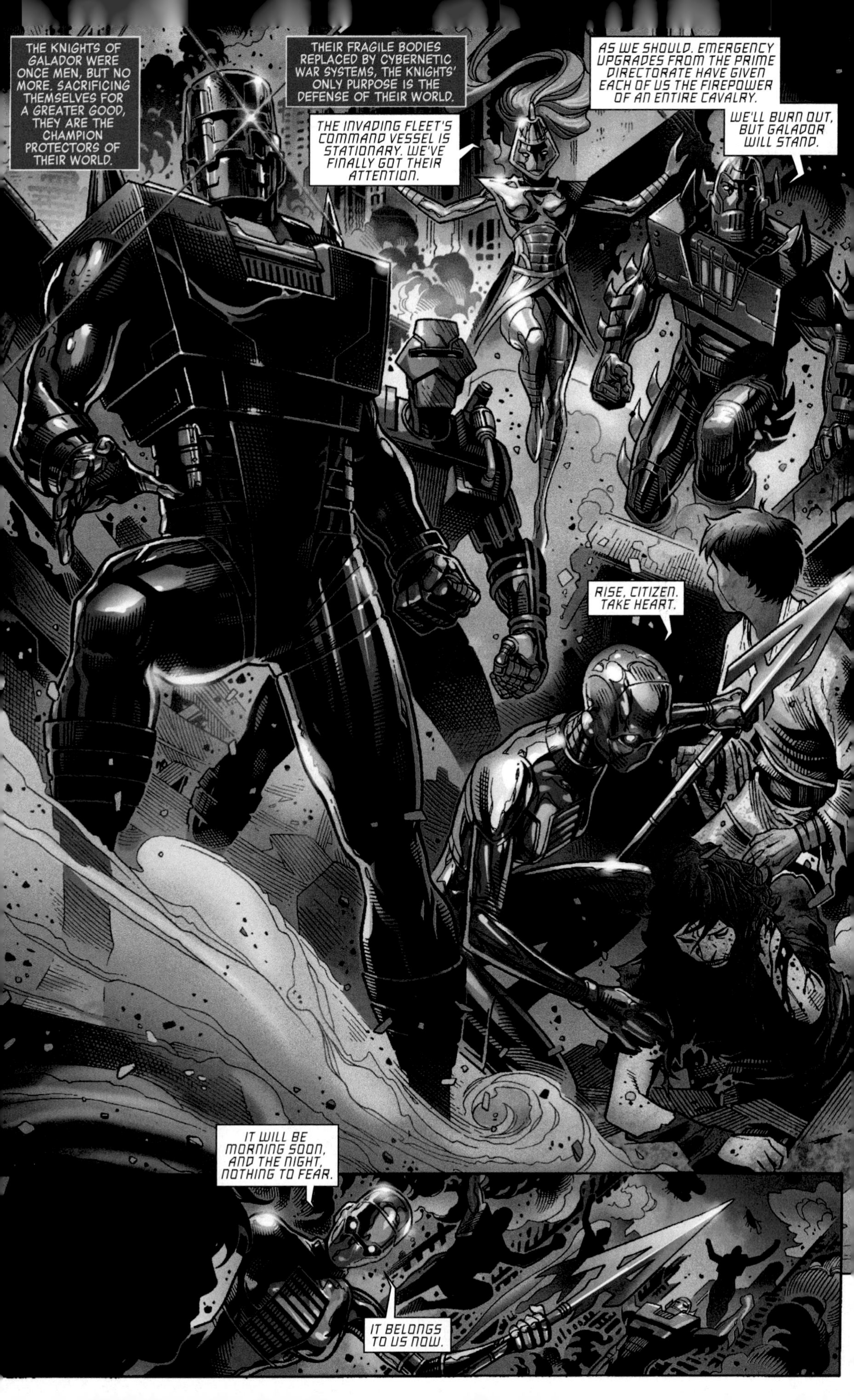
THE KNIGHTS OF GALADOR WERE ONCE MEN, BUT NO MORE. SACRIFICING THEMSELVES FOR A GREATER GOOD, THEY ARE THE CHAMPION PROTECTORS OF THEIR WORLD.
THEIR FRAGILE BODIES REPLACED BY CYBERNETIC WAR SYSTEMS, THE KNIGHTS' ONLY PURPOSE IS THE DEFENSE OF THEIR WORLD.
THE INVADING FLEET'S COMMAND VESSEL IS STATIONARY. WE'VE FINALLY GOT THEIR ATTENTION.
AS WE SHOULD. EMERGENCY UPGRADES FROM THE PRIME DIRECTORATE HAVE GIVEN EACH OF US THE FIREPOWER OF AN ENTIRE CAVALRY.
WE'LL BURN OUT, BUT GALADOR WILL STAND.
RISE, CITIZEN. TAKE HEART.
IT WILL BE MORNING SOON, AND THE NIGHT, NOTHING TO FEAR.
IT BELONGS TO US NOW.

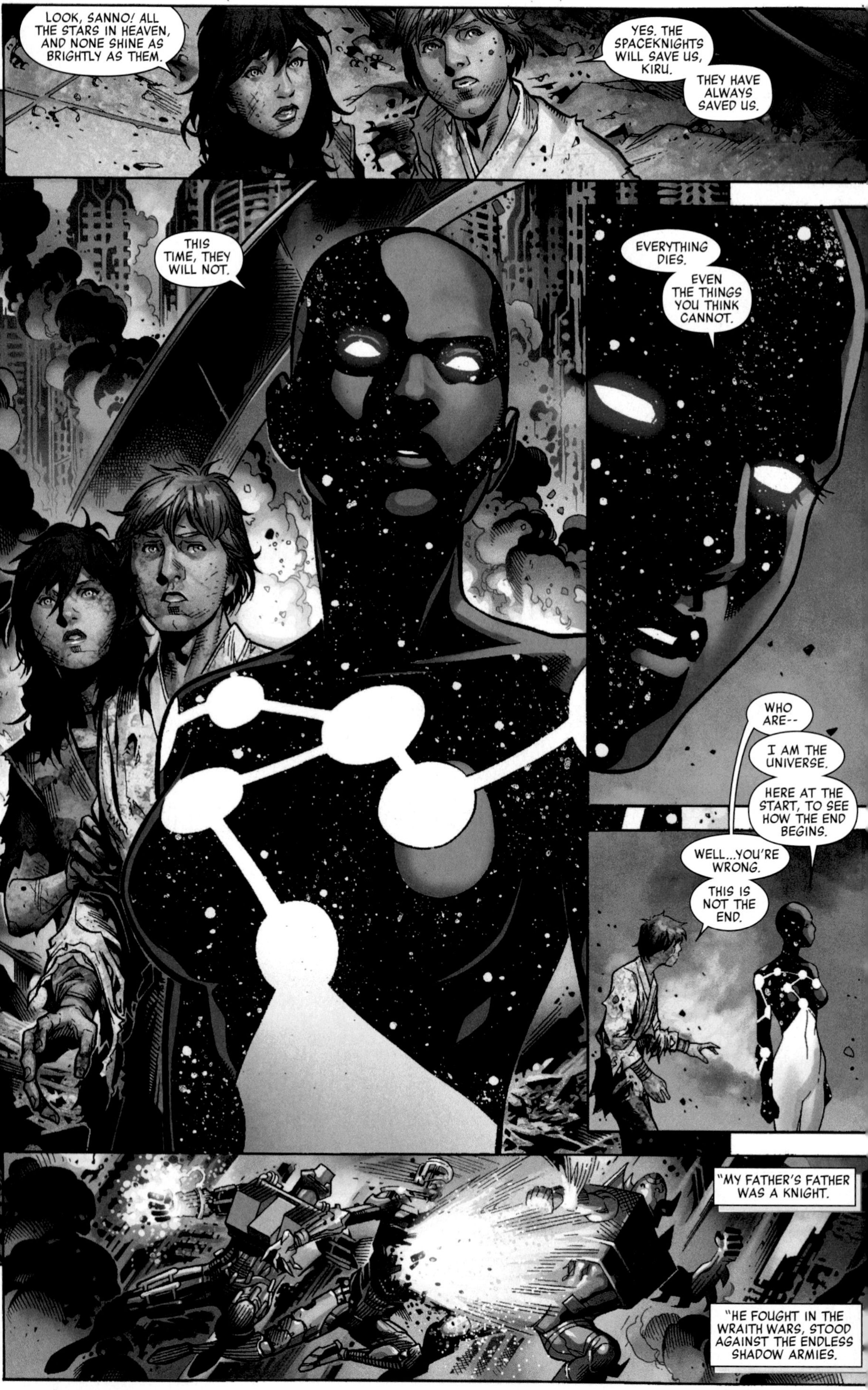

LOOK, SANNO! ALL THE STARS IN HEAVEN, AND NONE SHINE AS BRIGHTLY AS THEM.
YES. THE SPACEKNIGHTS WILL SAVE US, KIRU.
THEY HAVE ALWAYS SAVED US.
THIS TIME, THEY WILL NOT.
EVERYTHING DIES.
EVEN THE THINGS YOU THINK CANNOT.
WHO ARE--
I AM THE UNIVERSE.
HERE AT THE START, TO SEE HOW THE END BEGINS.
WELL...YOU'RE WRONG.
THIS IS NOT THE END.
"MY FATHER'S FATHER WAS A KNIGHT.
"HE FOUGHT IN THE WRAITH WARS, STOOD AGAINST THE ENDLESS SHADOW ARMIES.

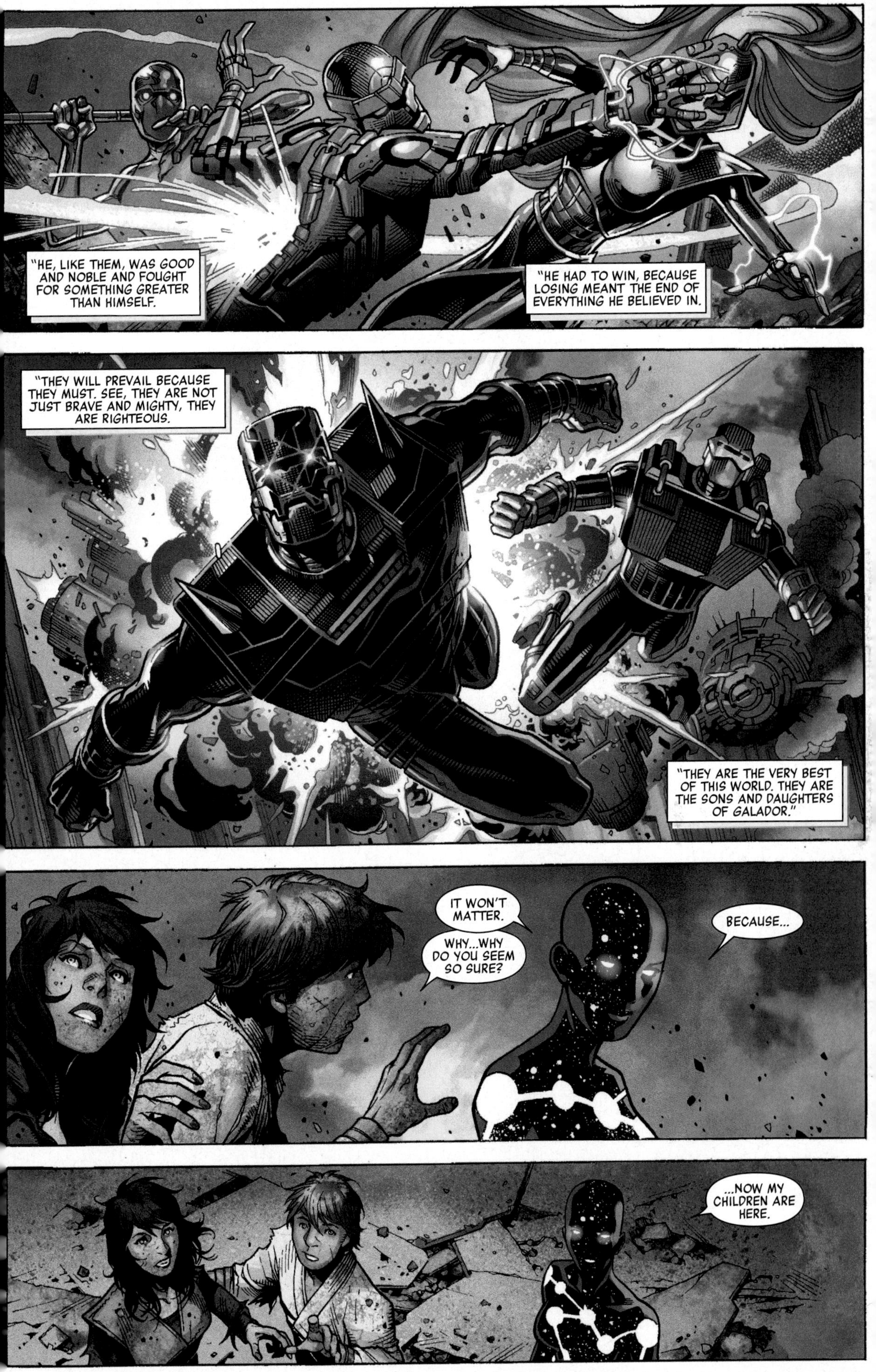
"HE, LIKE THEM, WAS GOOD AND NOBLE AND FOUGHT FOR SOMETHING GREATER THAN HIMSELF.
"HE HAD TO WIN, BECAUSE LOSING MEANT THE END OF EVERYTHING HE BELIEVED IN.
"THEY WILL PREVAIL BECAUSE THEY MUST. SEE, THEY ARE NOT JUST BRAVE AND MIGHTY, THEY ARE RIGHTEOUS.
"THEY ARE THE VERY BEST OF THIS WORLD. THEY ARE THE SONS AND DAUGHTERS OF GALADOR."
IT WON'T MATTER.
WHY...WHY DO YOU SEEM SO SURE?
BECAUSE...
...NOW MY CHILDREN ARE HERE.

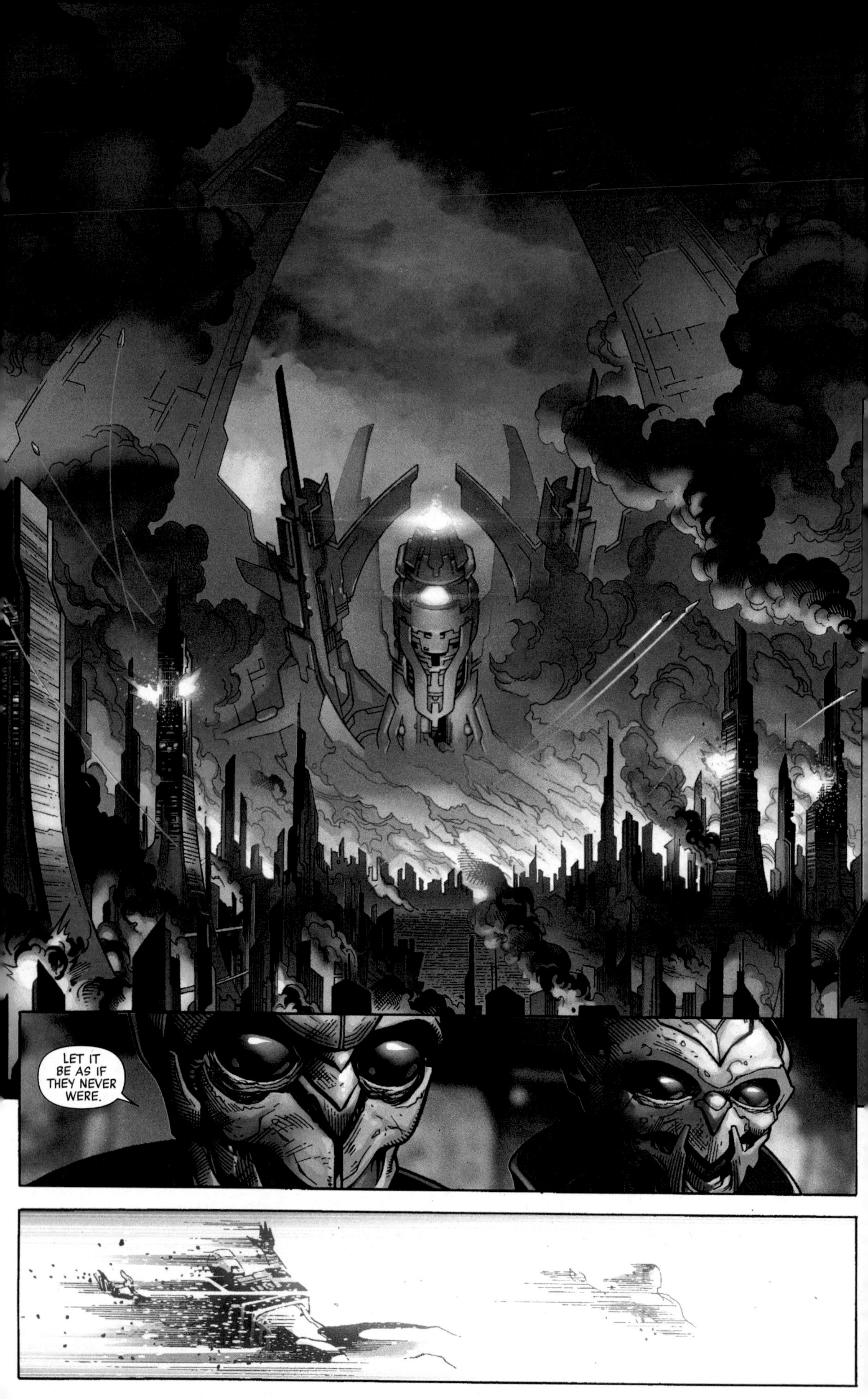
LET IT BE AS IF THEY NEVER WERE.

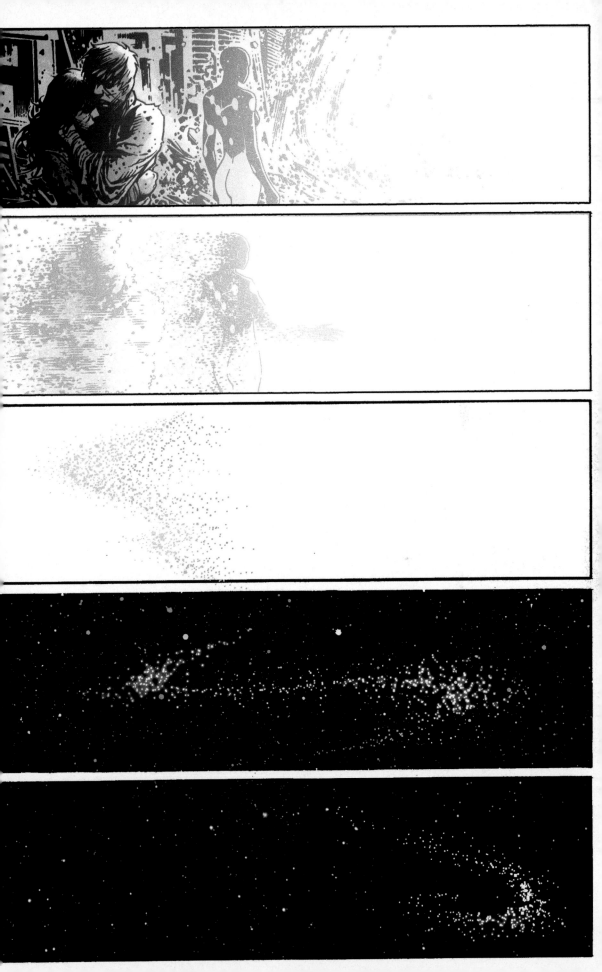

ORBITAL

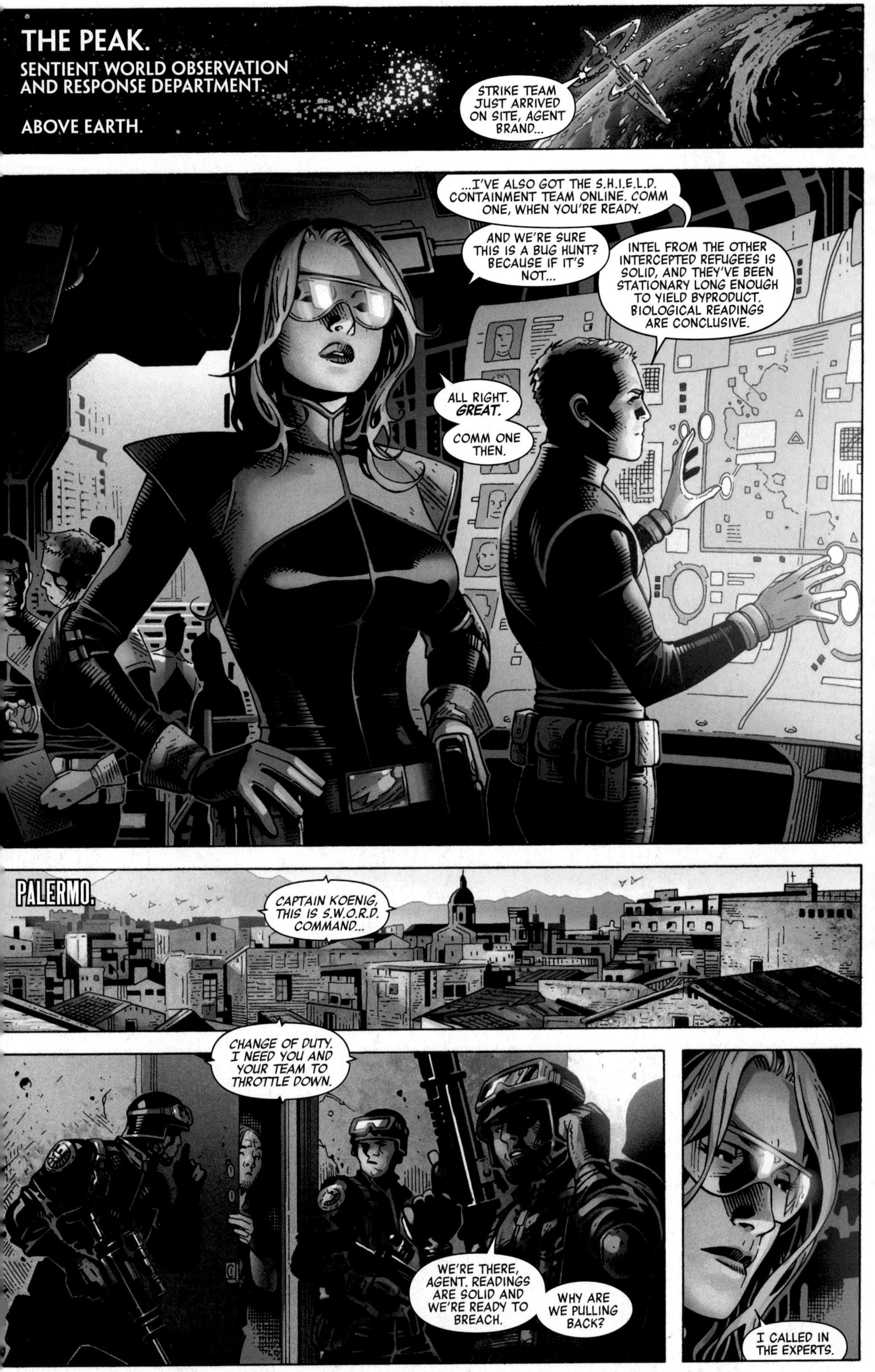
THE PEAK.
SENTIENT WORLD OBSERVATION AND RESPONSE DEPARTMENT.
ABOVE EARTH.
STRIKE TEAM JUST ARRIVED ON SITE, AGENT BRAND...
...I'VE ALSO GOT THE S.H.I.E.L.D. CONTAINMENT TEAM ONLINE. COMM ONE, WHEN YOU'RE READY.
AND WE'RE SURE THIS IS A BUG HUNT? BECAUSE IF IT'S NOT...
INTEL FROM THE OTHER INTERCEPTED REFUGEES IS SOLID, AND THEY'VE BEEN STATIONARY LONG ENOUGH TO YIELD BYPRODUCT. BIOLOGICAL READINGS ARE CONCLUSIVE.
ALL RIGHT. GREAT.
COMM ONE THEN.
PALERMO.
CAPTAIN KOENIG, THIS IS S.W.O.R.D. COMMAND...
CHANGE OF DUTY. I NEED YOU AND YOUR TEAM TO THROTTLE DOWN.
WE'RE THERE, AGENT. READINGS ARE SOLID AND WE'RE READY TO BREACH.
WHY ARE WE PULLING BACK?
I CALLED IN THE EXPERTS.

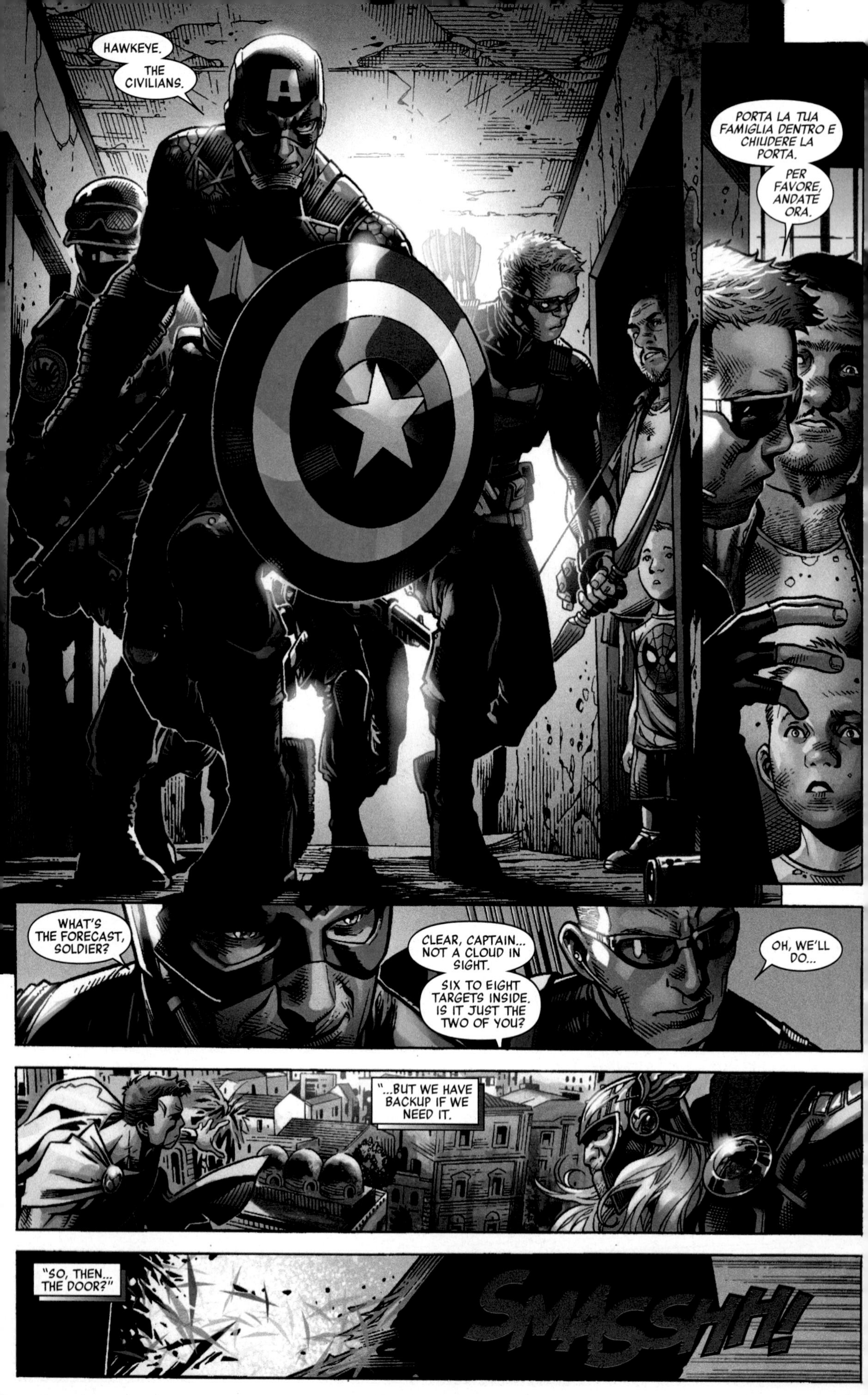
HAWKEYE.
THE CIVILIANS.
PORTA LA TUA FAMIGLIA DENTRO E CHIUDERE LA PORTA.
PER FAVORE, ANDATE ORA.
WHAT'S THE FORECAST, SOLDIER?
CLEAR, CAPTAIN... NOT A CLOUD IN SIGHT.
SIX TO EIGHT TARGETS INSIDE. IS IT JUST THE TWO OF YOU?
OH, WE'LL DO...
"...BUT WE HAVE BACKUP IF WE NEED IT.
"SO, THEN... THE DOOR?"
SMASHH!

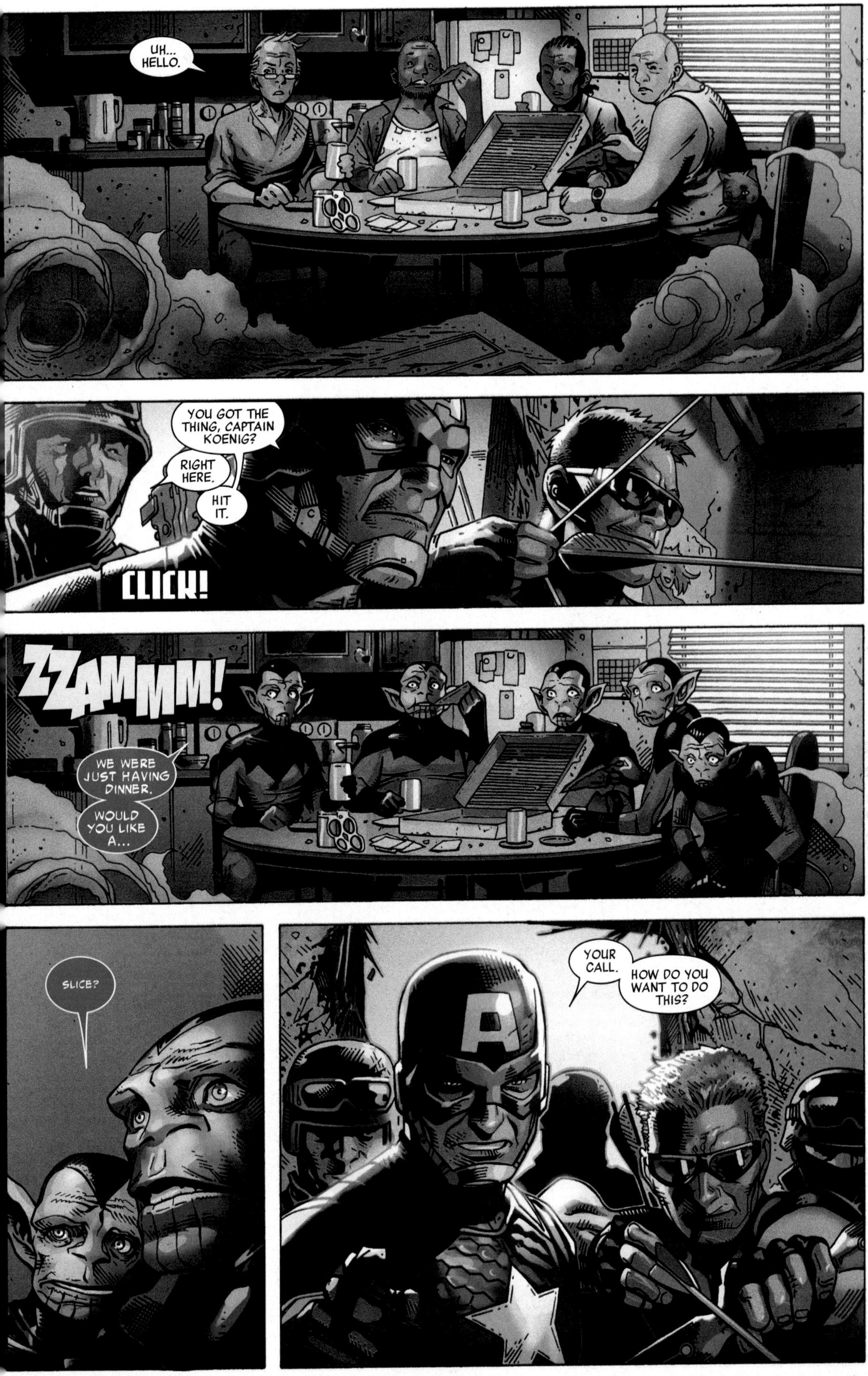
UH... HELLO.
YOU GOT THE THING, CAPTAIN KOENIG?
RIGHT HERE.
HIT IT.
CLICK!
ZZAMMMM!
WE WERE JUST HAVING DINNER.
WOULD YOU LIKE A...
SLICE?
YOUR CALL.
HOW DO YOU WANT TO DO THIS?

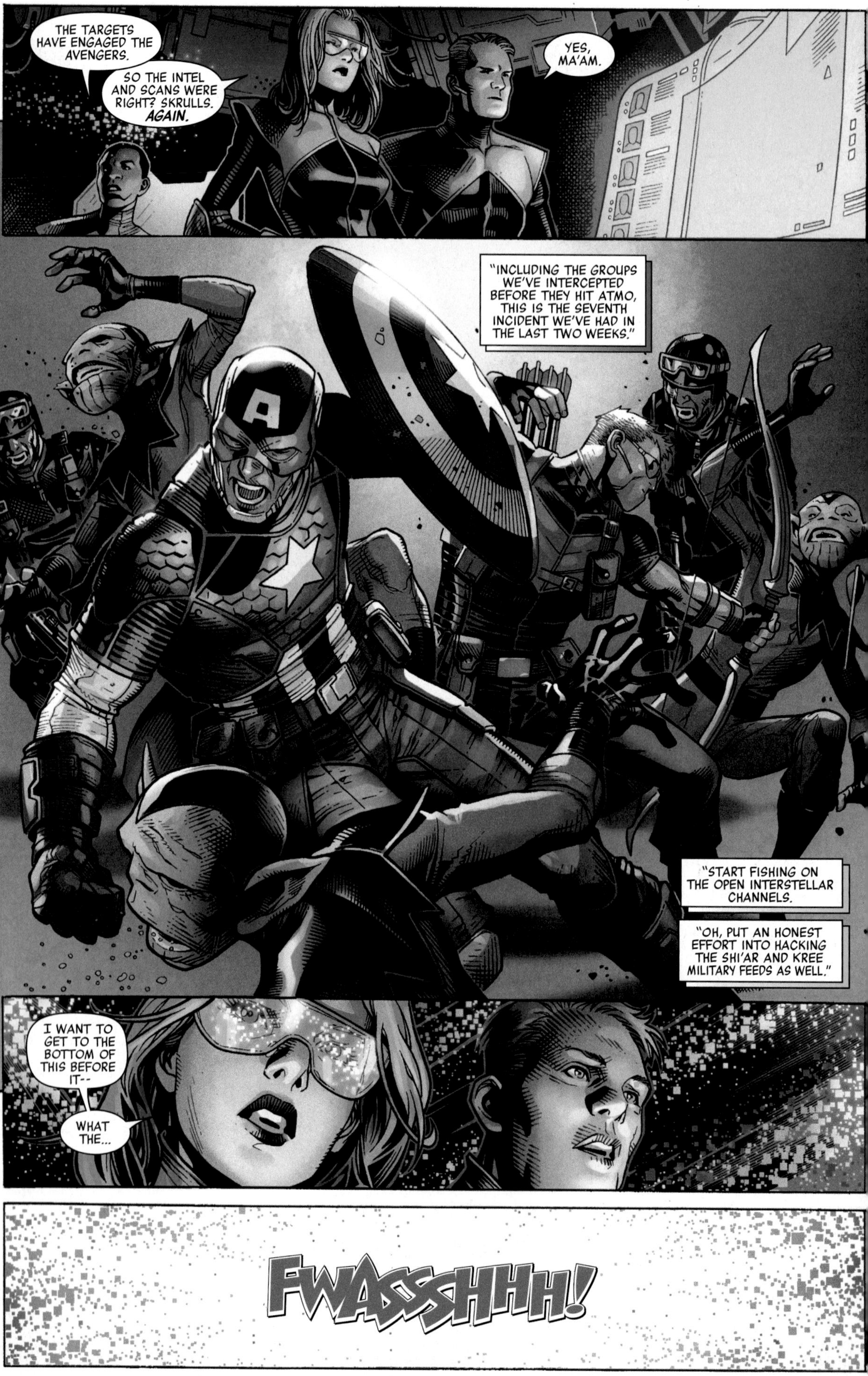

THE TARGETS HAVE ENGAGED THE AVENGERS.
SO THE INTEL AND SCANS WERE RIGHT? SKRULLS. AGAIN.
YES, MA'AM.
"INCLUDING THE GROUPS WE'VE INTERCEPTED BEFORE THEY HIT ATMO, THIS IS THE SEVENTH INCIDENT WE'VE HAD IN THE LAST TWO WEEKS."
"START FISHING ON THE OPEN INTERSTELLAR CHANNELS.
"OH, PUT AN HONEST EFFORT INTO HACKING THE SHI'AR AND KREE MILITARY FEEDS AS WELL."
I WANT TO GET TO THE BOTTOM OF THIS BEFORE IT--
WHAT THE...
FWASSHHH!

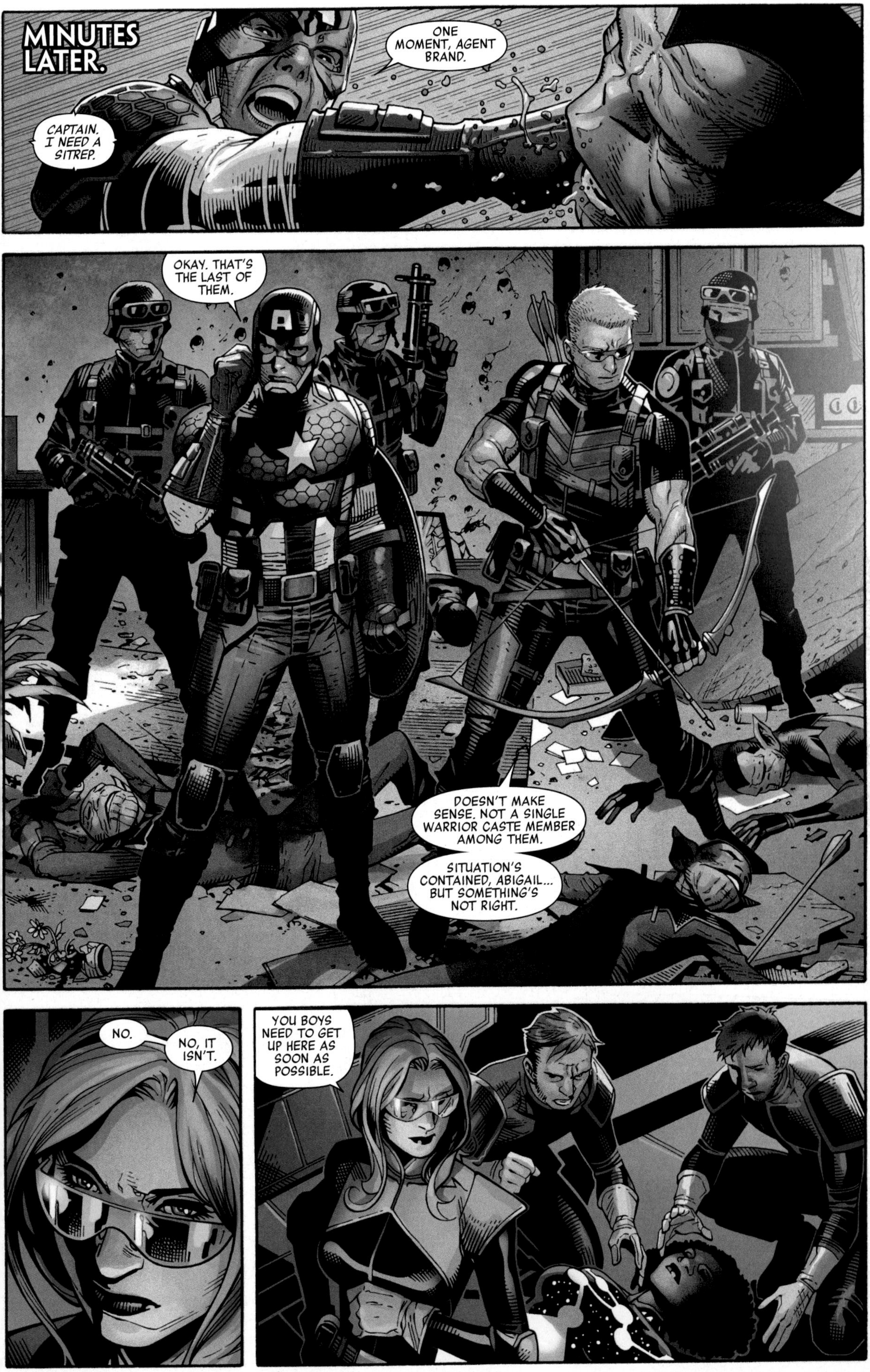
MINUTES LATER.
CAPTAIN. I NEED A SITREP.
ONE MOMENT, AGENT BRAND.
OKAY. THAT'S THE LAST OF THEM.
DOESN'T MAKE SENSE. NOT A SINGLE WARRIOR CASTE MEMBER AMONG THEM.
SITUATION'S CONTAINED, ABIGAIL... BUT SOMETHING'S NOT RIGHT.
NO.
NO, IT ISN'T.
YOU BOYS NEED TO GET UP HERE AS SOON AS POSSIBLE.

WHAT WAS HIDDEN, NOW UNCOVERED

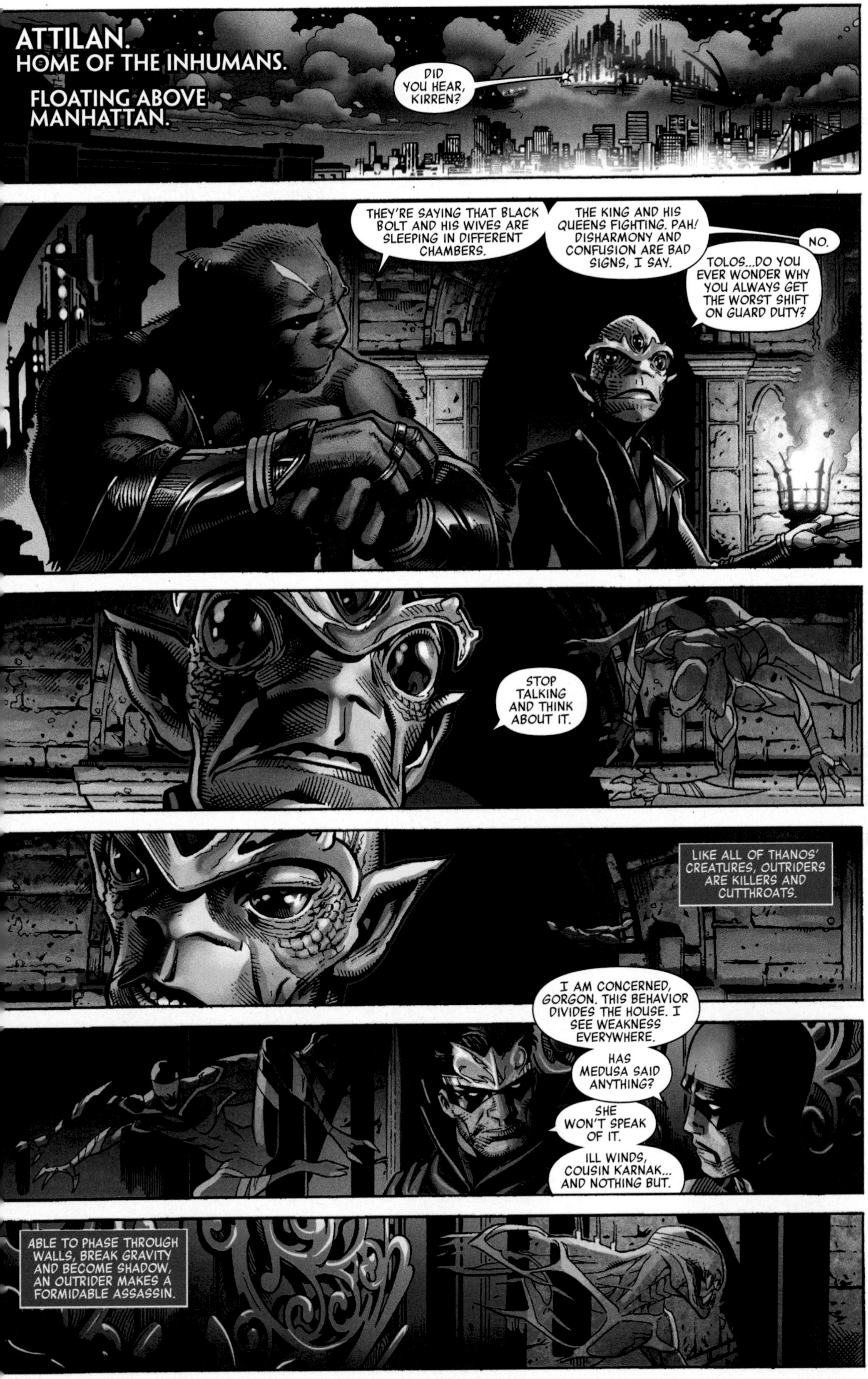
ATTILAN.
HOME OF THE INHUMANS.
FLOATING ABOVE MANHATTAN.
DID YOU HEAR, KIRREN?
THEY'RE SAYING THAT BLACK BOLT AND HIS WIVES ARE SLEEPING IN DIFFERENT CHAMBERS.
THE KING AND HIS QUEENS FIGHTING. PAH! DISHARMONY AND CONFUSION ARE BAD SIGNS, I SAY.
NO.
TOLOS...DO YOU EVER WONDER WHY YOU ALWAYS GET THE WORST SHIFT ON GUARD DUTY?
STOP TALKING AND THINK ABOUT IT.
LIKE ALL OF THANOS' CREATURES, OUTRIDERS ARE KILLERS AND CUTTHROATS.
I AM CONCERNED, GORGON. THIS BEHAVIOR DIVIDES THE HOUSE. I SEE WEAKNESS EVERYWHERE.
HAS MEDUSA SAID ANYTHING?
SHE WON'T SPEAK OF IT.
ILL WINDS, COUSIN KARNAK... AND NOTHING BUT.
ABLE TO PHASE THROUGH WALLS, BREAK GRAVITY AND BECOME SHADOW, AN OUTRIDER MAKES A FORMIDABLE ASSASSIN.

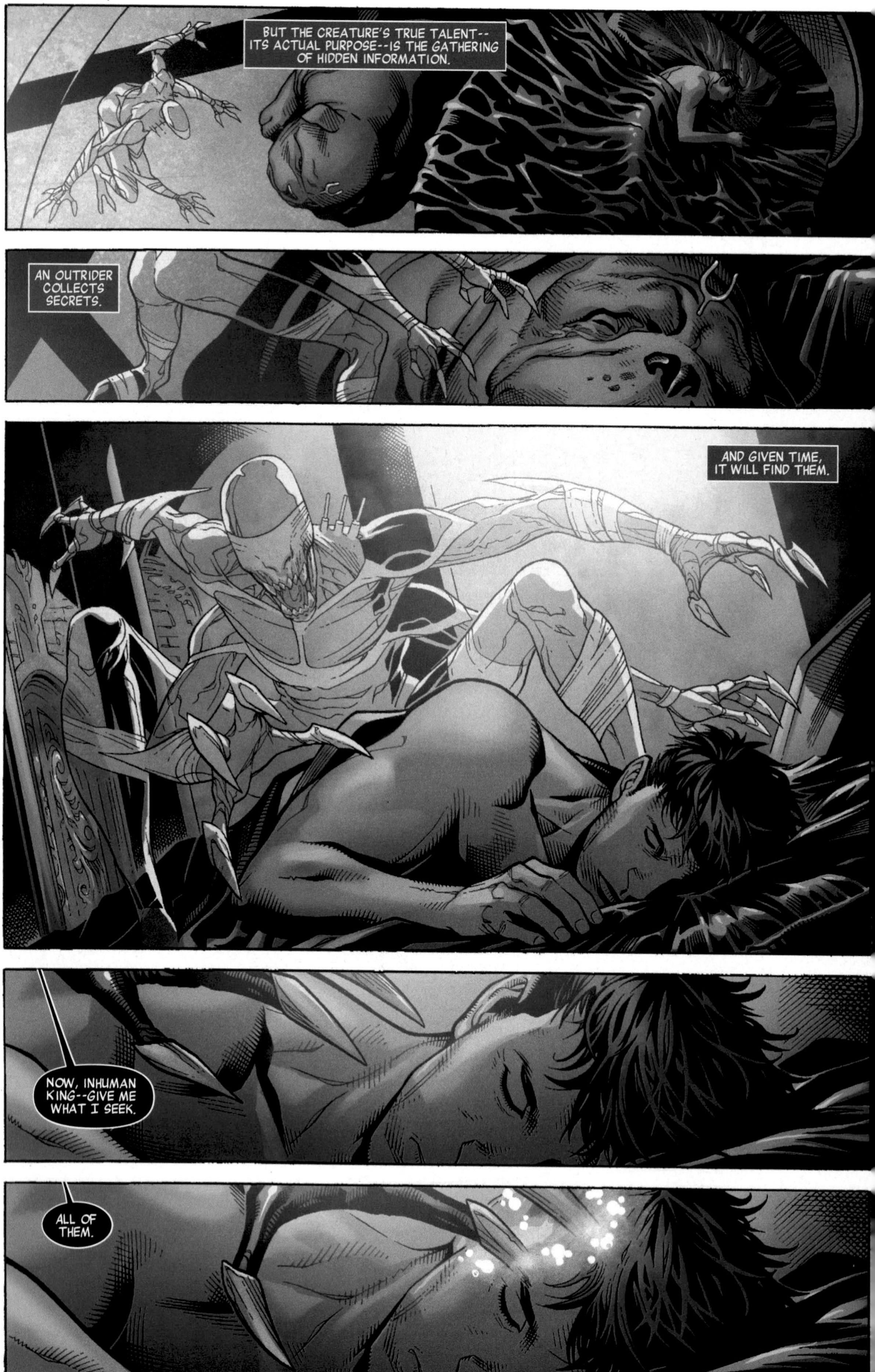
BUT THE CREATURE'S TRUE TALENT--ITS ACTUAL PURPOSE--IS THE GATHERING OF HIDDEN INFORMATION.
AN OUTRIDER COLLECTS SECRETS.
AND GIVEN TIME, IT WILL FIND THEM.
NOW, INHUMAN KING--GIVE ME WHAT I SEEK.
ALL OF THEM.

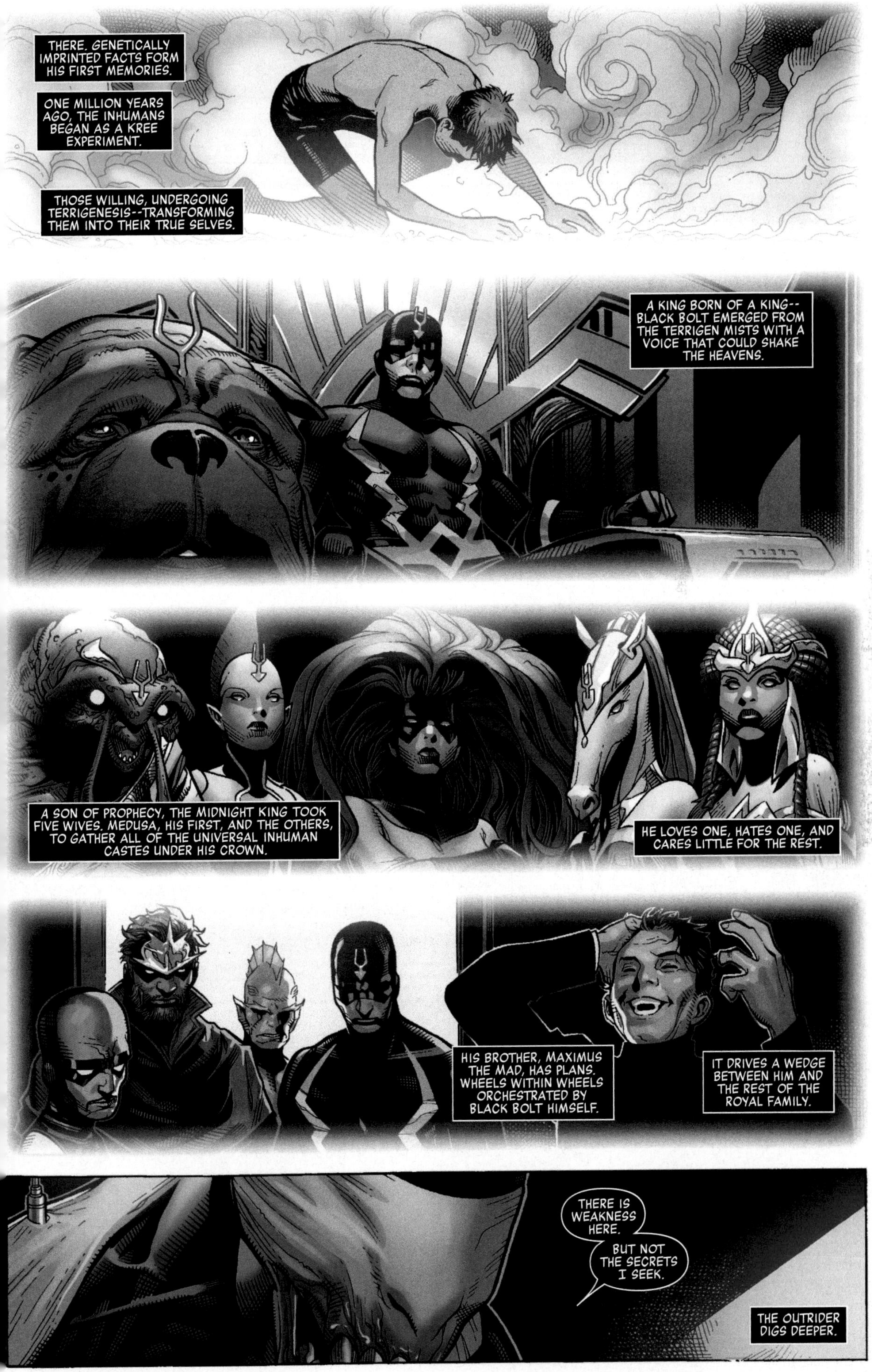

THERE. GENETICALLY IMPRINTED FACTS FORM HIS FIRST MEMORIES.
ONE MILLION YEARS AGO, THE INHUMANS BEGAN AS A KREE EXPERIMENT.
THOSE WILLING, UNDERGOING TERRIGENESIS--TRANSFORMING THEM INTO THEIR TRUE SELVES.
A KING BORN OF A KING--BLACK BOLT EMERGED FROM THE TERRIGEN MISTS WITH A VOICE THAT COULD SHAKE THE HEAVENS.
A SON OF PROPHECY, THE MIDNIGHT KING TOOK FIVE WIVES. MEDUSA, HIS FIRST, AND THE OTHERS, TO GATHER ALL OF THE UNIVERSAL INHUMAN CASTES UNDER HIS CROWN.
HE LOVES ONE, HATES ONE, AND CARES LITTLE FOR THE REST.
HIS BROTHER, MAXIMUS THE MAD, HAS PLANS. WHEELS WITHIN WHEELS ORCHESTRATED BY BLACK BOLT HIMSELF.
IT DRIVES A WEDGE BETWEEN HIM AND THE REST OF THE ROYAL FAMILY.
THERE IS WEAKNESS HERE.
BUT NOT THE SECRETS I SEEK.
THE OUTRIDER DIGS DEEPER.

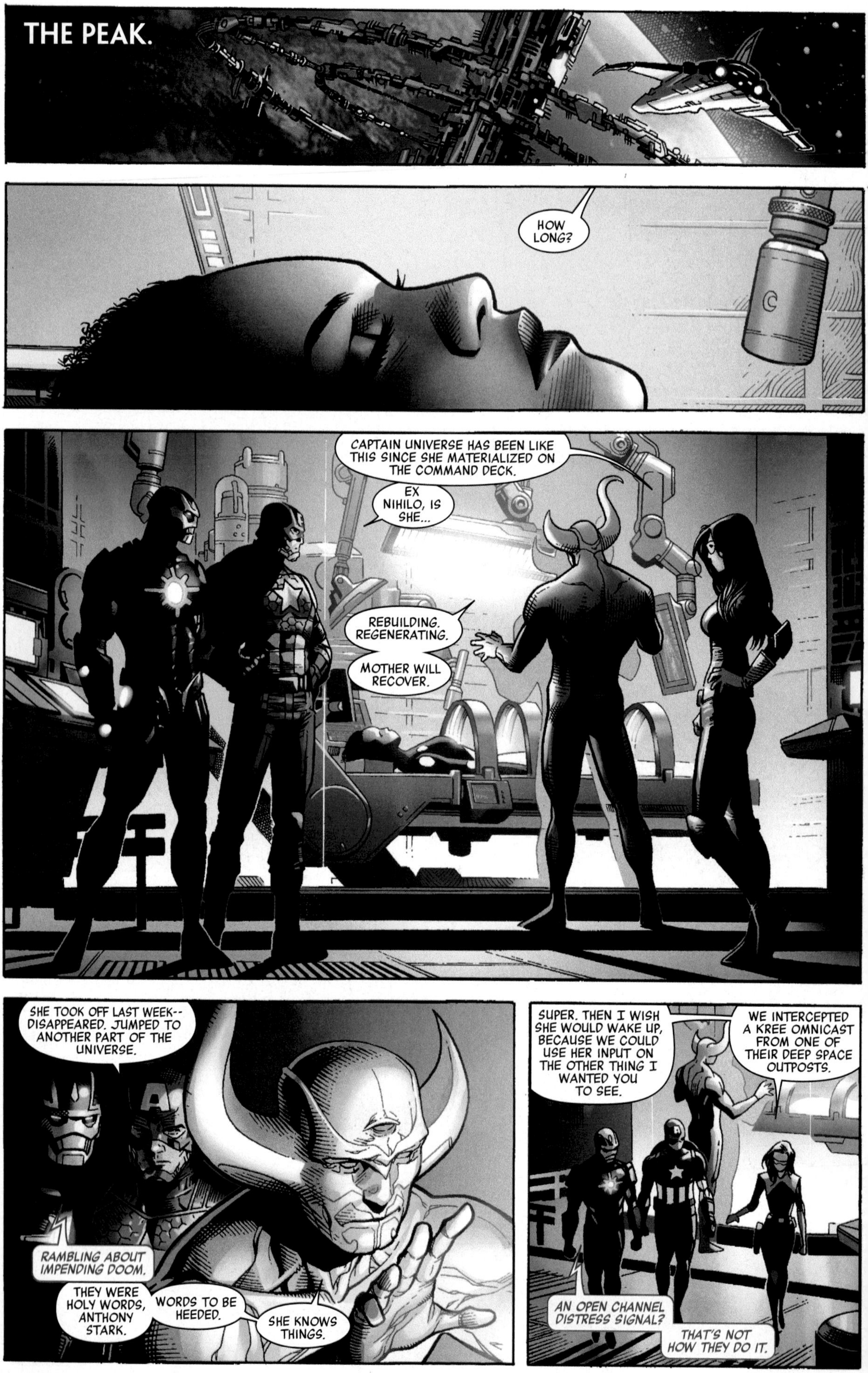
THE PEAK.
HOW LONG?
CAPTAIN UNIVERSE HAS BEEN LIKE THIS SINCE SHE MATERIALIZED ON THE COMMAND DECK.
EX NIHILO, IS SHE...
REBUILDING. REGENERATING.
MOTHER WILL RECOVER.
SHE TOOK OFF LAST WEEK-- DISAPPEARED. JUMPED TO ANOTHER PART OF THE UNIVERSE.
RAMBLING ABOUT IMPENDING DOOM.
THEY WERE HOLY WORDS, ANTHONY STARK.
WORDS TO BE HEEDED.
SHE KNOWS THINGS.
SUPER. THEN I WISH SHE WOULD WAKE UP, BECAUSE WE COULD USE HER INPUT ON THE OTHER THING I WANTED YOU TO SEE.
WE INTERCEPTED A KREE OMNICAST FROM ONE OF THEIR DEEP SPACE OUTPOSTS.
AN OPEN CHANNEL DISTRESS SIGNAL?
THAT'S NOT HOW THEY DO IT.

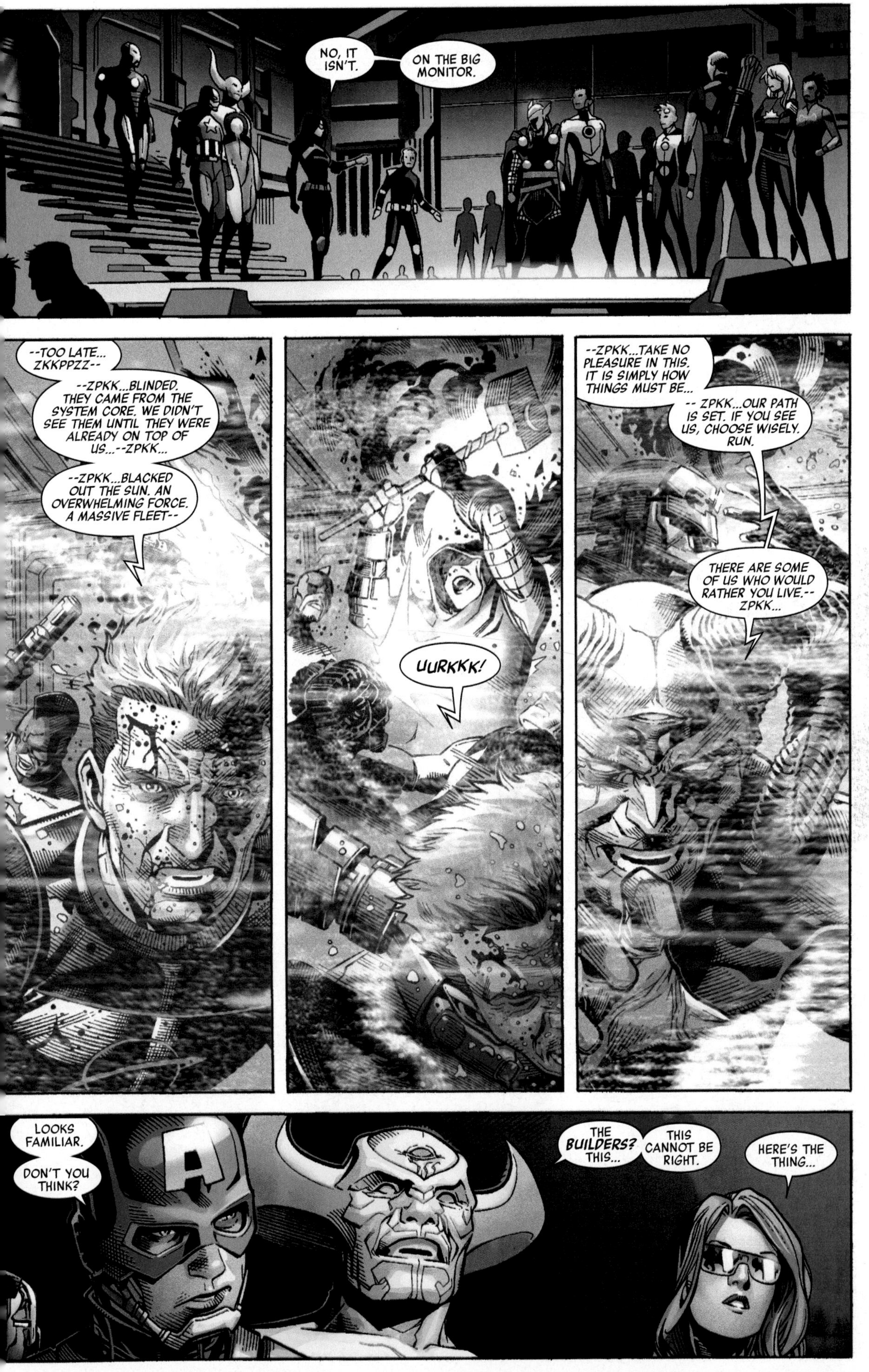
NO, IT ISN'T.
ON THE BIG MONITOR.
--TOO LATE... ZKKPPZZ--
--ZPKK...BLINDED. THEY CAME FROM THE SYSTEM CORE. WE DIDN'T SEE THEM UNTIL THEY WERE ALREADY ON TOP OF US...--ZPKK...
--ZPKK...BLACKED OUT THE SUN. AN OVERWHELMING FORCE. A MASSIVE FLEET--
UURKKK!
--ZPKK...TAKE NO PLEASURE IN THIS. IT IS SIMPLY HOW THINGS MUST BE...
-- ZPKK...OUR PATH IS SET. IF YOU SEE US, CHOOSE WISELY. RUN.
THERE ARE SOME OF US WHO WOULD RATHER YOU LIVE.--ZPKK...
LOOKS FAMILIAR.
DON'T YOU THINK?
THE BUILDERS? THIS...
THIS CANNOT BE RIGHT.
HERE'S THE THING...

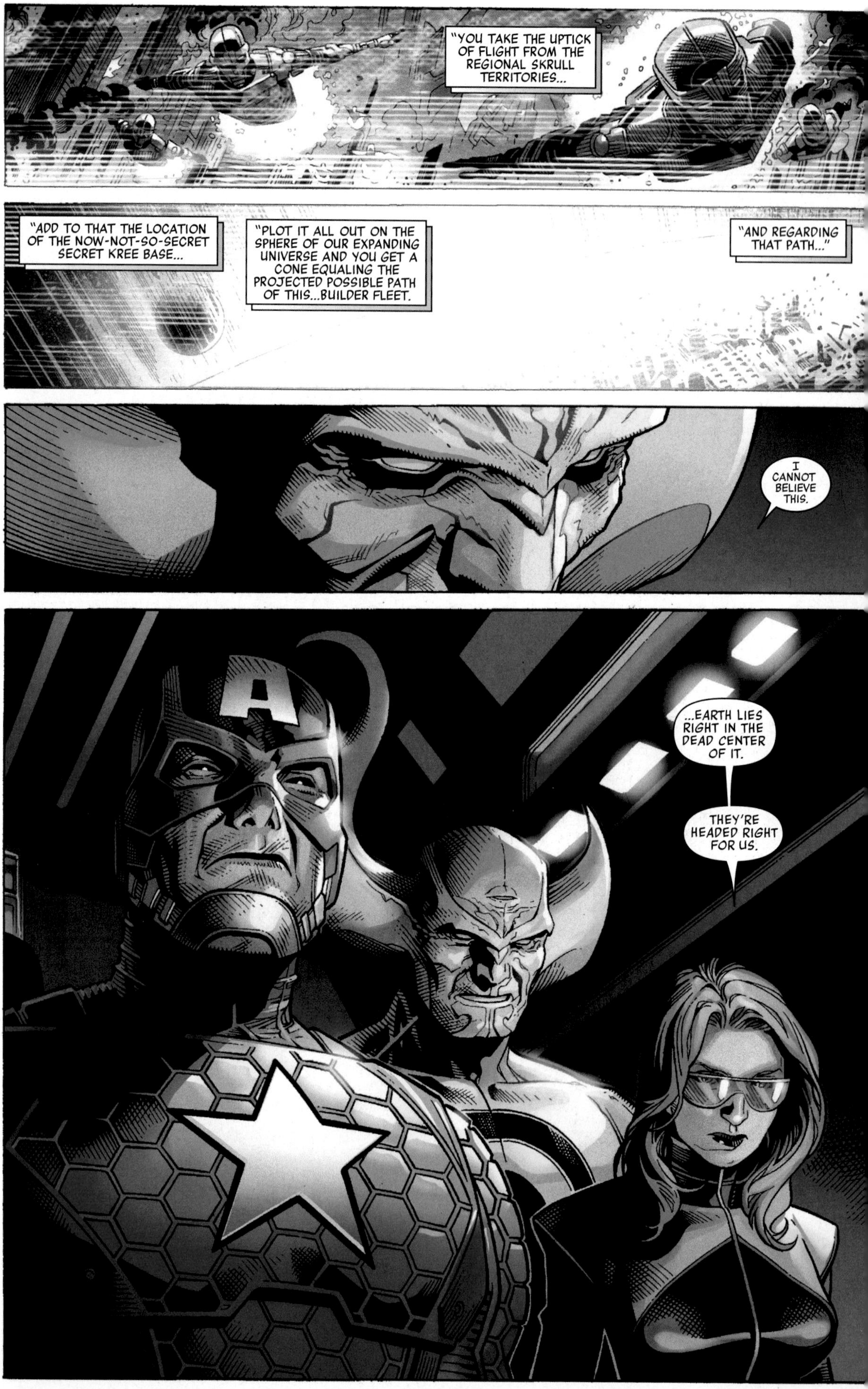
"YOU TAKE THE UPTICK OF FLIGHT FROM THE REGIONAL SKRULL TERRITORIES...
"ADD TO THAT THE LOCATION OF THE NOW-NOT-SO-SECRET SECRET KREE BASE...
"PLOT IT ALL OUT ON THE SPHERE OF OUR EXPANDING UNIVERSE AND YOU GET A CONE EQUALING THE PROJECTED POSSIBLE PATH OF THIS...BUILDER FLEET.
"AND REGARDING THAT PATH..."
I CANNOT BELIEVE THIS.
...EARTH LIES RIGHT IN THE DEAD CENTER OF IT.
THEY'RE HEADED RIGHT FOR US.

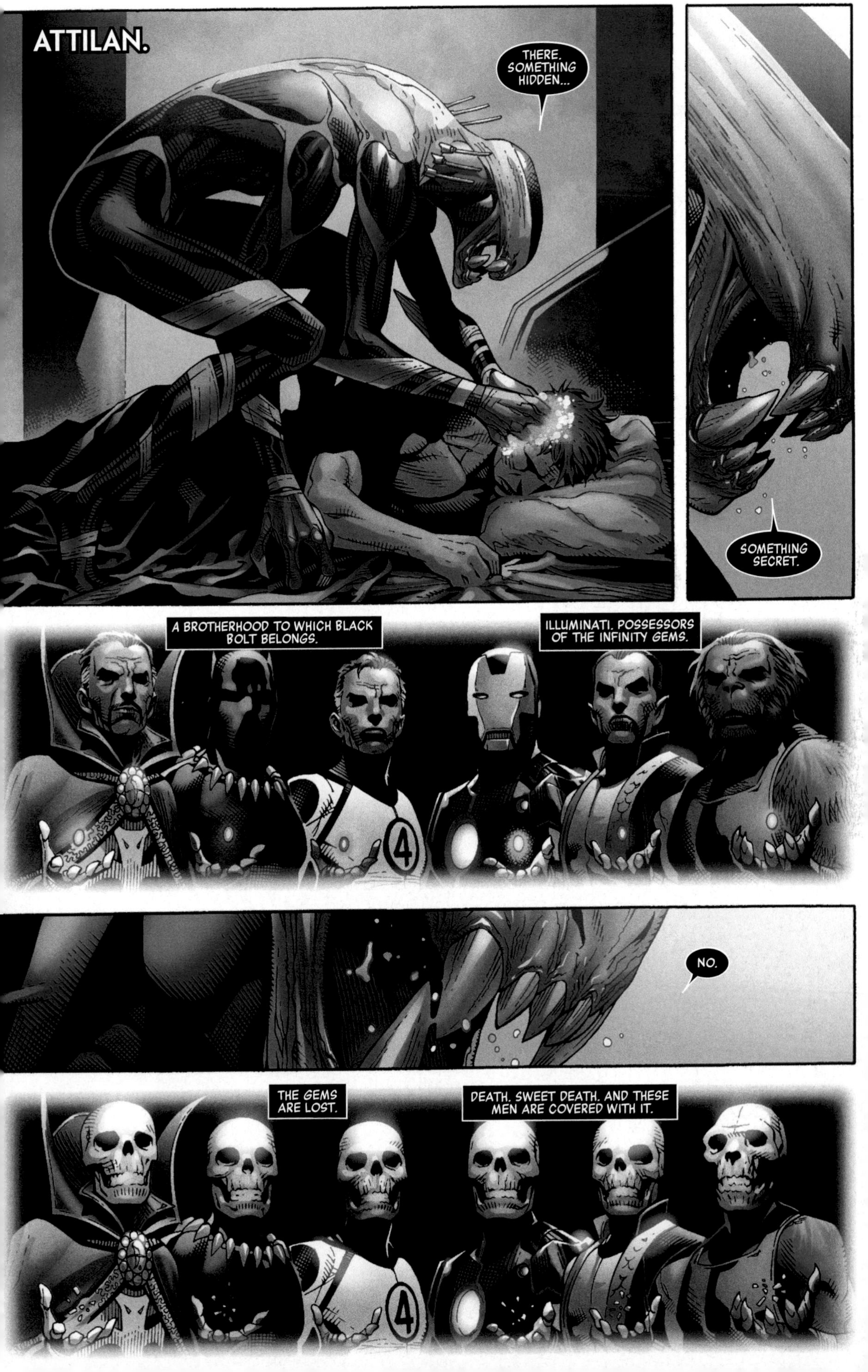
ATTILAN.
THERE. SOMETHING HIDDEN...
SOMETHING SECRET.
A BROTHERHOOD TO WHICH BLACK BOLT BELONGS.
ILLUMINATI. POSSESSORS OF THE INFINITY GEMS.
NO.
THE GEMS ARE LOST.
DEATH. SWEET DEATH. AND THESE MEN ARE COVERED WITH IT.

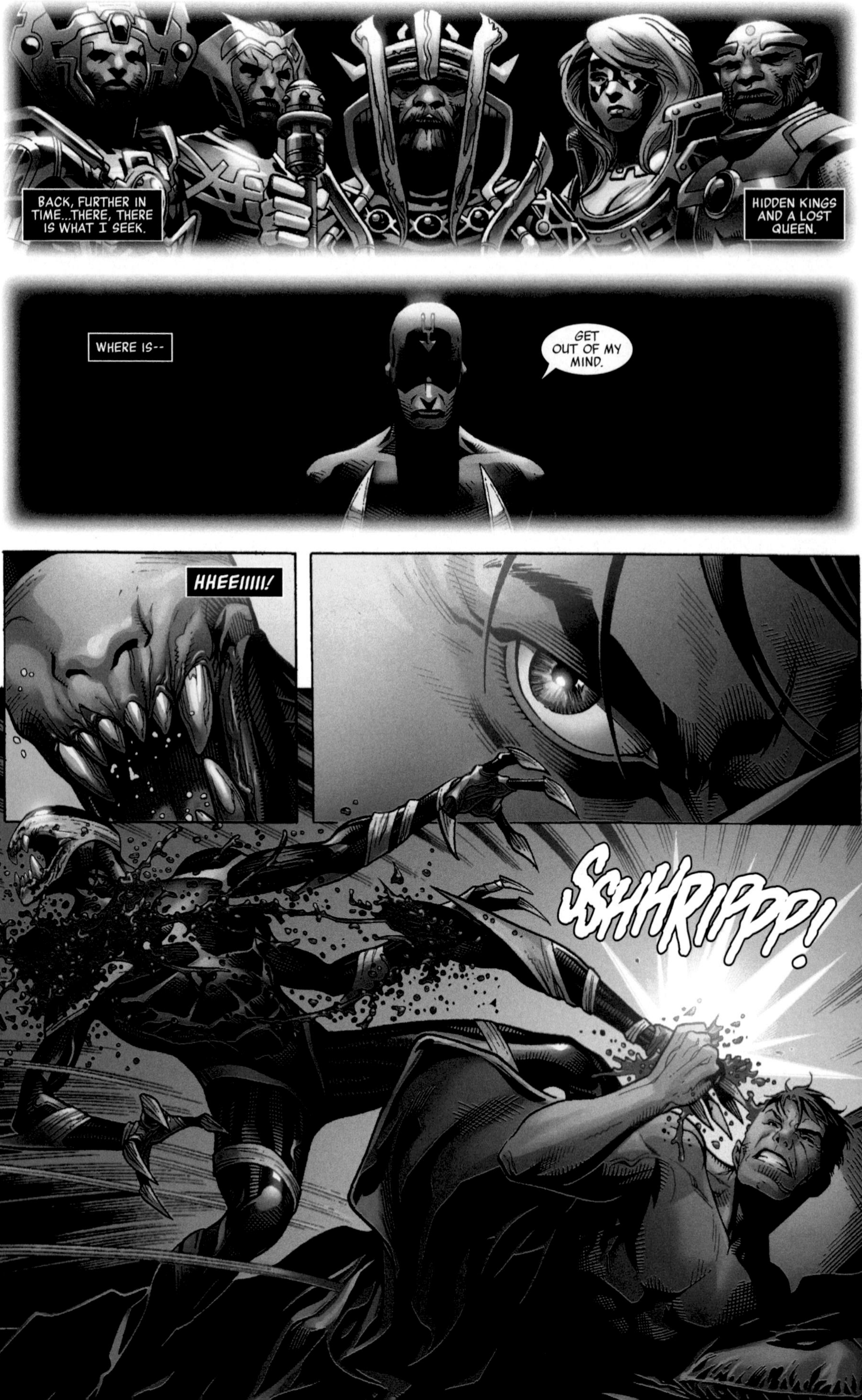
BACK, FURTHER IN TIME...THERE, THERE IS WHAT I SEEK.
HIDDEN KINGS AND A LOST QUEEN.
WHERE IS--
GET OUT OF MY MIND.
HHEEIIIII!
SSHHRIPPP!

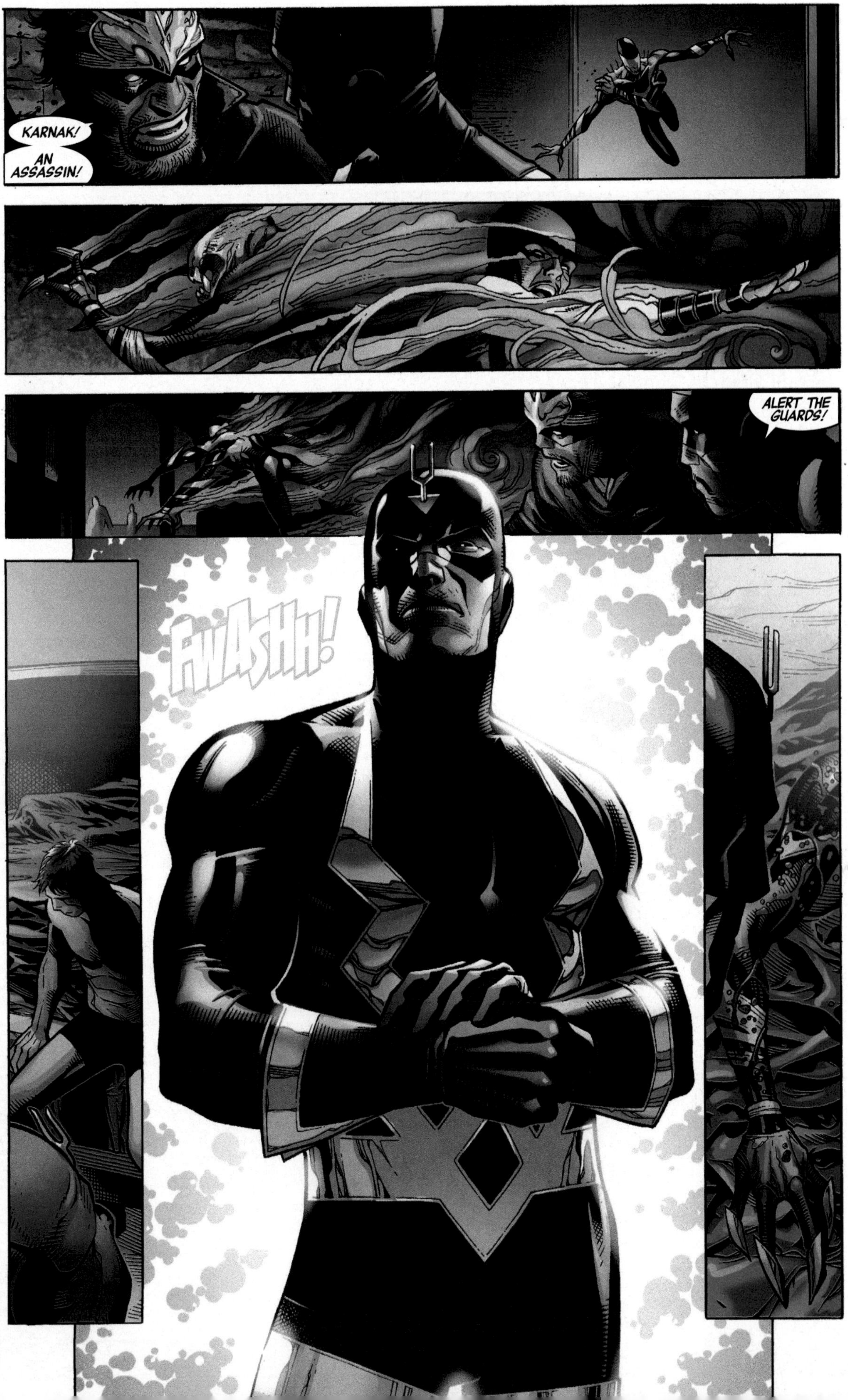
KARNAK!
AN ASSASSIN!
ALERT THE GUARDS!
FWASHH!

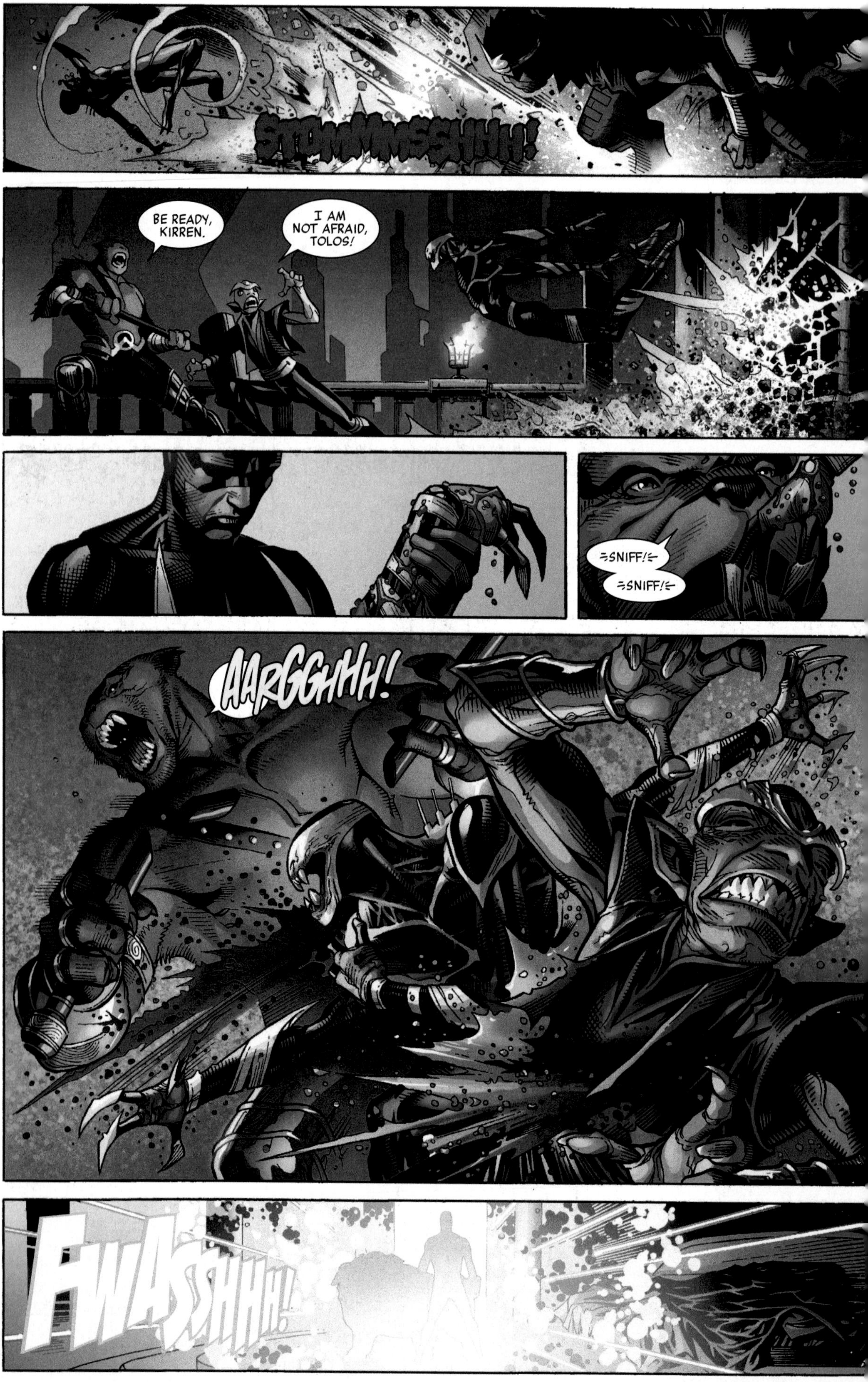

STOMMMSSHHH!
BE READY, KIRREN.
I AM NOT AFRAID, TOLOS!
=SNIFF!=
=SNIFF!=
AARGGHHH!
FWASSHHH!

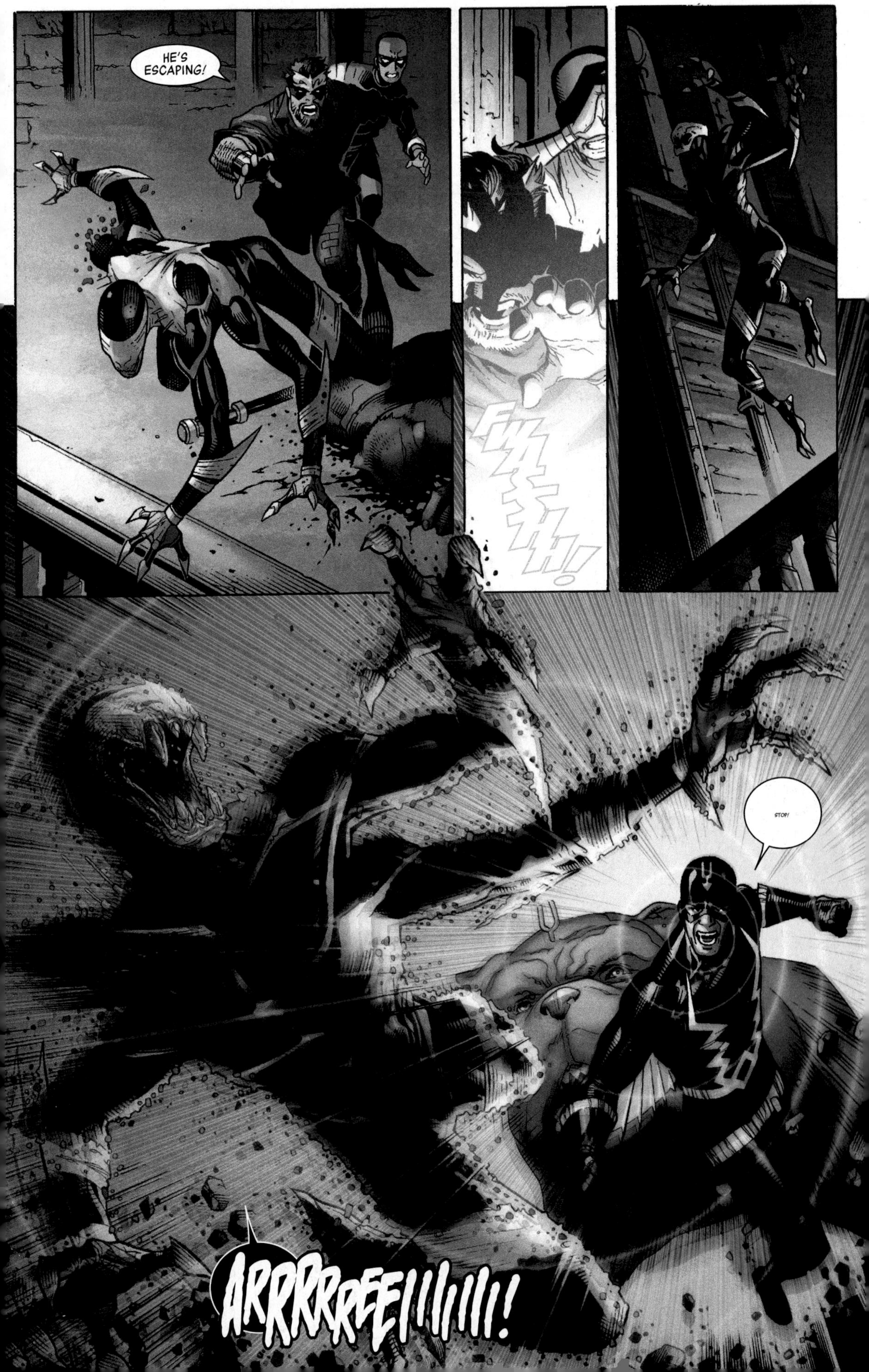
HE'S ESCAPING!
FWASSHH!
STOP!
ARRRRREEIIIIIII!

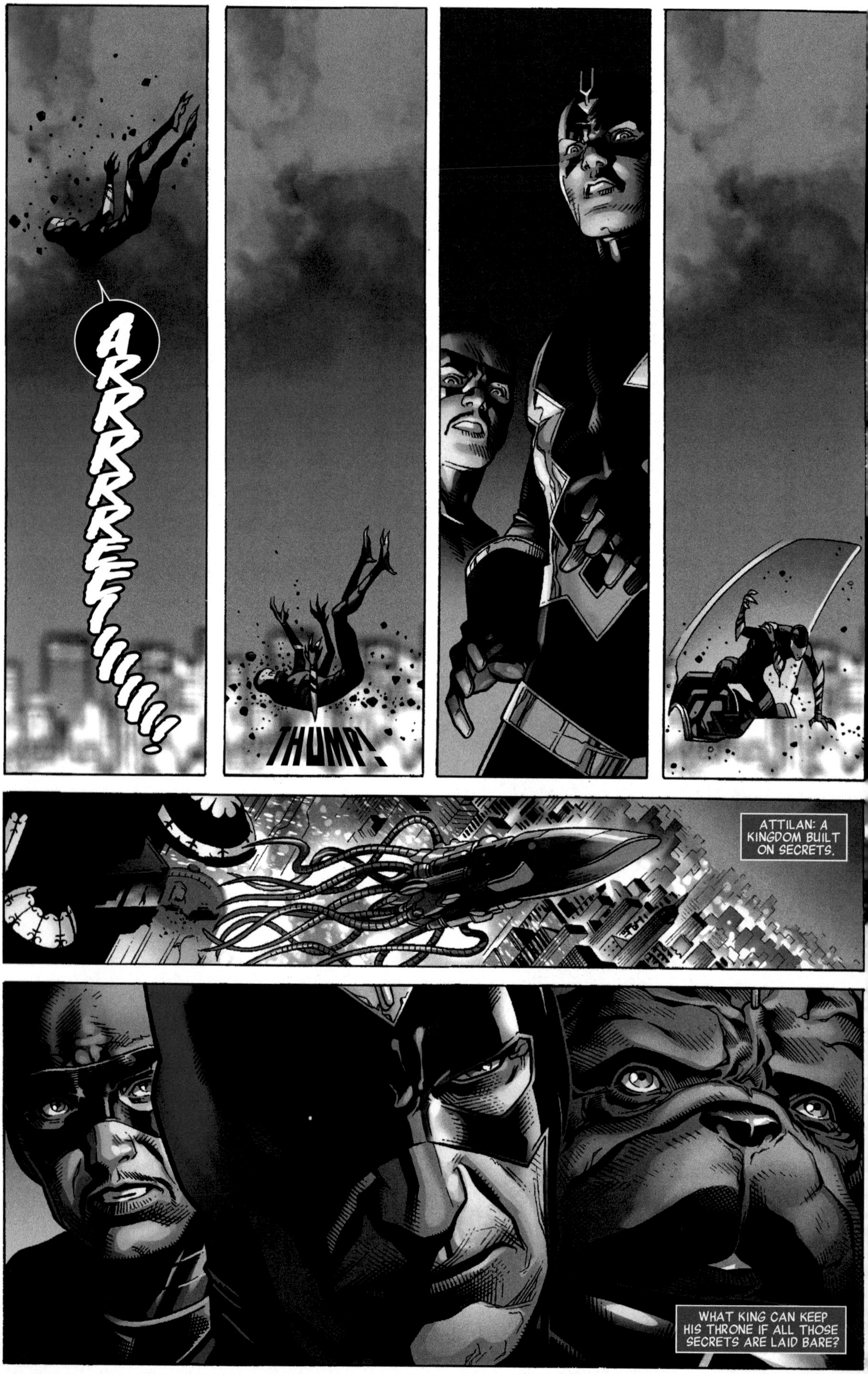
ARRRRREE!!!!!!!!!
THUMP!
ATTILAN: A KINGDOM BUILT ON SECRETS.
WHAT KING CAN KEEP HIS THRONE IF ALL THOSE SECRETS ARE LAID BARE?

OUTBOUND

◆

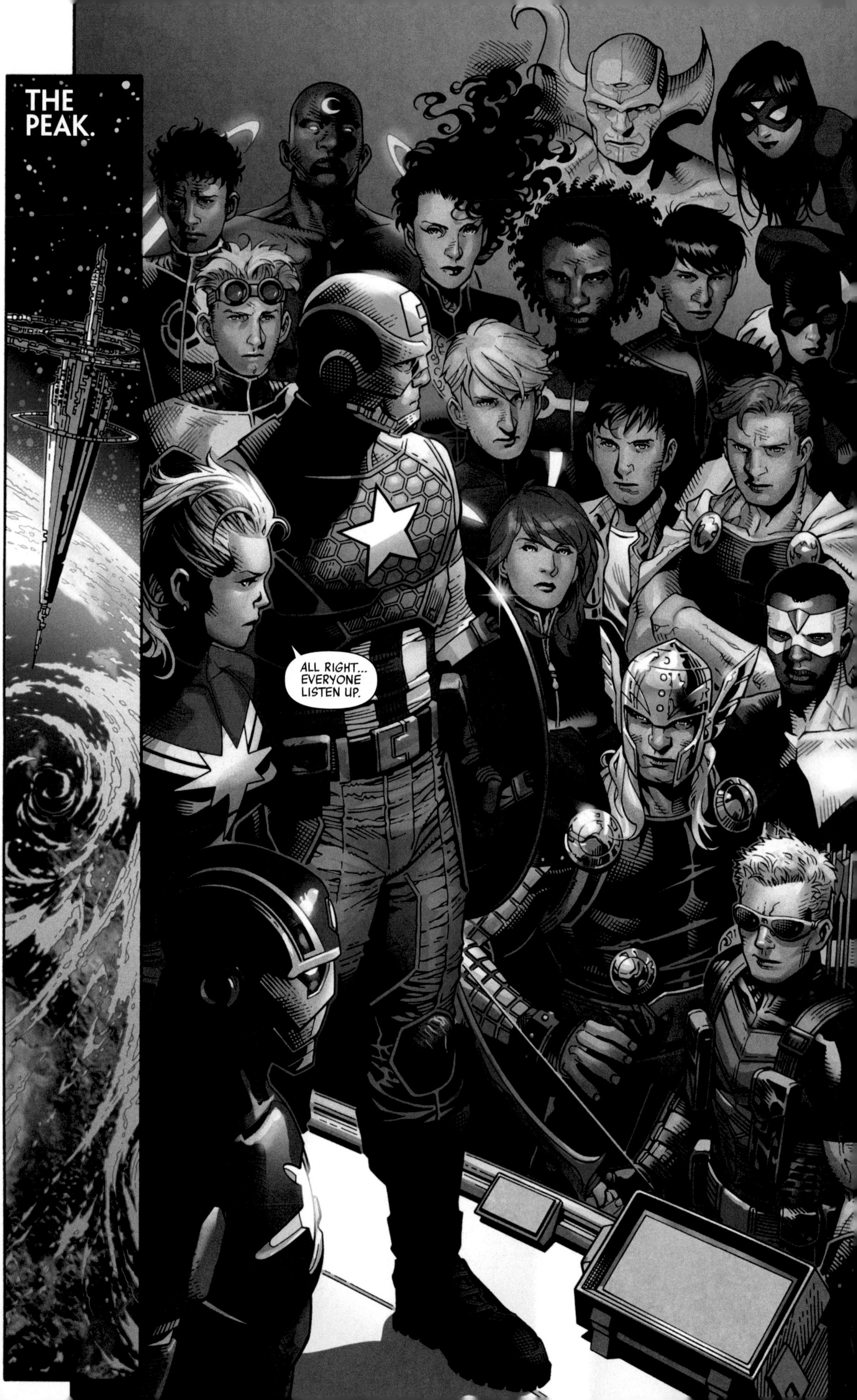
THE PEAK.
ALL RIGHT... EVERYONE LISTEN UP.

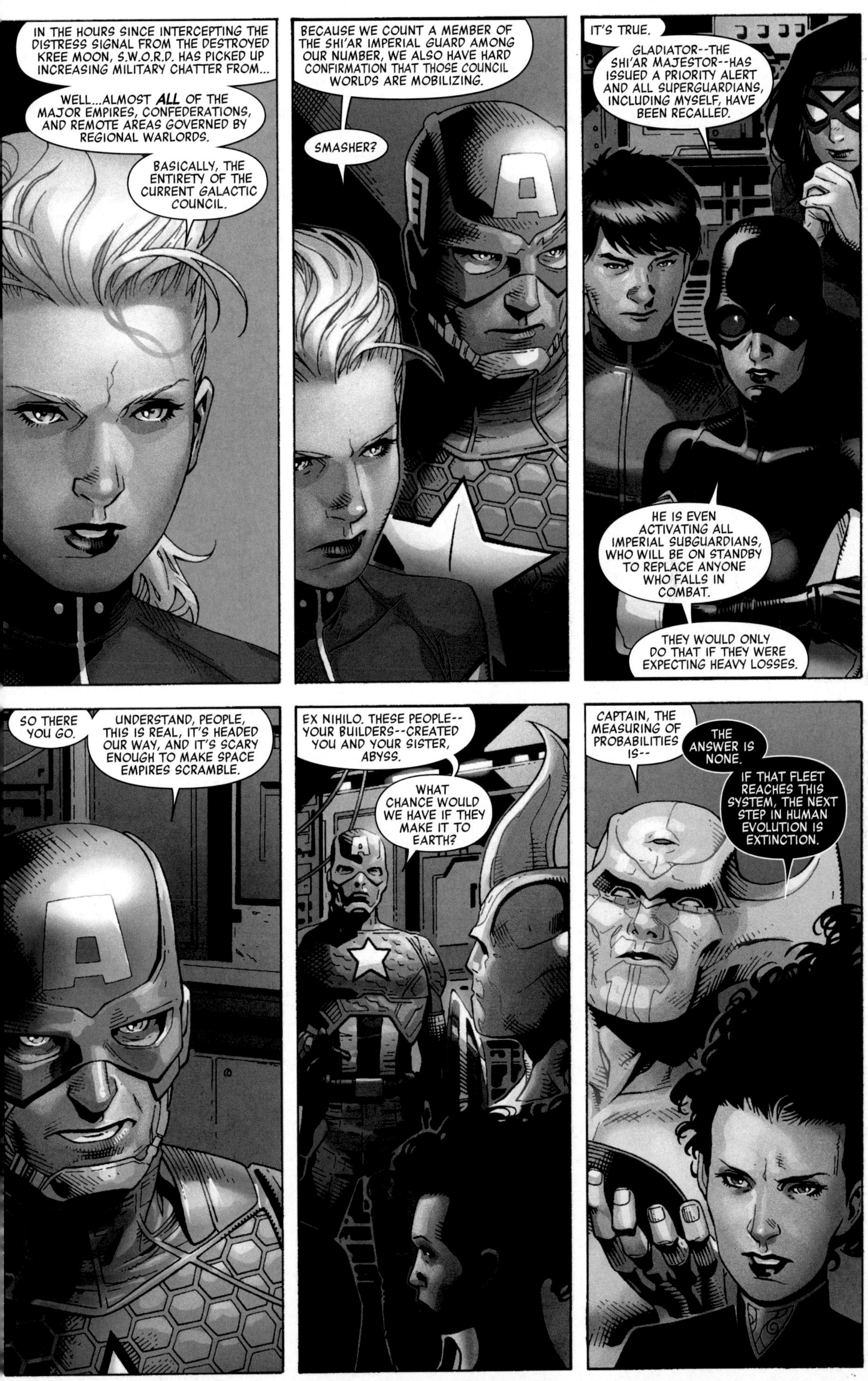

IN THE HOURS SINCE INTERCEPTING THE DISTRESS SIGNAL FROM THE DESTROYED KREE MOON, S.W.O.R.D. HAS PICKED UP INCREASING MILITARY CHATTER FROM...
WELL...ALMOST **ALL** OF THE MAJOR EMPIRES, CONFEDERATIONS, AND REMOTE AREAS GOVERNED BY REGIONAL WARLORDS.
BASICALLY, THE ENTIRETY OF THE CURRENT GALACTIC COUNCIL.
BECAUSE WE COUNT A MEMBER OF THE SHI'AR IMPERIAL GUARD AMONG OUR NUMBER, WE ALSO HAVE HARD CONFIRMATION THAT THOSE COUNCIL WORLDS ARE MOBILIZING.
SMASHER?
IT'S TRUE.
GLADIATOR--THE SHI'AR MAJESTOR--HAS ISSUED A PRIORITY ALERT AND ALL SUPERGUARDIANS, INCLUDING MYSELF, HAVE BEEN RECALLED.
HE IS EVEN ACTIVATING ALL IMPERIAL SUBGUARDIANS, WHO WILL BE ON STANDBY TO REPLACE ANYONE WHO FALLS IN COMBAT.
THEY WOULD ONLY DO THAT IF THEY WERE EXPECTING HEAVY LOSSES.
SO THERE YOU GO.
UNDERSTAND, PEOPLE, THIS IS REAL, IT'S HEADED OUR WAY, AND IT'S SCARY ENOUGH TO MAKE SPACE EMPIRES SCRAMBLE.
EX NIHILO. THESE PEOPLE-- YOUR BUILDERS--CREATED YOU AND YOUR SISTER, ABYSS.
WHAT CHANCE WOULD WE HAVE IF THEY MAKE IT TO EARTH?
CAPTAIN, THE MEASURING OF PROBABILITIES IS--
THE ANSWER IS NONE.
IF THAT FLEET REACHES THIS SYSTEM, THE NEXT STEP IN HUMAN EVOLUTION IS EXTINCTION.

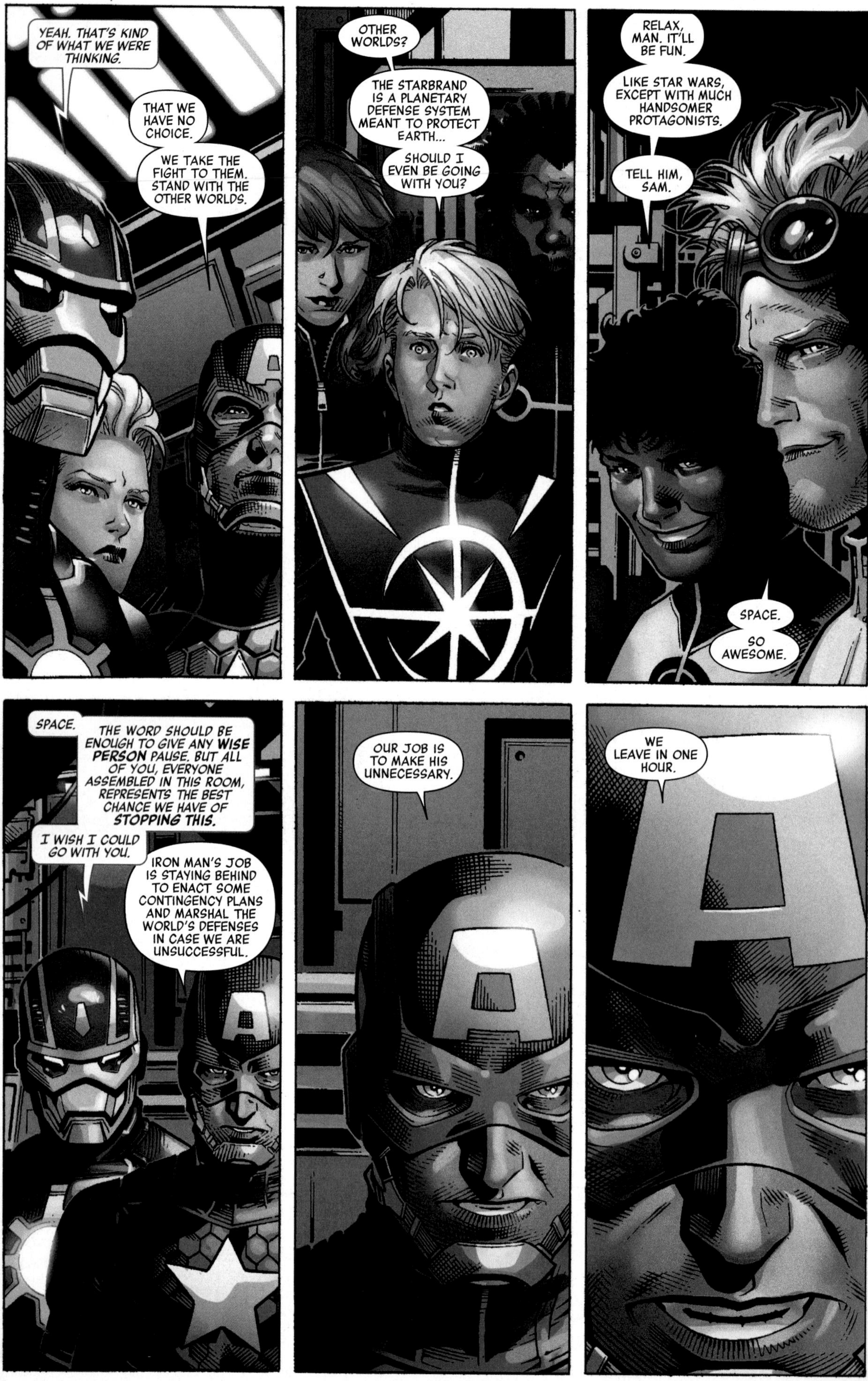

YEAH. THAT'S KIND OF WHAT WE WERE THINKING.
THAT WE HAVE NO CHOICE.
WE TAKE THE FIGHT TO THEM. STAND WITH THE OTHER WORLDS.
OTHER WORLDS?
THE STARBRAND IS A PLANETARY DEFENSE SYSTEM MEANT TO PROTECT EARTH...
SHOULD I EVEN BE GOING WITH YOU?
RELAX, MAN. IT'LL BE FUN.
LIKE STAR WARS, EXCEPT WITH MUCH HANDSOMER PROTAGONISTS.
TELL HIM, SAM.
SPACE.
SO AWESOME.
SPACE.
THE WORD SHOULD BE ENOUGH TO GIVE ANY WISE PERSON PAUSE. BUT ALL OF YOU, EVERYONE ASSEMBLED IN THIS ROOM, REPRESENTS THE BEST CHANCE WE HAVE OF STOPPING THIS.
I WISH I COULD GO WITH YOU.
IRON MAN'S JOB IS STAYING BEHIND TO ENACT SOME CONTINGENCY PLANS AND MARSHAL THE WORLD'S DEFENSES IN CASE WE ARE UNSUCCESSFUL.
OUR JOB IS TO MAKE HIS UNNECESSARY.
WE LEAVE IN ONE HOUR.

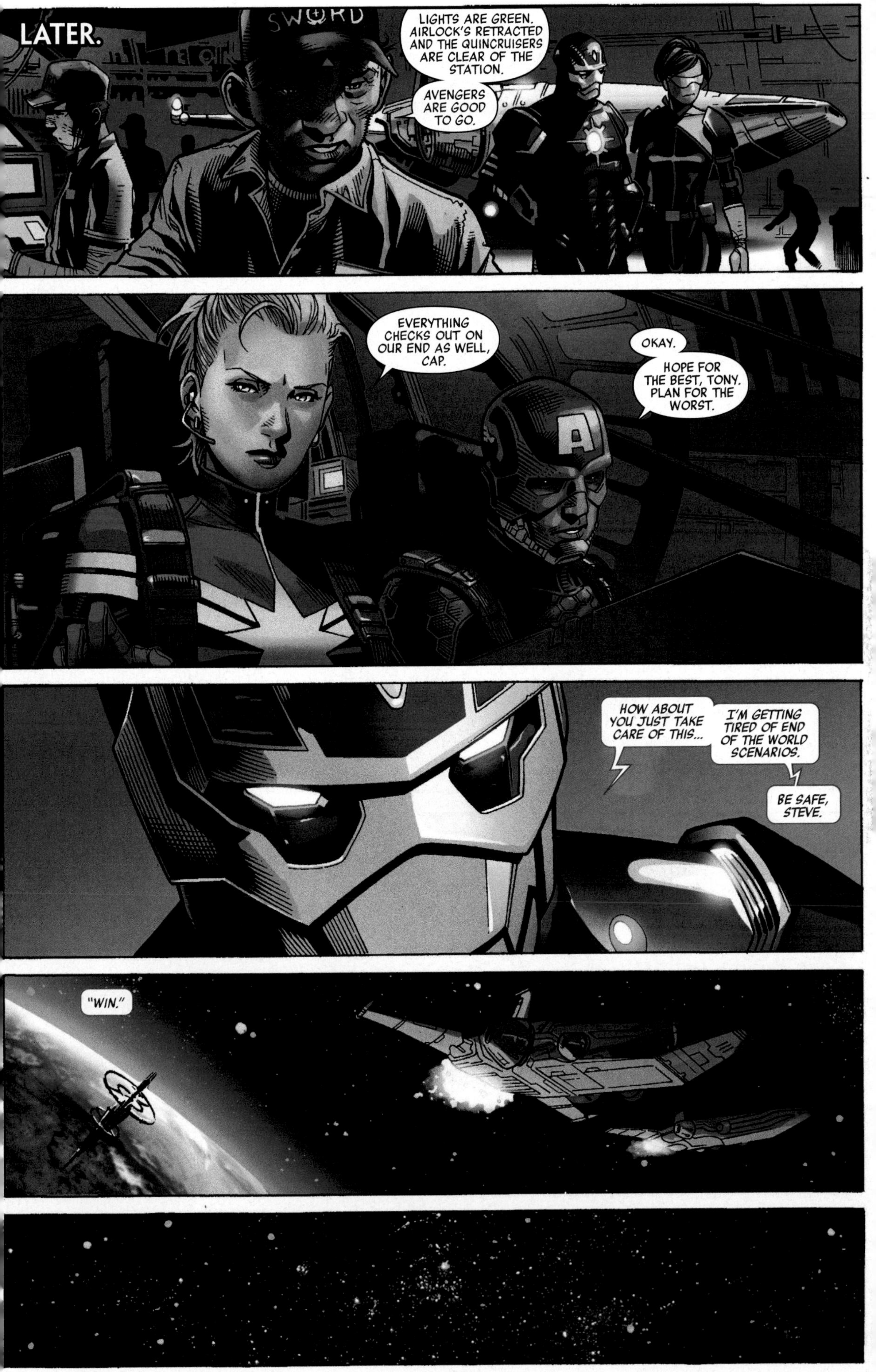

LATER.
LIGHTS ARE GREEN. AIRLOCK'S RETRACTED AND THE QUINCRUISERS ARE CLEAR OF THE STATION.
AVENGERS ARE GOOD TO GO.
EVERYTHING CHECKS OUT ON OUR END AS WELL, CAP.
OKAY.
HOPE FOR THE BEST, TONY. PLAN FOR THE WORST.
HOW ABOUT YOU JUST TAKE CARE OF THIS...
I'M GETTING TIRED OF END OF THE WORLD SCENARIOS.
BE SAFE, STEVE.
"WIN."

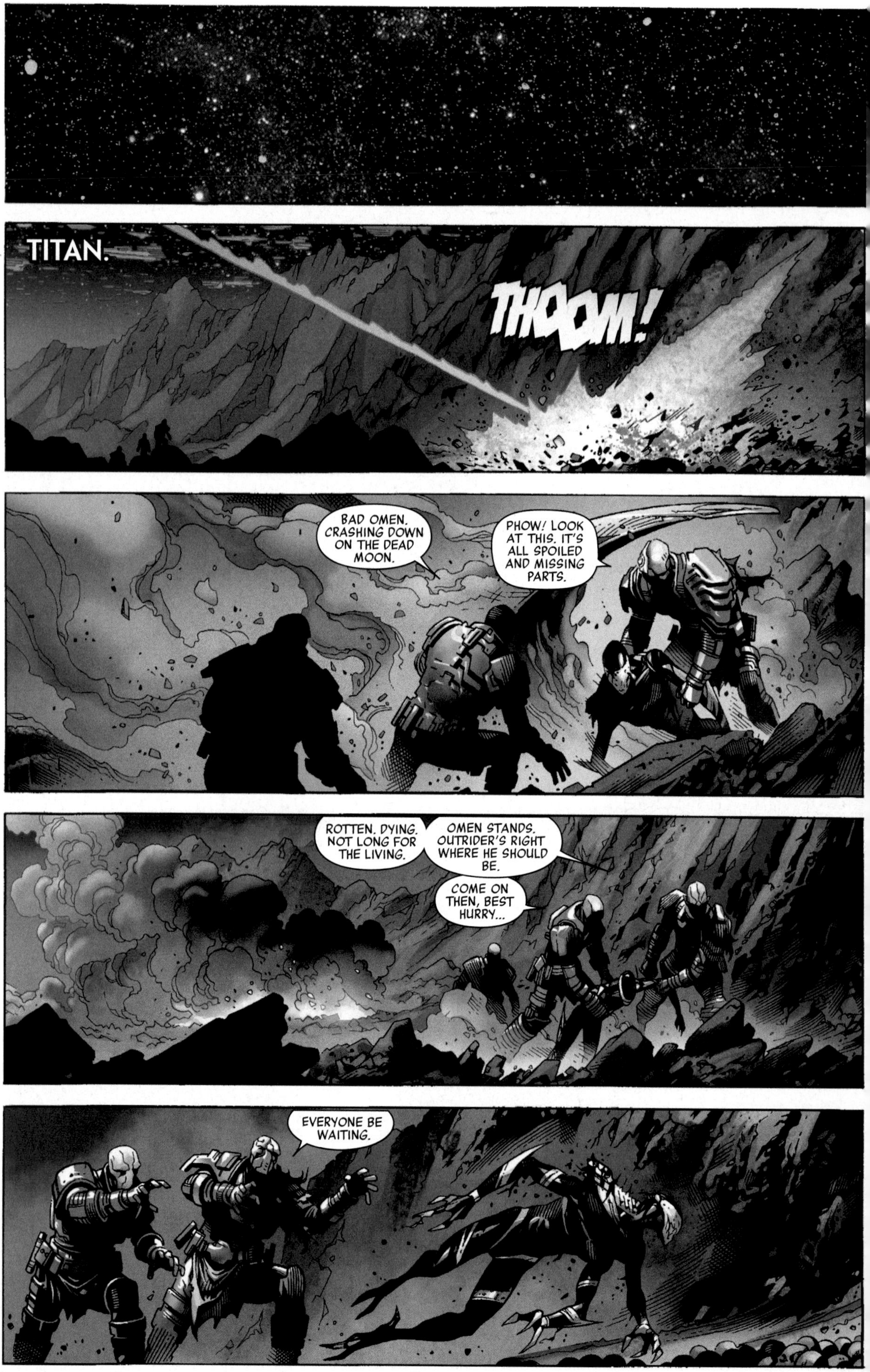
TITAN.
THOOM!
BAD OMEN. CRASHING DOWN ON THE DEAD MOON.
PHOW! LOOK AT THIS. IT'S ALL SPOILED AND MISSING PARTS.
ROTTEN. DYING. NOT LONG FOR THE LIVING.
OMEN STANDS. OUTRIDER'S RIGHT WHERE HE SHOULD BE.
COME ON THEN, BEST HURRY...
EVERYONE BE WAITING.

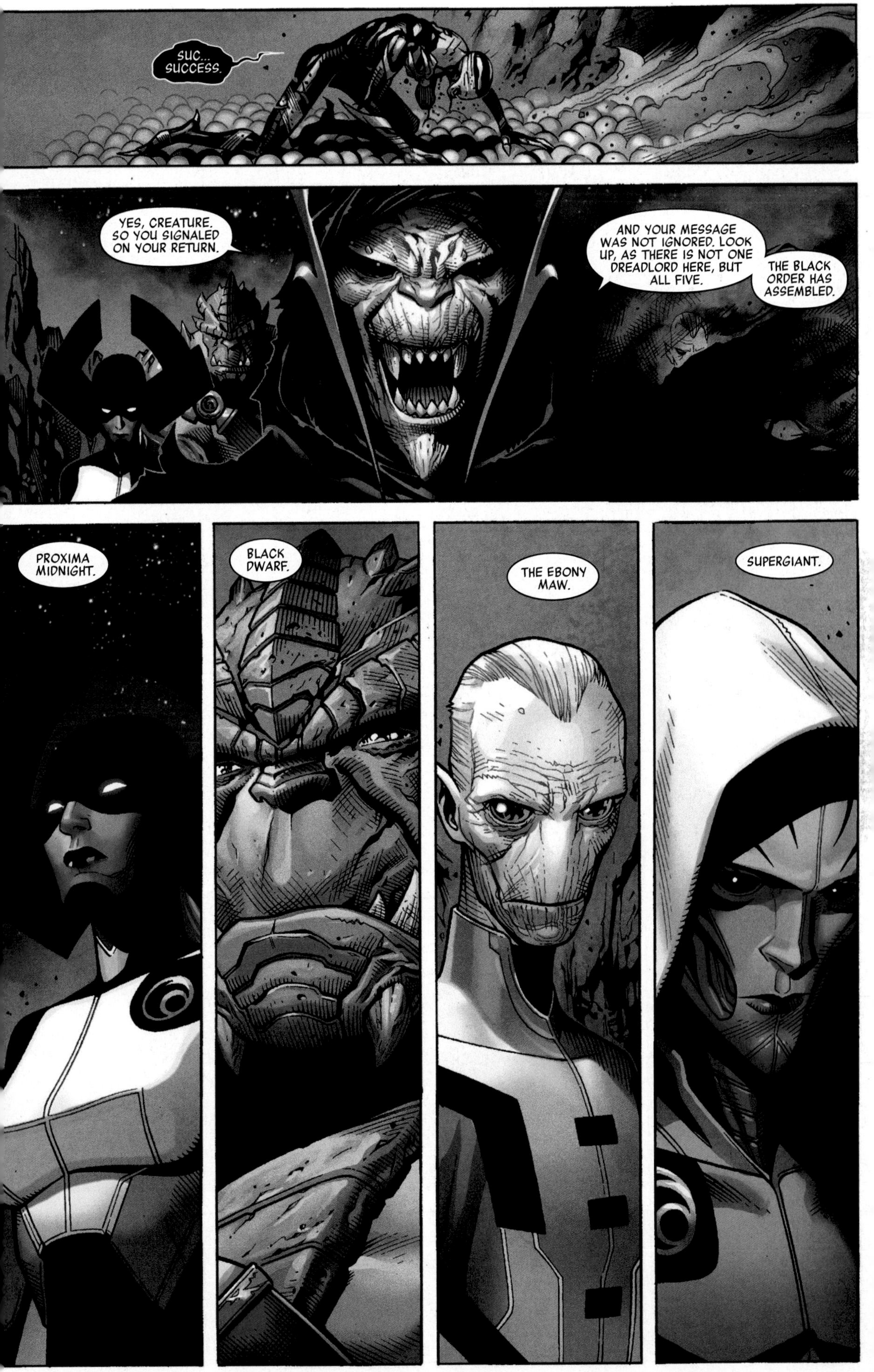
SUC... SUCCESS.
YES, CREATURE. SO YOU SIGNALED ON YOUR RETURN.
AND YOUR MESSAGE WAS NOT IGNORED. LOOK UP, AS THERE IS NOT ONE DREADLORD HERE, BUT ALL FIVE.
THE BLACK ORDER HAS ASSEMBLED.
PROXIMA MIDNIGHT.
BLACK DWARF.
THE EBONY MAW.
SUPERGIANT.

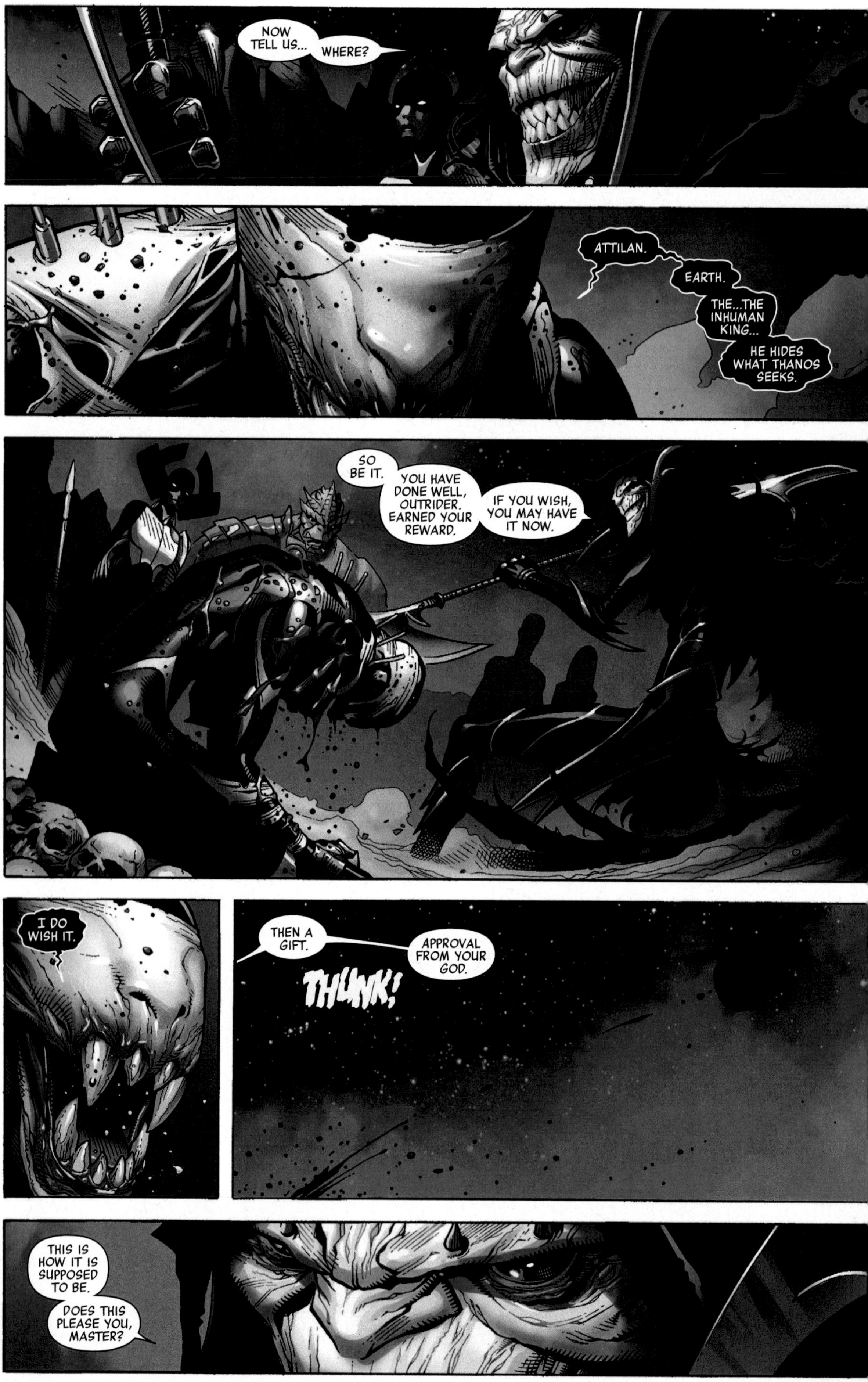
NOW TELL US...
WHERE?
ATTILAN.
EARTH.
THE...THE INHUMAN KING...
HE HIDES WHAT THANOS SEEKS.
SO BE IT.
YOU HAVE DONE WELL, OUTRIDER. EARNED YOUR REWARD.
IF YOU WISH, YOU MAY HAVE IT NOW.
I DO WISH IT.
THEN A GIFT.
APPROVAL FROM YOUR GOD.
THUNK!
THIS IS HOW IT IS SUPPOSED TO BE.
DOES THIS PLEASE YOU, MASTER?

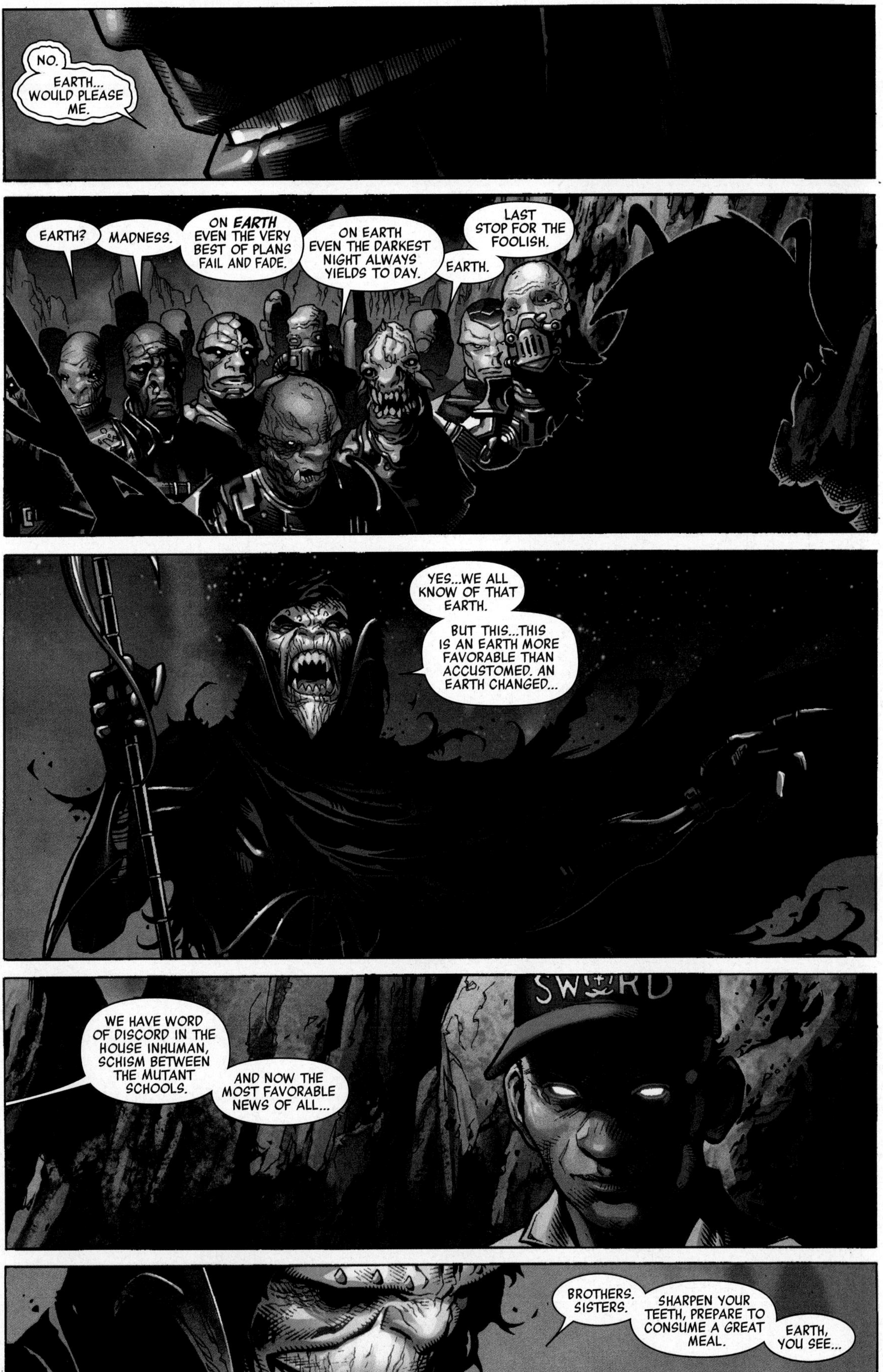
NO.
EARTH... WOULD PLEASE ME.
EARTH?
MADNESS.
ON EARTH EVEN THE VERY BEST OF PLANS FAIL AND FADE.
ON EARTH EVEN THE DARKEST NIGHT ALWAYS YIELDS TO DAY.
EARTH.
LAST STOP FOR THE FOOLISH.
YES...WE ALL KNOW OF THAT EARTH.
BUT THIS...THIS IS AN EARTH MORE FAVORABLE THAN ACCUSTOMED. AN EARTH CHANGED...
SWORD
WE HAVE WORD OF DISCORD IN THE HOUSE INHUMAN, SCHISM BETWEEN THE MUTANT SCHOOLS.
AND NOW THE MOST FAVORABLE NEWS OF ALL...
BROTHERS. SISTERS.
SHARPEN YOUR TEETH, PREPARE TO CONSUME A GREAT MEAL.
EARTH, YOU SEE...

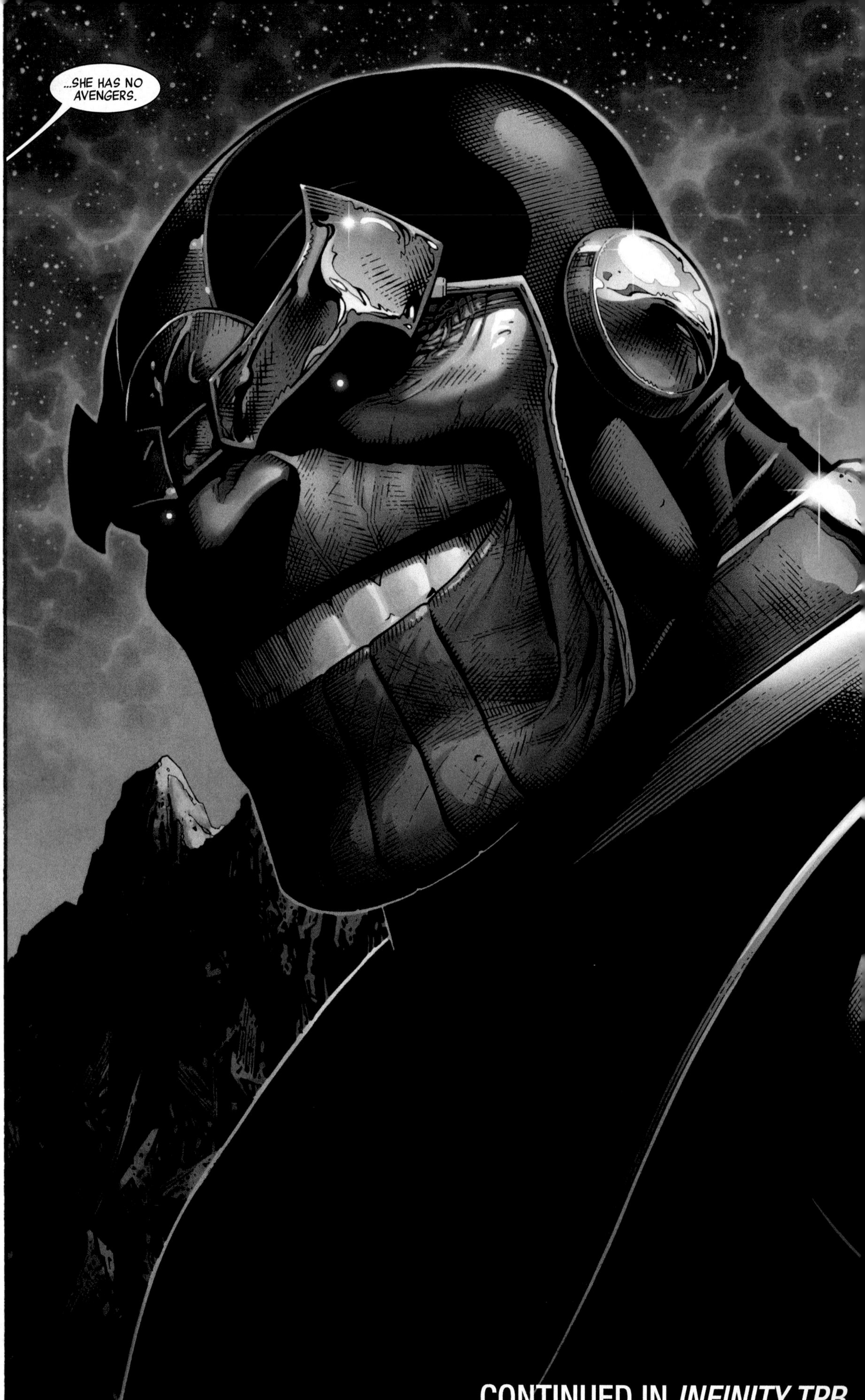
...SHE HAS NO AVENGERS.

CONTINUED IN *INFINITY TPB*.

DELVE INTO THE MAD TITAN'S PAST AS HE JOINS HIMSELF ON A TIME-BENDING JOURNEY OF DISCOVERY — ONE THAT SETS THE STAGE FOR HIS NEXT COSMIC ODYSSEY!

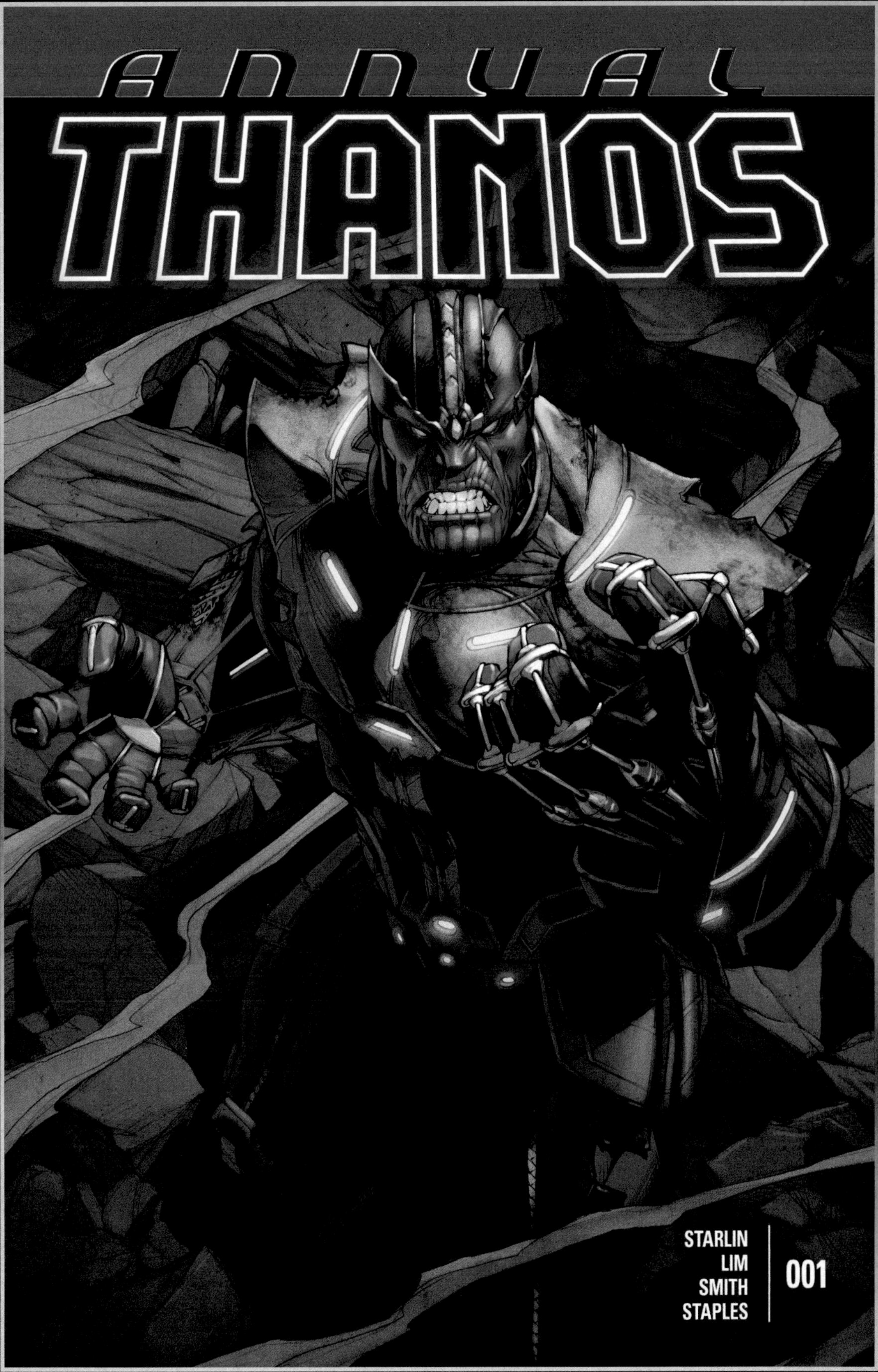
ANNUAL
THANOS
STARLIN
LIM
SMITH
STAPLES
001

The Mad Titan known as THANOS is obsessed with two things: power and death, the former of which he uses to bring about the latter.

In pursuit of these obsessions, Thanos gained control of the Infinity Gauntlet – a weapon of unimaginable power – which briefly made him the equivalent of a god. Ever since, his life has often been intertwined with the Gauntlet and its Gems in one way or another.

Currently Thanos is imprisoned on Earth, trapped in a "living death" by the very person he came there to kill: his son Thane. But it is only a matter of time before the Mad Titan is free once more!

The following details a key moment in Thanos' life when he was faced with a future that may lead beyond death itself…

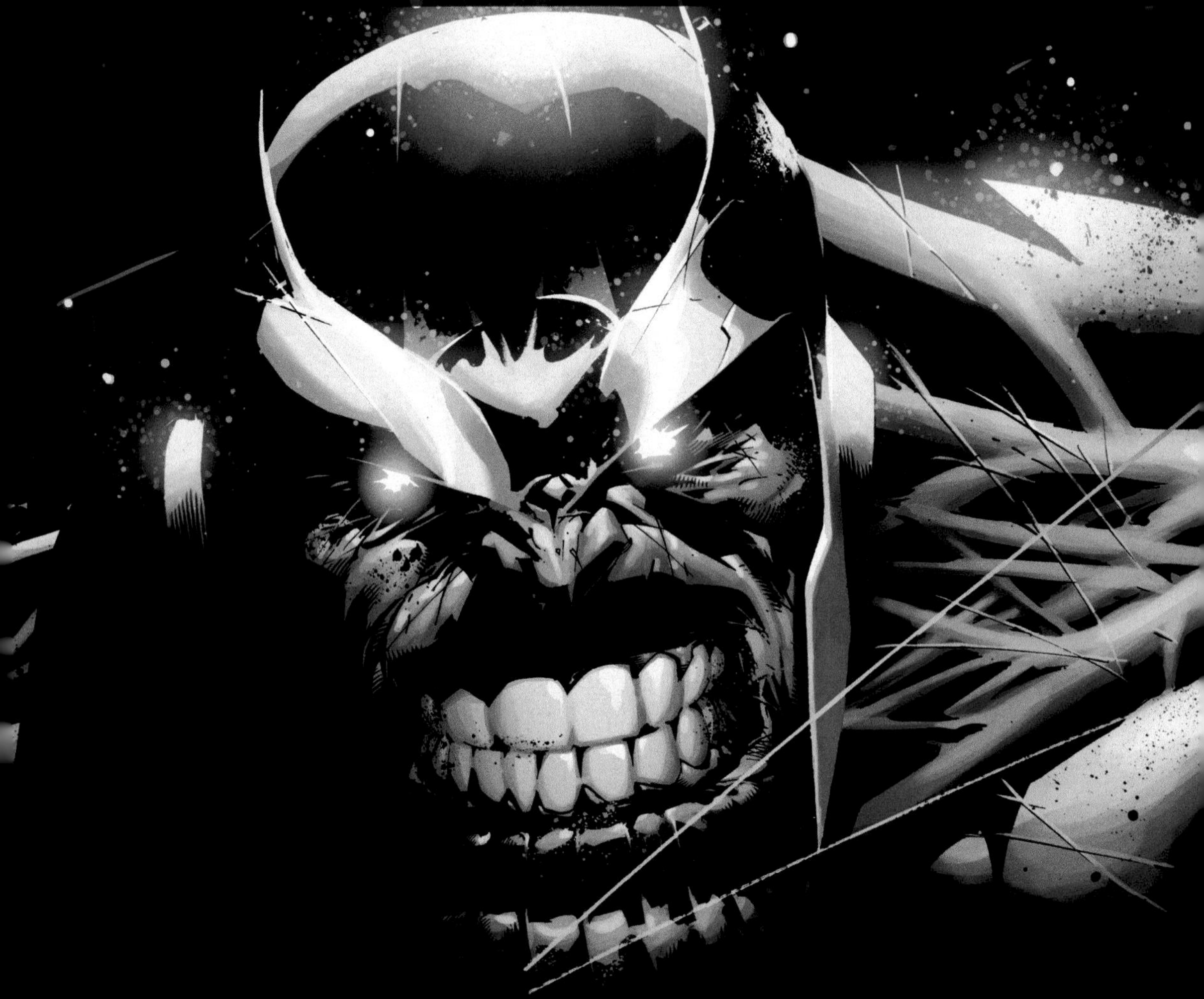

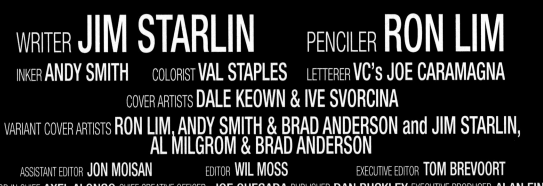

WRITER **JIM STARLIN** PENCILER **RON LIM**

INKER **ANDY SMITH** COLORIST **VAL STAPLES** LETTERER **VC's JOE CARAMAGNA**

COVER ARTISTS **DALE KEOWN & IVE SVORCINA**

VARIANT COVER ARTISTS **RON LIM, ANDY SMITH & BRAD ANDERSON and JIM STARLIN, AL MILGROM & BRAD ANDERSON**

ASSISTANT EDITOR **JON MOISAN** EDITOR **WIL MOSS** EXECUTIVE EDITOR **TOM BREVOORT**

EDITOR IN CHIEF **AXEL ALONSO** CHIEF CREATIVE OFFICER **JOE QUESADA** PUBLISHER **DAN BUCKLEY** EXECUTIVE PRODUCER **ALAN FINE**

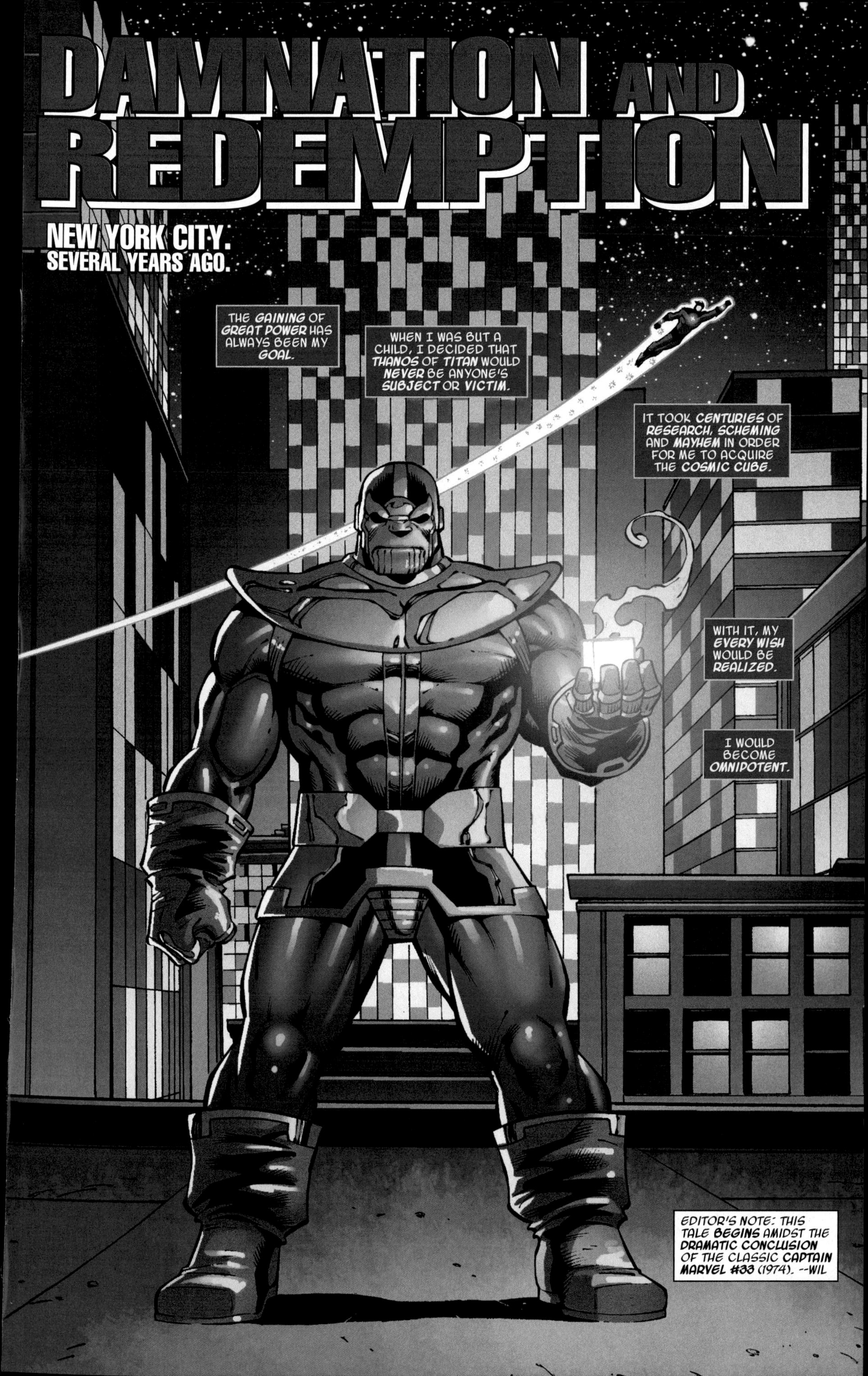
DAMNATION AND REDEMPTION
NEW YORK CITY.
SEVERAL YEARS AGO.
THE GAINING OF GREAT POWER HAS ALWAYS BEEN MY GOAL.
WHEN I WAS BUT A CHILD, I DECIDED THAT THANOS OF TITAN WOULD NEVER BE ANYONE'S SUBJECT OR VICTIM.
IT TOOK CENTURIES OF RESEARCH, SCHEMING AND MAYHEM IN ORDER FOR ME TO ACQUIRE THE COSMIC CUBE.
WITH IT, MY EVERY WISH WOULD BE REALIZED.
I WOULD BECOME OMNIPOTENT.
EDITOR'S NOTE: THIS TALE BEGINS AMIDST THE DRAMATIC CONCLUSION OF THE CLASSIC CAPTAIN MARVEL #33 (1974). --WIL

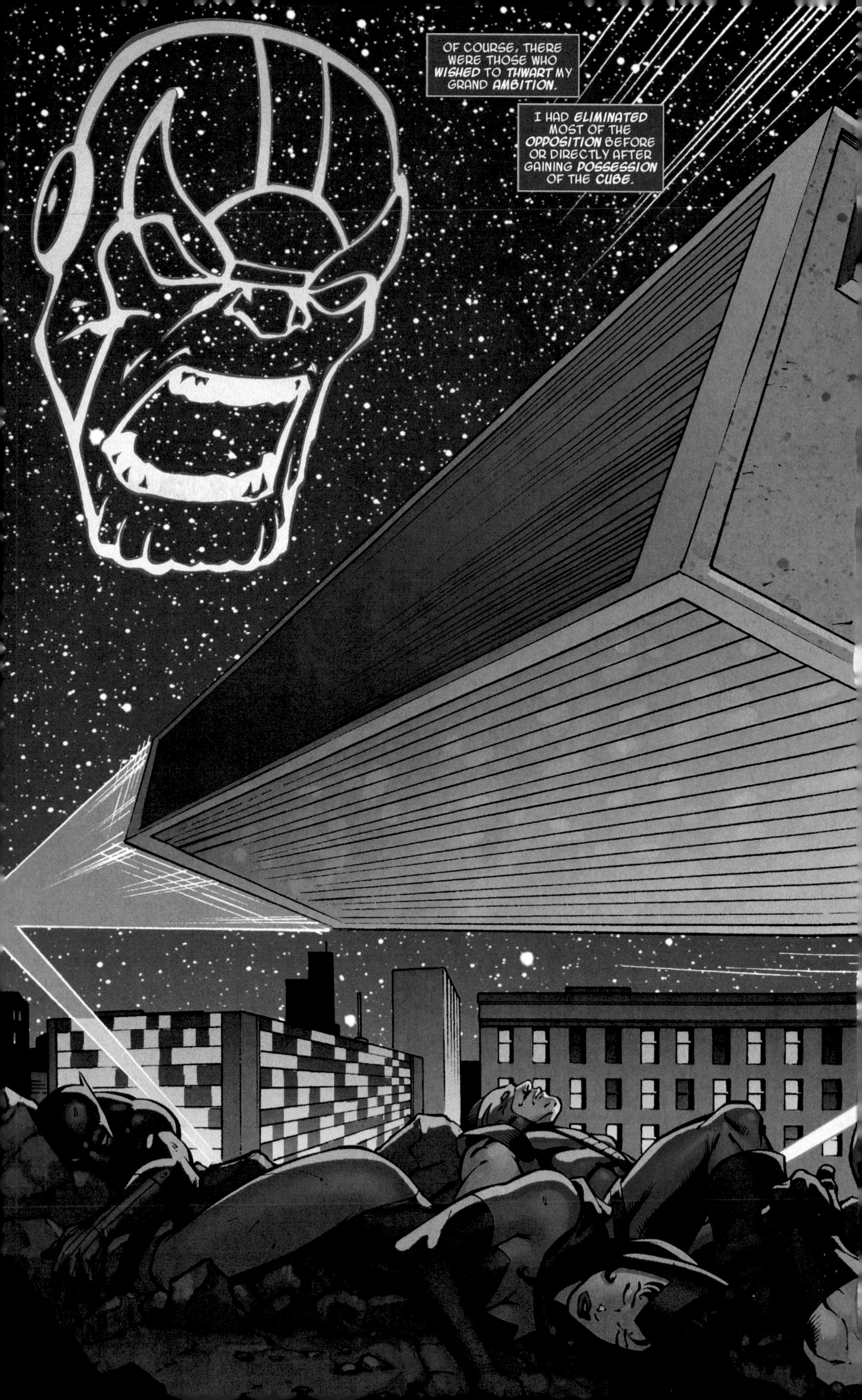
OF COURSE, THERE WERE THOSE WHO WISHED TO THWART MY GRAND AMBITION.
I HAD ELIMINATED MOST OF THE OPPOSITION BEFORE OR DIRECTLY AFTER GAINING POSSESSION OF THE CUBE.

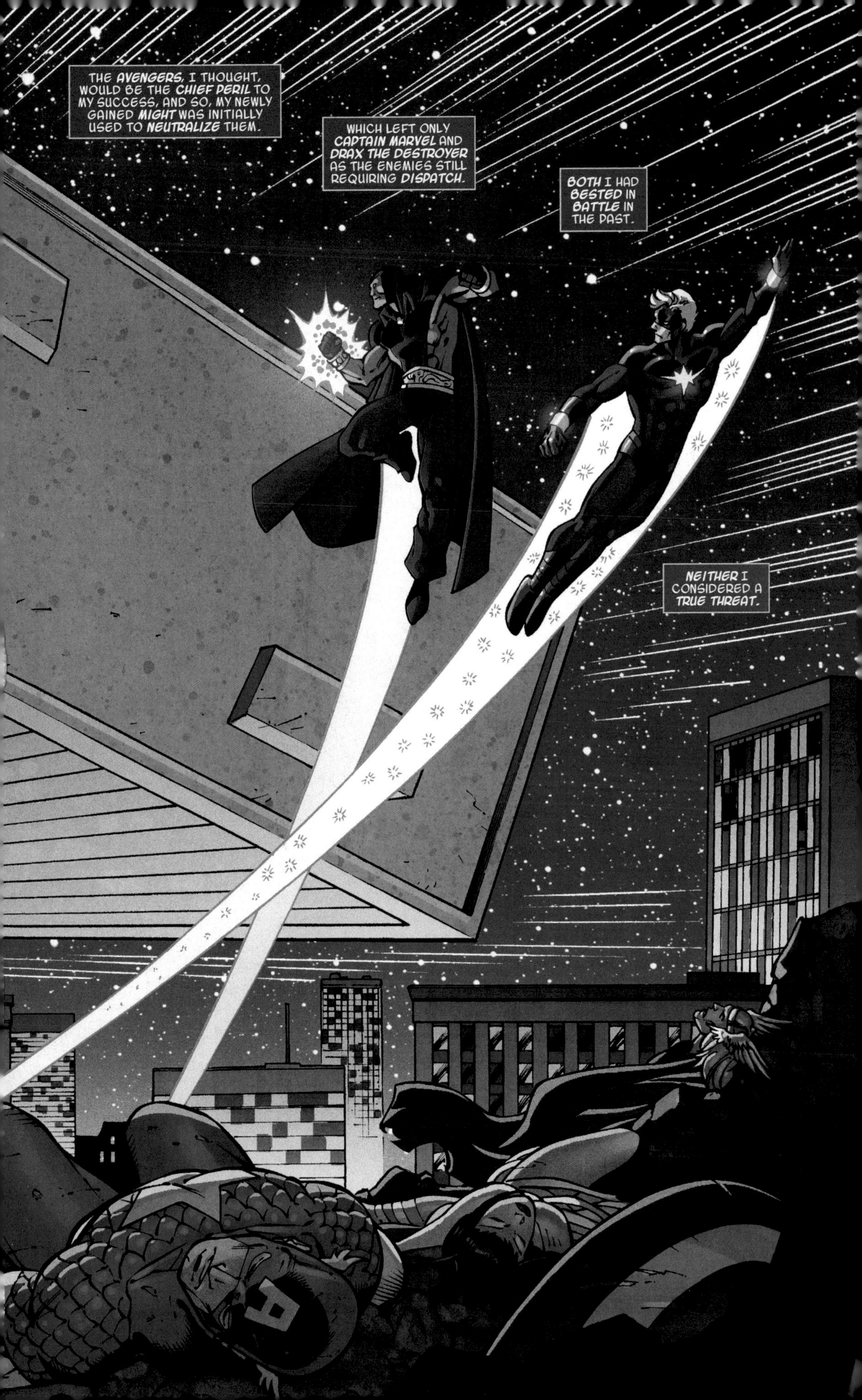
THE AVENGERS, I THOUGHT, WOULD BE THE CHIEF PERIL TO MY SUCCESS, AND SO, MY NEWLY GAINED MIGHT WAS INITIALLY USED TO NEUTRALIZE THEM.
WHICH LEFT ONLY CAPTAIN MARVEL AND DRAX THE DESTROYER AS THE ENEMIES STILL REQUIRING DISPATCH.
BOTH I HAD BESTED IN BATTLE IN THE PAST.
NEITHER I CONSIDERED A TRUE THREAT.

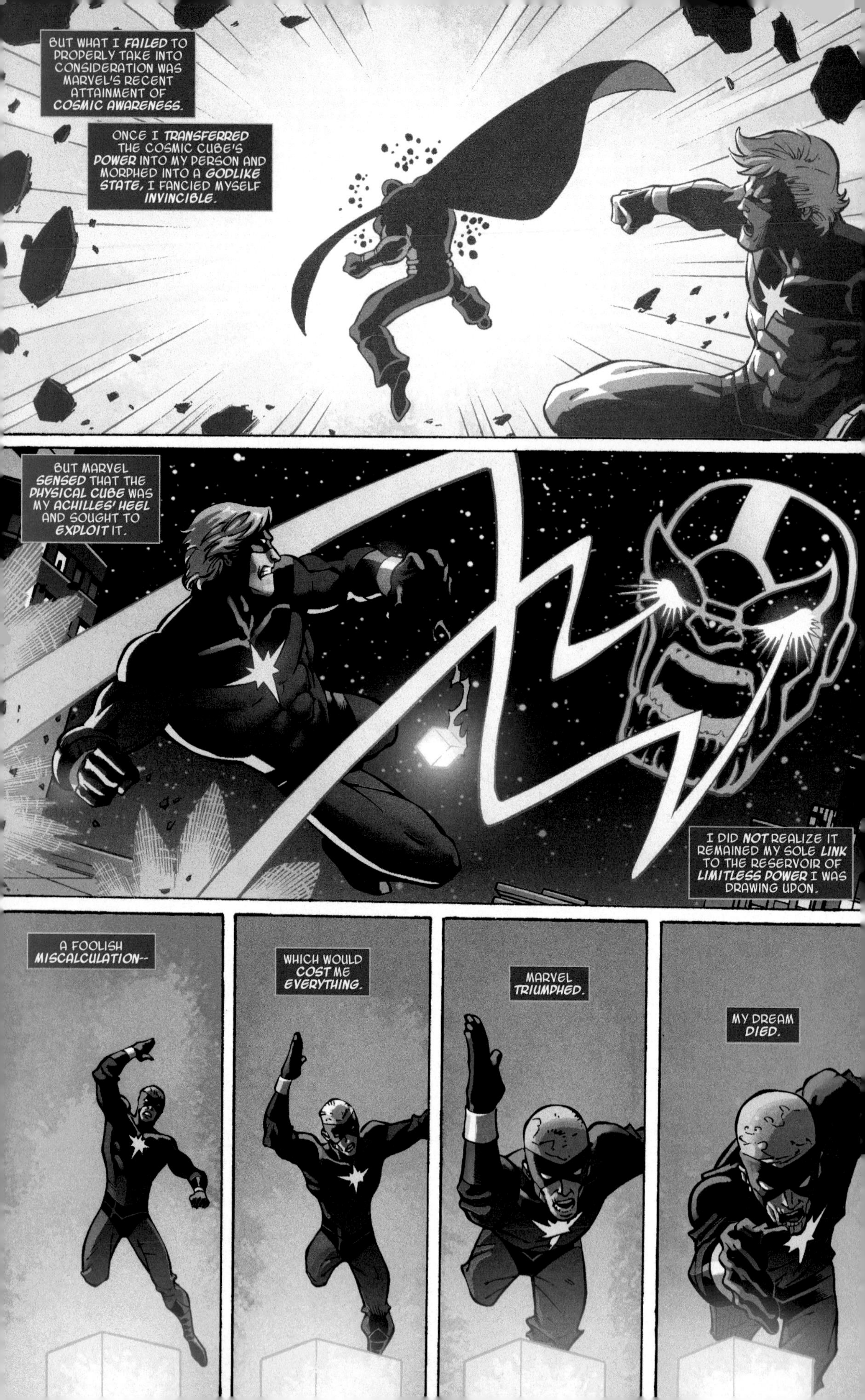
BUT WHAT I FAILED TO PROPERLY TAKE INTO CONSIDERATION WAS MARVEL'S RECENT ATTAINMENT OF COSMIC AWARENESS.
ONCE I TRANSFERRED THE COSMIC CUBE'S POWER INTO MY PERSON AND MORPHED INTO A GODLIKE STATE, I FANCIED MYSELF INVINCIBLE.
BUT MARVEL SENSED THAT THE PHYSICAL CUBE WAS MY ACHILLES' HEEL AND SOUGHT TO EXPLOIT IT.
I DID NOT REALIZE IT REMAINED MY SOLE LINK TO THE RESERVOIR OF LIMITLESS POWER I WAS DRAWING UPON.
A FOOLISH MISCALCULATION--
WHICH WOULD COST ME EVERYTHING.
MARVEL TRIUMPHED.
MY DREAM DIED.

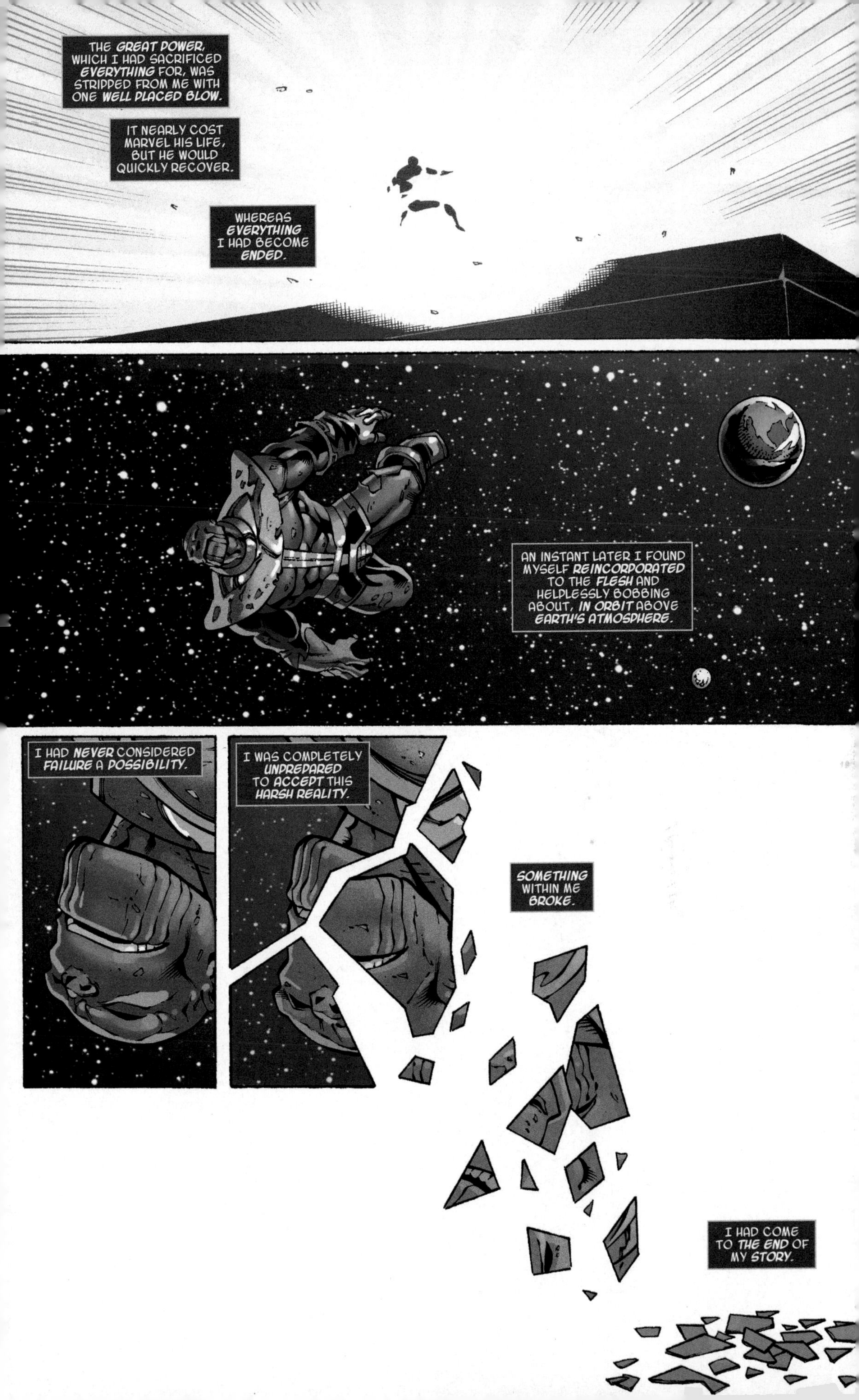
THE GREAT POWER, WHICH I HAD SACRIFICED EVERYTHING FOR, WAS STRIPPED FROM ME WITH ONE WELL PLACED BLOW.
IT NEARLY COST MARVEL HIS LIFE, BUT HE WOULD QUICKLY RECOVER.
WHEREAS EVERYTHING I HAD BECOME ENDED.
AN INSTANT LATER I FOUND MYSELF REINCORPORATED TO THE FLESH AND HELPLESSLY BOBBING ABOUT, IN ORBIT ABOVE EARTH'S ATMOSPHERE.
I HAD NEVER CONSIDERED FAILURE A POSSIBILITY.
I WAS COMPLETELY UNPREPARED TO ACCEPT THIS HARSH REALITY.
SOMETHING WITHIN ME BROKE.
I HAD COME TO THE END OF MY STORY.

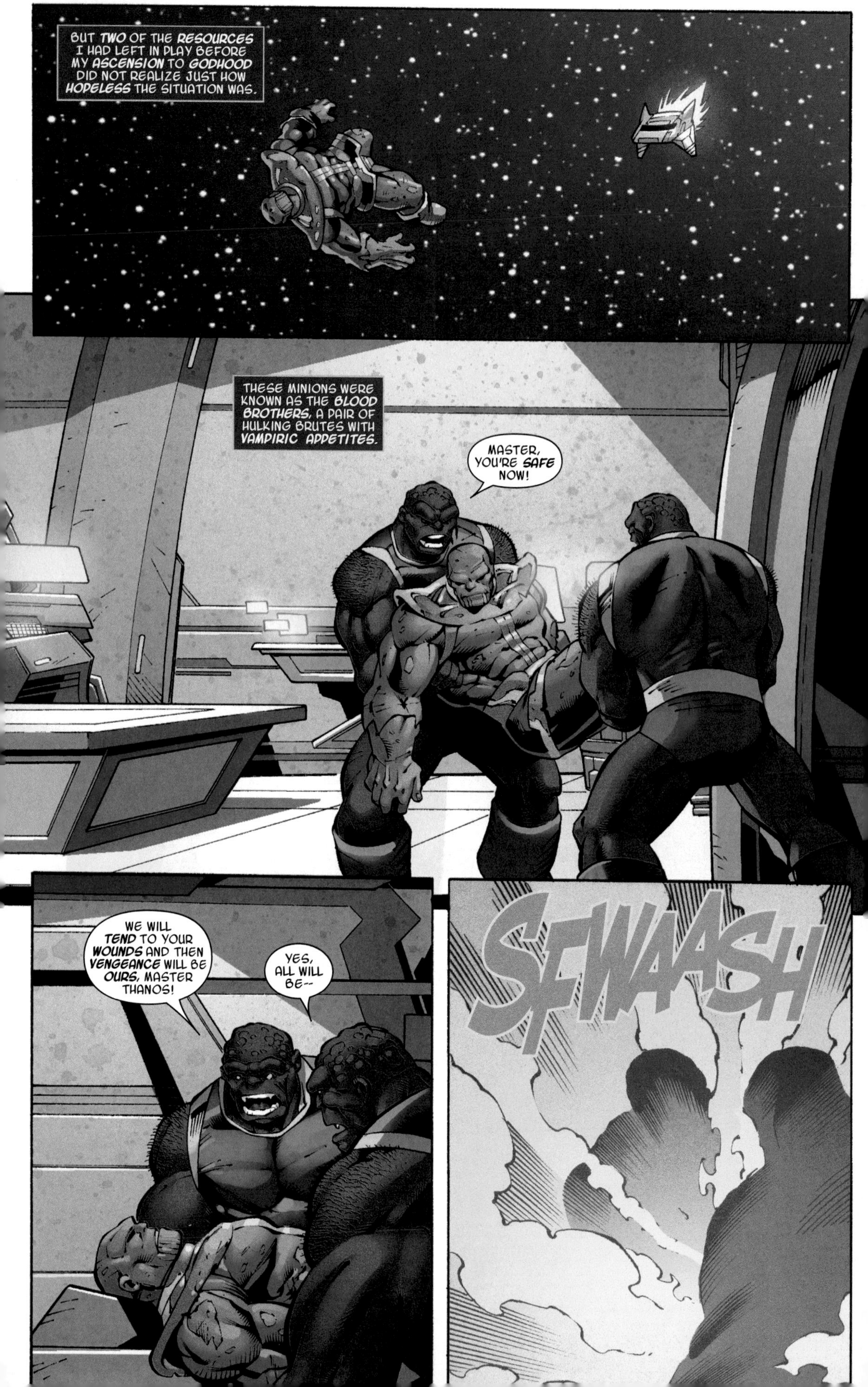
BUT TWO OF THE RESOURCES I HAD LEFT IN PLAY BEFORE MY ASCENSION TO GODHOOD DID NOT REALIZE JUST HOW HOPELESS THE SITUATION WAS.
THESE MINIONS WERE KNOWN AS THE BLOOD BROTHERS, A PAIR OF HULKING BRUTES WITH VAMPIRIC APPETITES.
MASTER, YOU'RE SAFE NOW!
WE WILL TEND TO YOUR WOUNDS AND THEN VENGEANCE WILL BE OURS, MASTER THANOS!
YES, ALL WILL BE--
SFWAASH

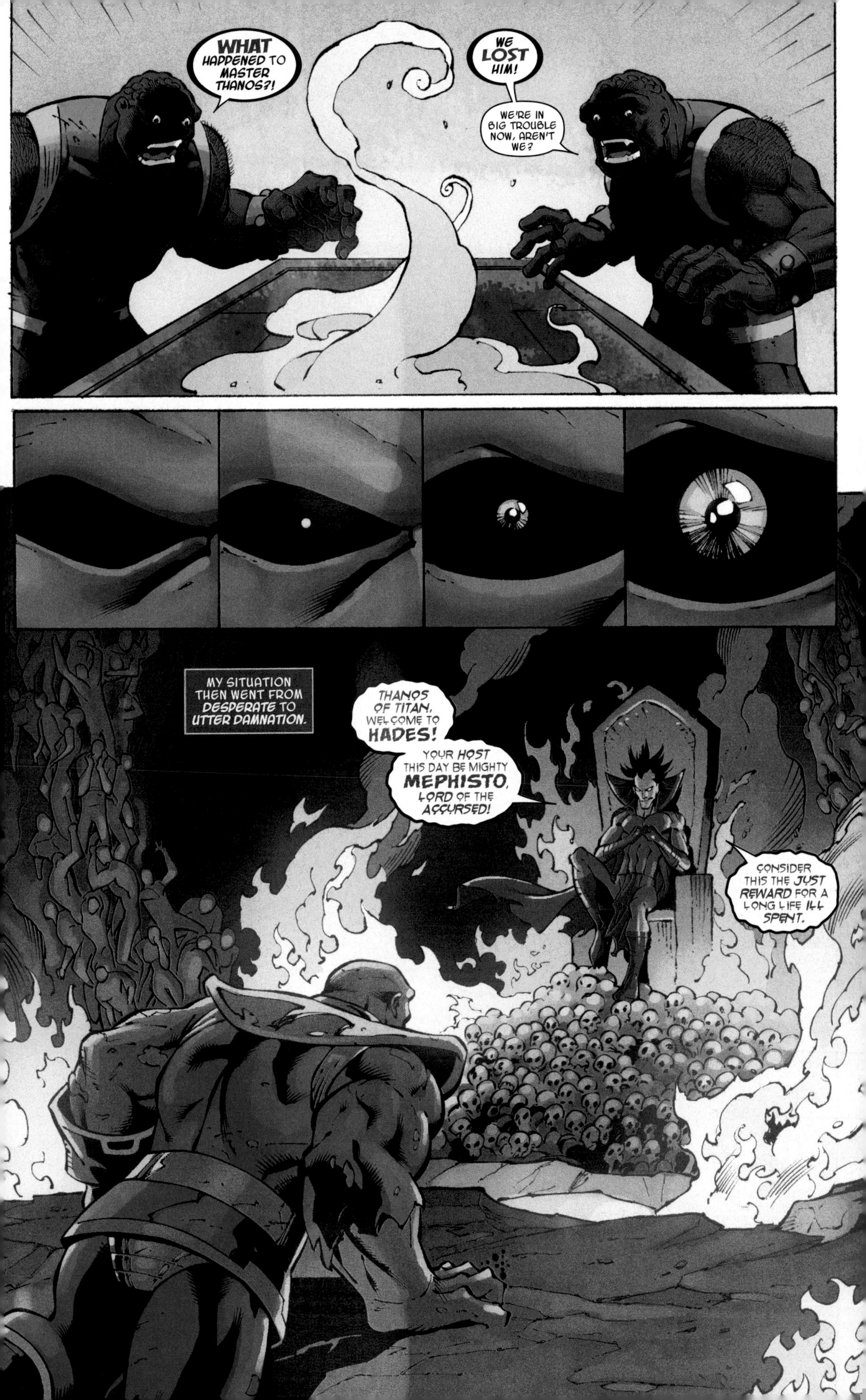
WHAT HAPPENED TO MASTER THANOS?!
WE LOST HIM!
WE'RE IN BIG TROUBLE NOW, AREN'T WE?
MY SITUATION THEN WENT FROM DESPERATE TO UTTER DAMNATION.
THANOS OF TITAN, WELCOME TO HADES!
YOUR HOST THIS DAY BE MIGHTY MEPHISTO, LORD OF THE ACCURSED!
CONSIDER THIS THE JUST REWARD FOR A LONG LIFE ILL SPENT.

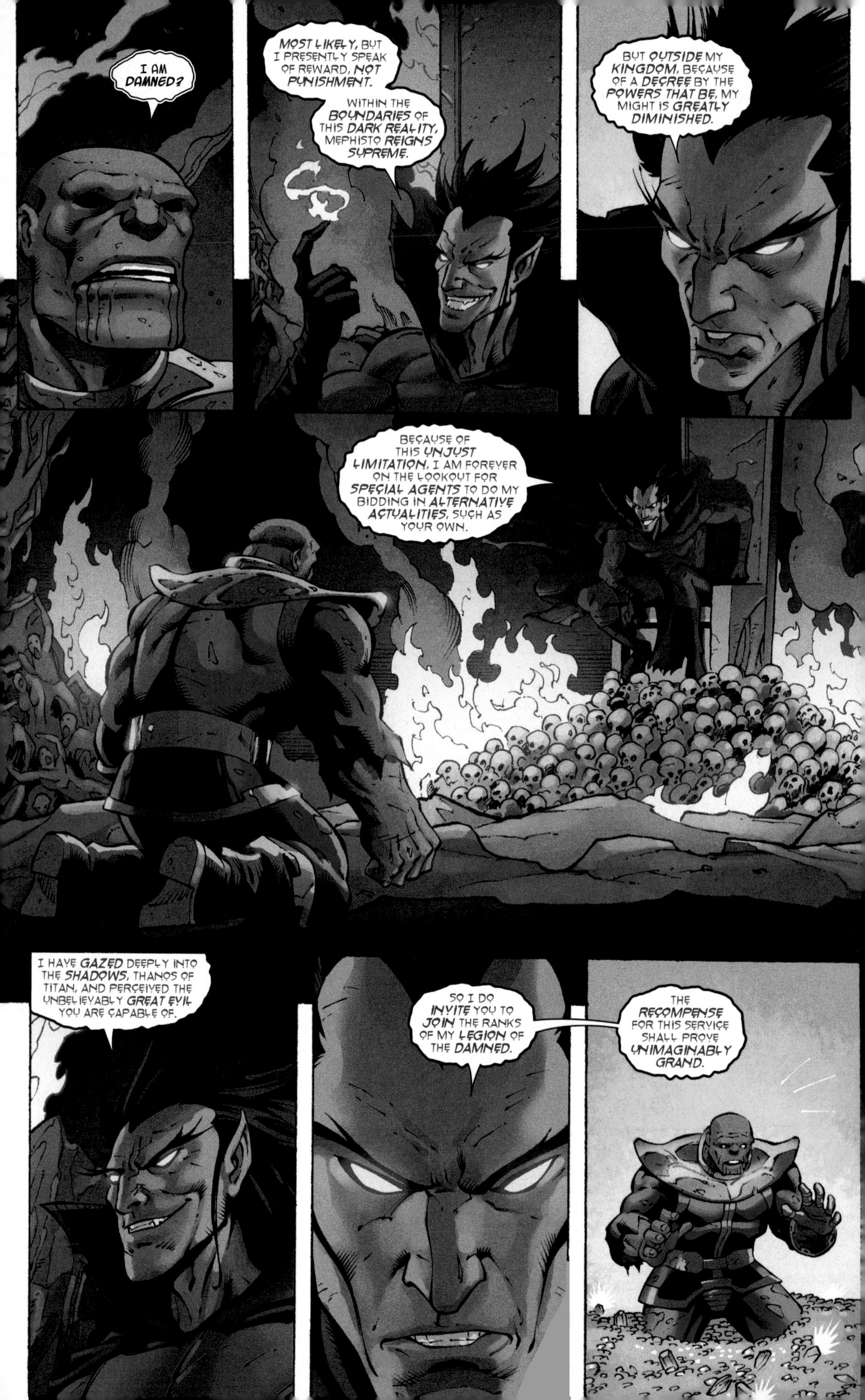
I AM DAMNED?
MOST LIKELY, BUT I PRESENTLY SPEAK OF REWARD, NOT PUNISHMENT.
WITHIN THE BOUNDARIES OF THIS DARK REALITY, MEPHISTO REIGNS SUPREME.
BUT OUTSIDE MY KINGDOM, BECAUSE OF A DECREE BY THE POWERS THAT BE, MY MIGHT IS GREATLY DIMINISHED.
BECAUSE OF THIS UNJUST LIMITATION, I AM FOREVER ON THE LOOKOUT FOR SPECIAL AGENTS TO DO MY BIDDING IN ALTERNATIVE ACTUALITIES, SUCH AS YOUR OWN.
I HAVE GAZED DEEPLY INTO THE SHADOWS, THANOS OF TITAN, AND PERCEIVED THE UNBELIEVABLY GREAT EVIL YOU ARE CAPABLE OF.
SO I DO INVITE YOU TO JOIN THE RANKS OF MY LEGION OF THE DAMNED.
THE RECOMPENSE FOR THIS SERVICE SHALL PROVE UNIMAGINABLY GRAND.

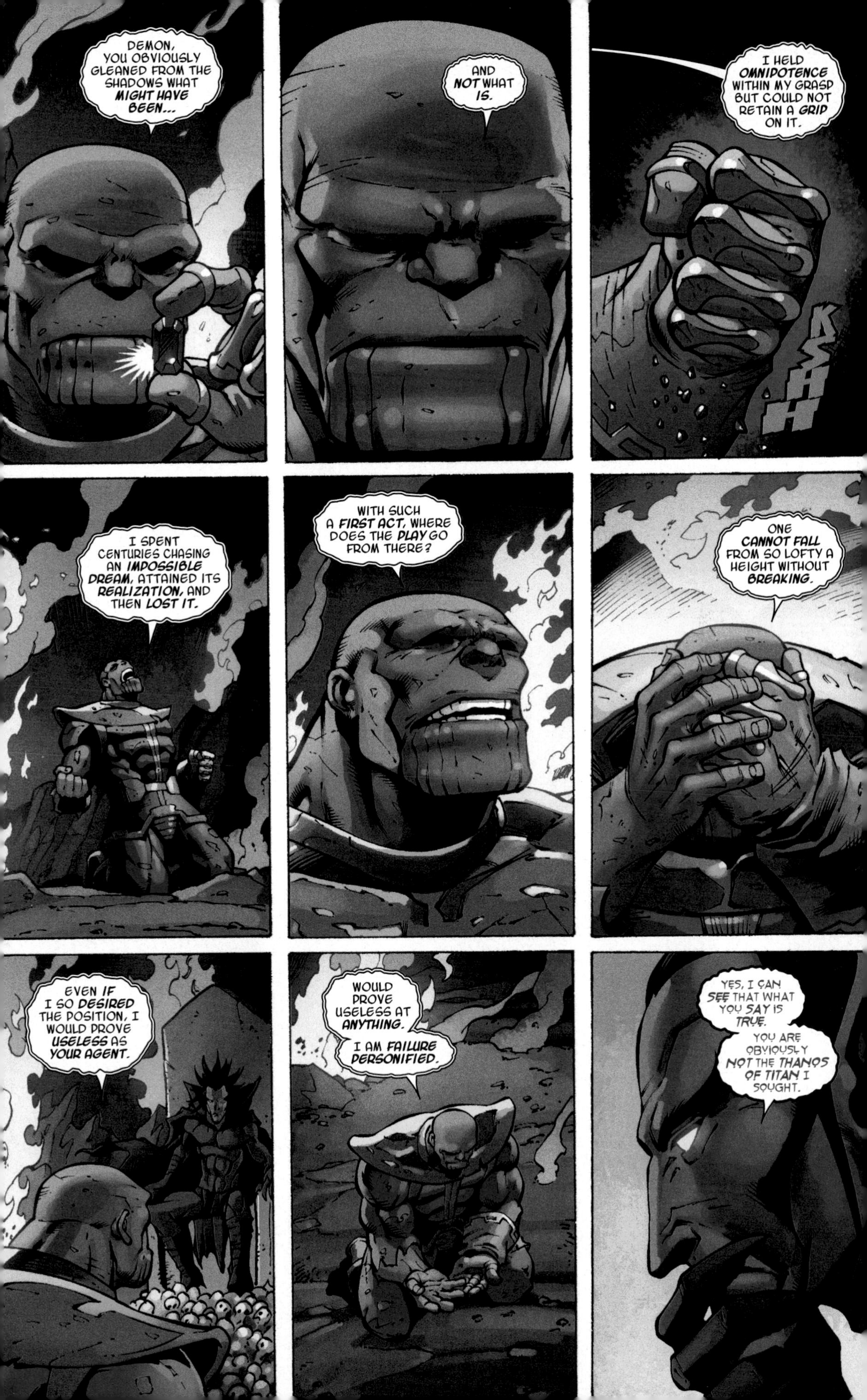
DEMON, YOU OBVIOUSLY GLEANED FROM THE SHADOWS WHAT MIGHT HAVE BEEN...
AND NOT WHAT IS.
I HELD OMNIPOTENCE WITHIN MY GRASP BUT COULD NOT RETAIN A GRID ON IT.
KSHH
I SPENT CENTURIES CHASING AN IMPOSSIBLE DREAM, ATTAINED ITS REALIZATION, AND THEN LOST IT.
WITH SUCH A FIRST ACT, WHERE DOES THE PLAY GO FROM THERE?
ONE CANNOT FALL FROM SO LOFTY A HEIGHT WITHOUT BREAKING.
EVEN IF I SO DESIRED THE POSITION, I WOULD PROVE USELESS AS YOUR AGENT.
WOULD PROVE USELESS AT ANYTHING.
I AM FAILURE PERSONIFIED.
YES, I CAN SEE THAT WHAT YOU SAY IS TRUE.
YOU ARE OBVIOUSLY NOT THE THANOS OF TITAN I SOUGHT.

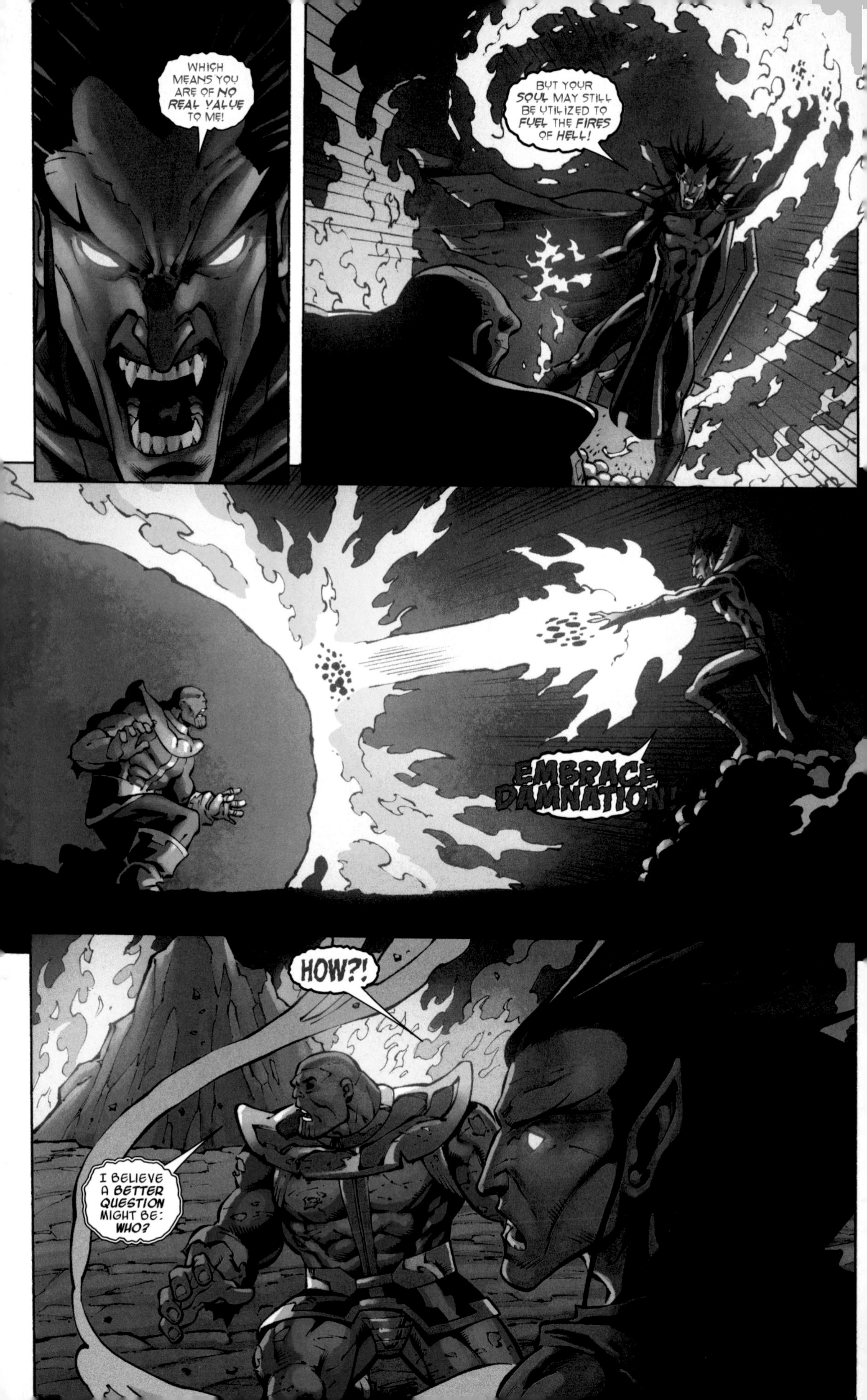
WHICH MEANS YOU ARE OF NO REAL VALUE TO ME!
BUT YOUR SOUL MAY STILL BE UTILIZED TO FUEL THE FIRES OF HELL!
EMBRACE DAMNATION!
HOW?!
I BELIEVE A BETTER QUESTION MIGHT BE: WHO?

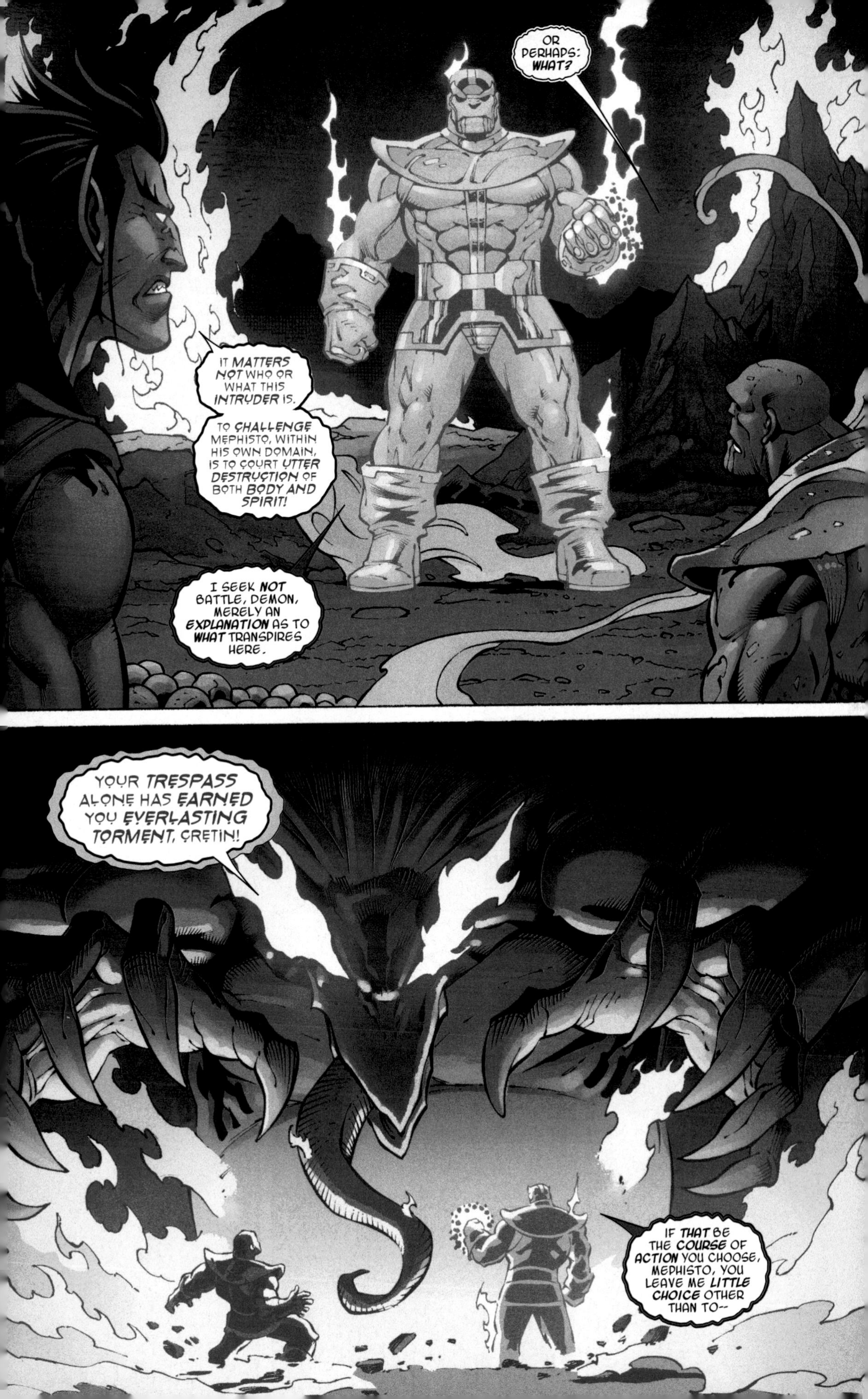
OR PERHAPS: WHAT?
IT MATTERS NOT WHO OR WHAT THIS INTRUDER IS.
TO CHALLENGE MEPHISTO, WITHIN HIS OWN DOMAIN, IS TO COURT UTTER DESTRUCTION OF BOTH BODY AND SPIRIT!
I SEEK NOT BATTLE, DEMON, MERELY AN EXPLANATION AS TO WHAT TRANSPIRES HERE.
YOUR TRESPASS ALONE HAS EARNED YOU EVERLASTING TORMENT, CRETIN!
IF THAT BE THE COURSE OF ACTION YOU CHOOSE, MEPHISTO, YOU LEAVE ME LITTLE CHOICE OTHER THAN TO--

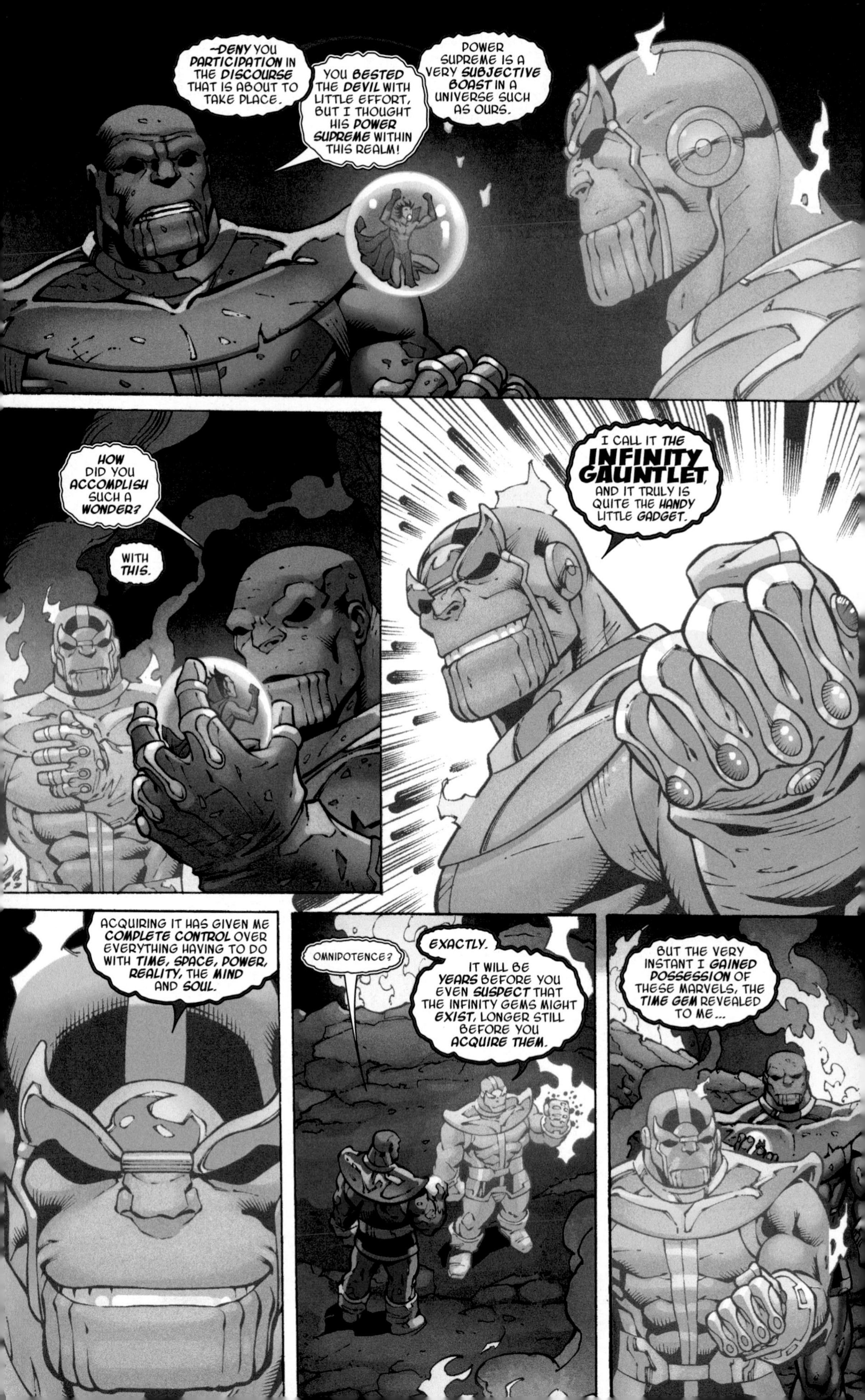

–DENY YOU PARTICIPATION IN THE DISCOURSE THAT IS ABOUT TO TAKE PLACE.
YOU BESTED THE DEVIL WITH LITTLE EFFORT, BUT I THOUGHT HIS POWER SUPREME WITHIN THIS REALM!
POWER SUPREME IS A VERY SUBJECTIVE BOAST IN A UNIVERSE SUCH AS OURS.
HOW DID YOU ACCOMPLISH SUCH A WONDER?
WITH THIS.
I CALL IT THE INFINITY GAUNTLET, AND IT TRULY IS QUITE THE HANDY LITTLE GADGET.
ACQUIRING IT HAS GIVEN ME COMPLETE CONTROL OVER EVERYTHING HAVING TO DO WITH TIME, SPACE, POWER, REALITY, THE MIND AND SOUL.
OMNIPOTENCE?
EXACTLY.
IT WILL BE YEARS BEFORE YOU EVEN SUSPECT THAT THE INFINITY GEMS MIGHT EXIST, LONGER STILL BEFORE YOU ACQUIRE THEM.
BUT THE VERY INSTANT I GAINED POSSESSION OF THESE MARVELS, THE TIME GEM REVEALED TO ME...

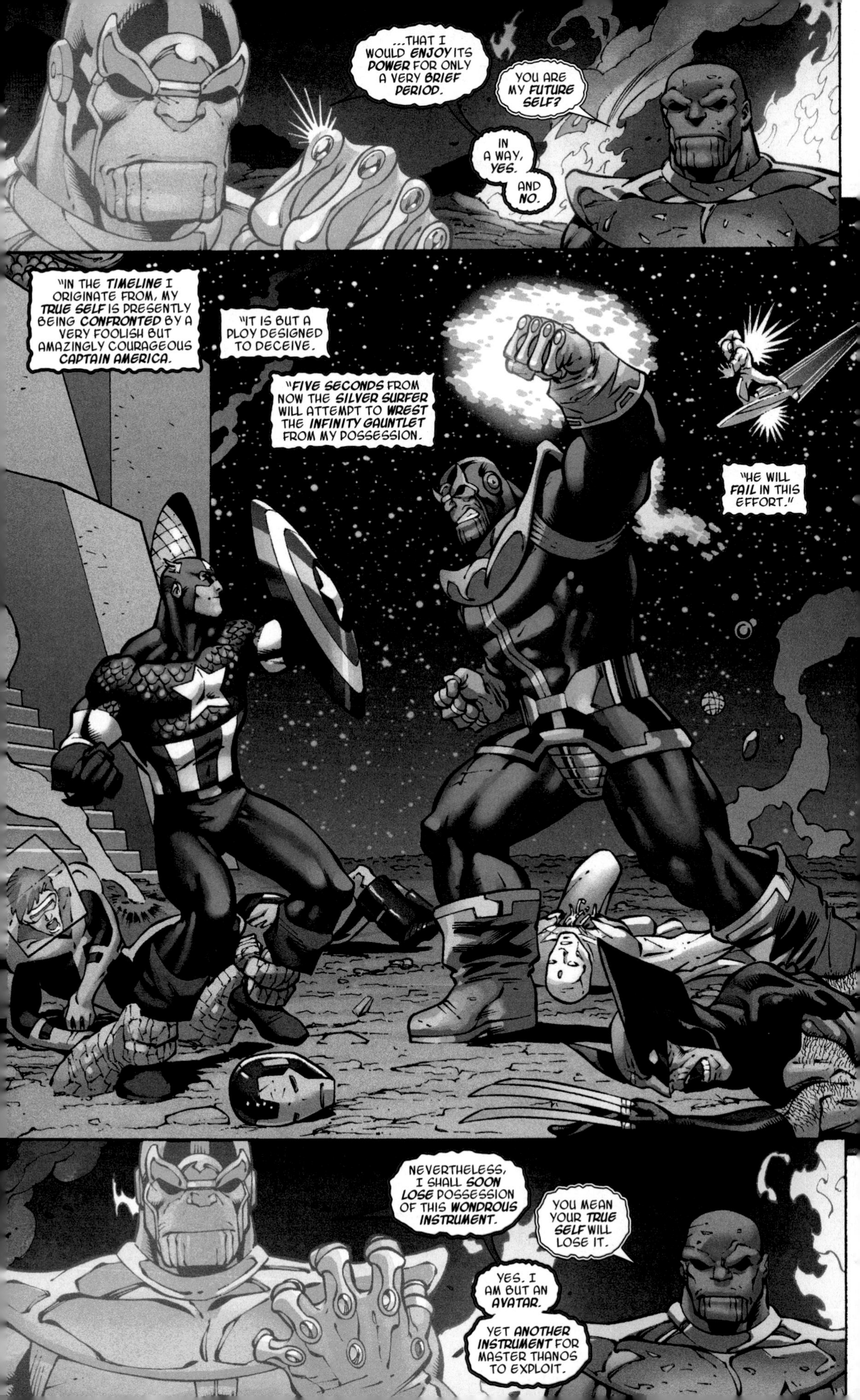
...THAT I WOULD ENJOY ITS POWER FOR ONLY A VERY BRIEF PERIOD.
YOU ARE MY FUTURE SELF?
IN A WAY, YES.
AND NO.
"IN THE TIMELINE I ORIGINATE FROM, MY TRUE SELF IS PRESENTLY BEING CONFRONTED BY A VERY FOOLISH BUT AMAZINGLY COURAGEOUS CAPTAIN AMERICA.
"IT IS BUT A PLOY DESIGNED TO DECEIVE.
"FIVE SECONDS FROM NOW THE SILVER SURFER WILL ATTEMPT TO WREST THE INFINITY GAUNTLET FROM MY POSSESSION.
"HE WILL FAIL IN THIS EFFORT."
NEVERTHELESS, I SHALL SOON LOSE POSSESSION OF THIS WONDROUS INSTRUMENT.
YOU MEAN YOUR TRUE SELF WILL LOSE IT.
YES. I AM BUT AN AVATAR.
YET ANOTHER INSTRUMENT FOR MASTER THANOS TO EXPLOIT.

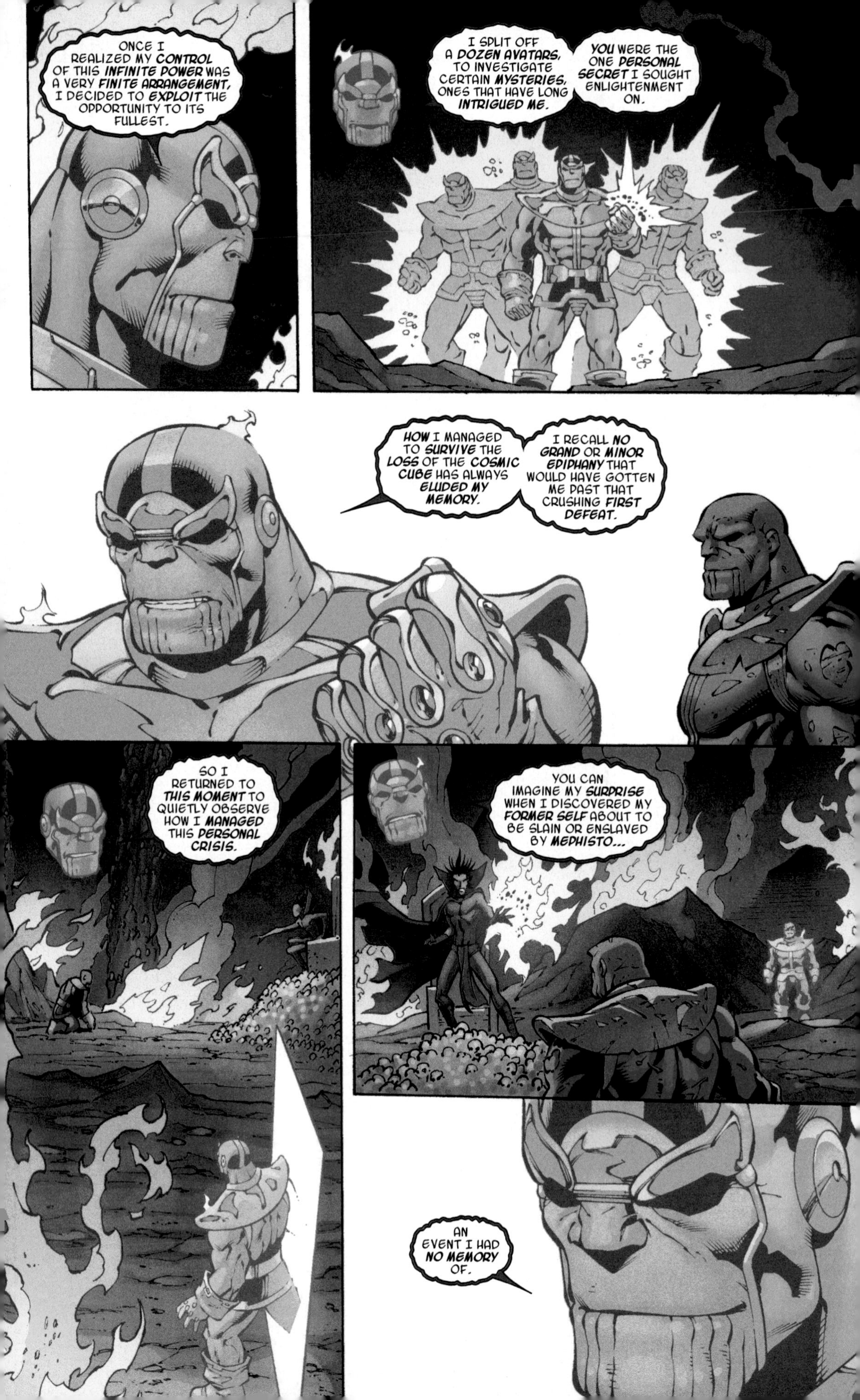
ONCE I REALIZED MY CONTROL OF THIS INFINITE POWER WAS A VERY FINITE ARRANGEMENT, I DECIDED TO EXPLOIT THE OPPORTUNITY TO ITS FULLEST.
I SPLIT OFF A DOZEN AVATARS, TO INVESTIGATE CERTAIN MYSTERIES, ONES THAT HAVE LONG INTRIGUED ME.
YOU WERE THE ONE PERSONAL SECRET I SOUGHT ENLIGHTENMENT ON.
HOW I MANAGED TO SURVIVE THE LOSS OF THE COSMIC CUBE HAS ALWAYS ELUDED MY MEMORY.
I RECALL NO GRAND OR MINOR EPIPHANY THAT WOULD HAVE GOTTEN ME PAST THAT CRUSHING FIRST DEFEAT.
SO I RETURNED TO THIS MOMENT TO QUIETLY OBSERVE HOW I MANAGED THIS PERSONAL CRISIS.
YOU CAN IMAGINE MY SURPRISE WHEN I DISCOVERED MY FORMER SELF ABOUT TO BE SLAIN OR ENSLAVED BY MEPHISTO...
AN EVENT I HAD NO MEMORY OF.

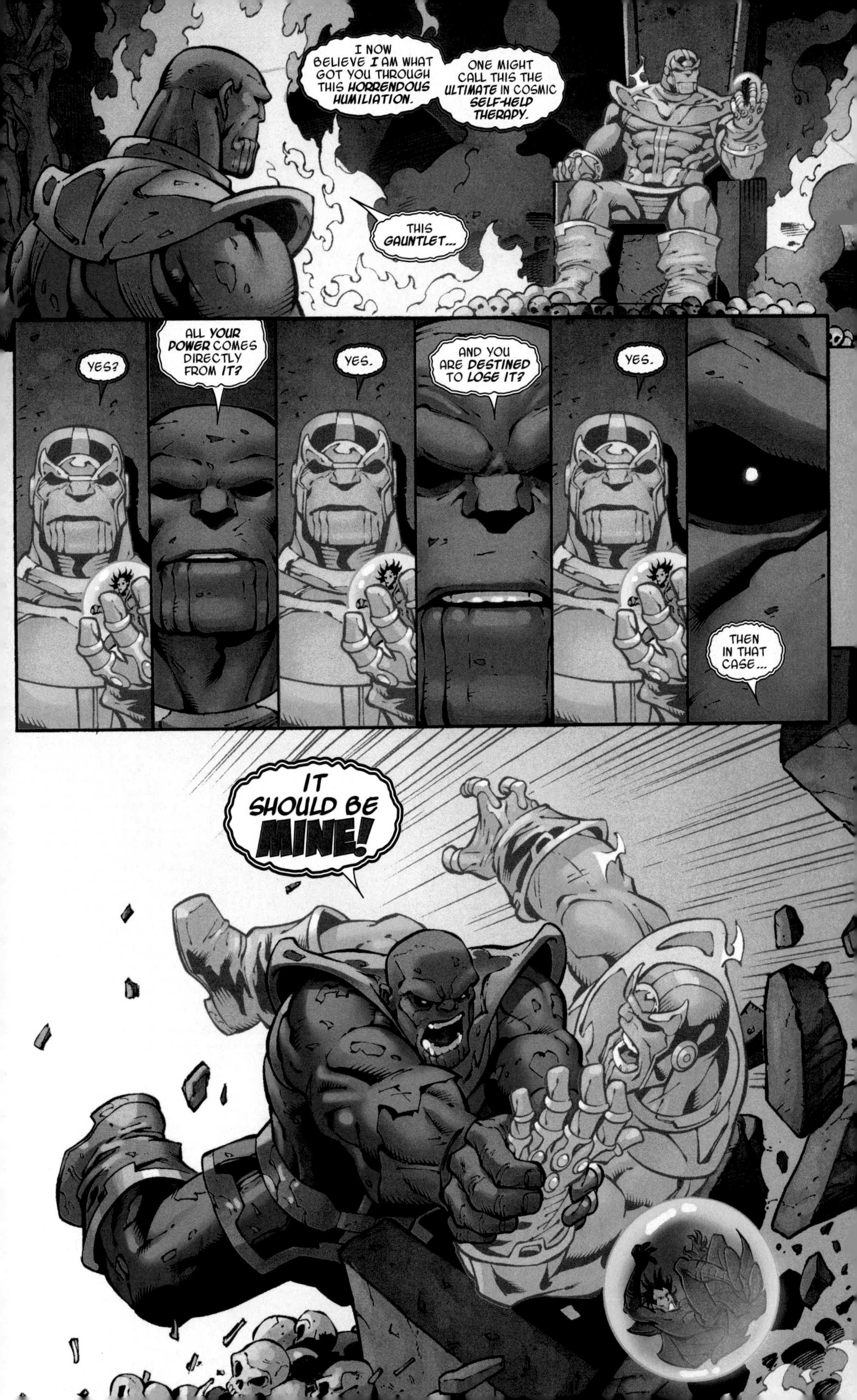
I NOW BELIEVE I AM WHAT GOT YOU THROUGH THIS HORRENDOUS HUMILIATION.
ONE MIGHT CALL THIS THE ULTIMATE IN COSMIC SELF-HELP THERAPY.
THIS GAUNTLET...
YES?
ALL YOUR POWER COMES DIRECTLY FROM IT?
YES.
AND YOU ARE DESTINED TO LOSE IT?
YES.
THEN IN THAT CASE...
IT SHOULD BE MINE!

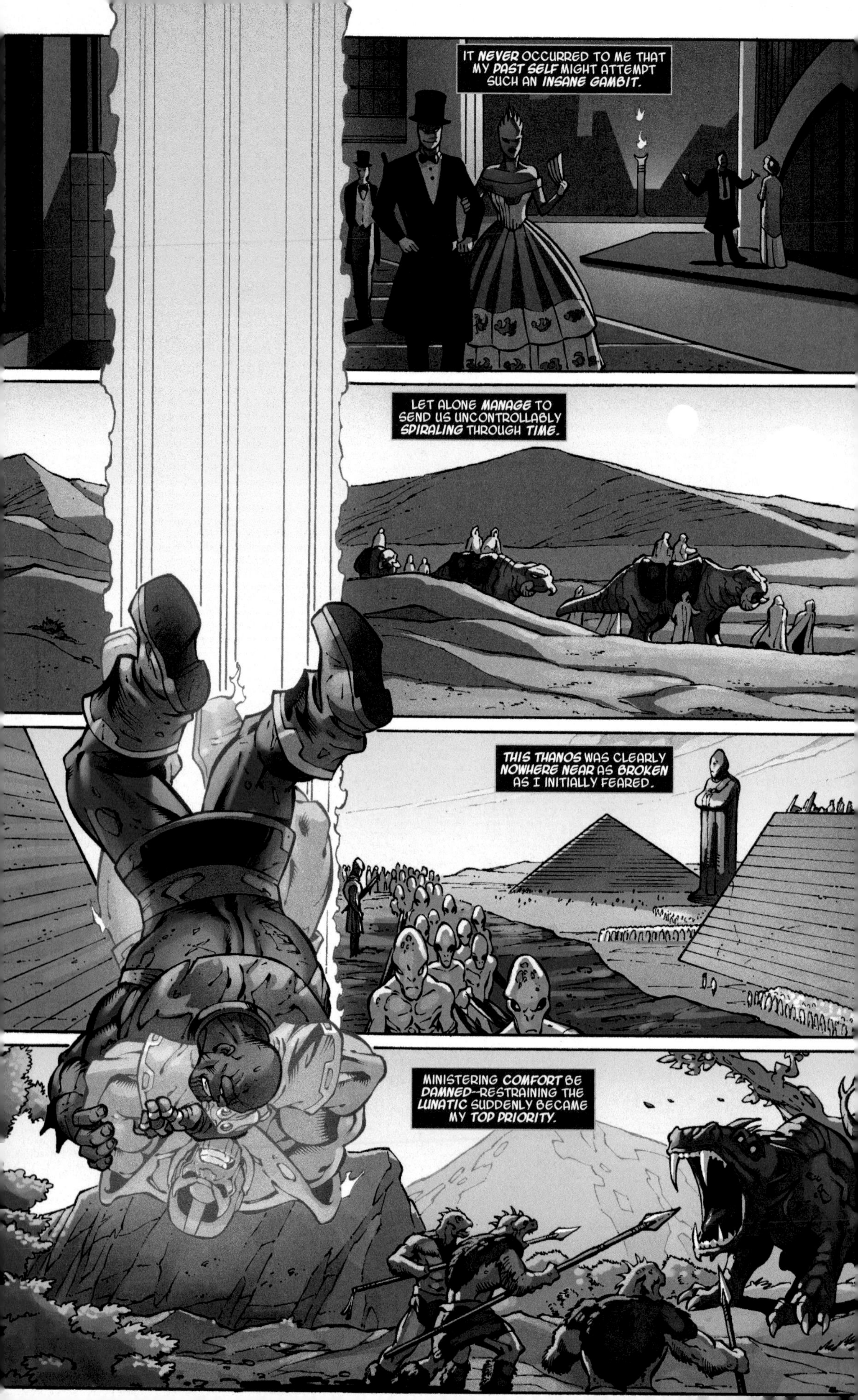
IT NEVER OCCURRED TO ME THAT MY PAST SELF MIGHT ATTEMPT SUCH AN INSANE GAMBIT.
LET ALONE MANAGE TO SEND US UNCONTROLLABLY SPIRALING THROUGH TIME.
THIS THANOS WAS CLEARLY NOWHERE NEAR AS BROKEN AS I INITIALLY FEARED.
MINISTERING COMFORT BE DAMNED--RESTRAINING THE LUNATIC SUDDENLY BECAME MY TOP PRIORITY.

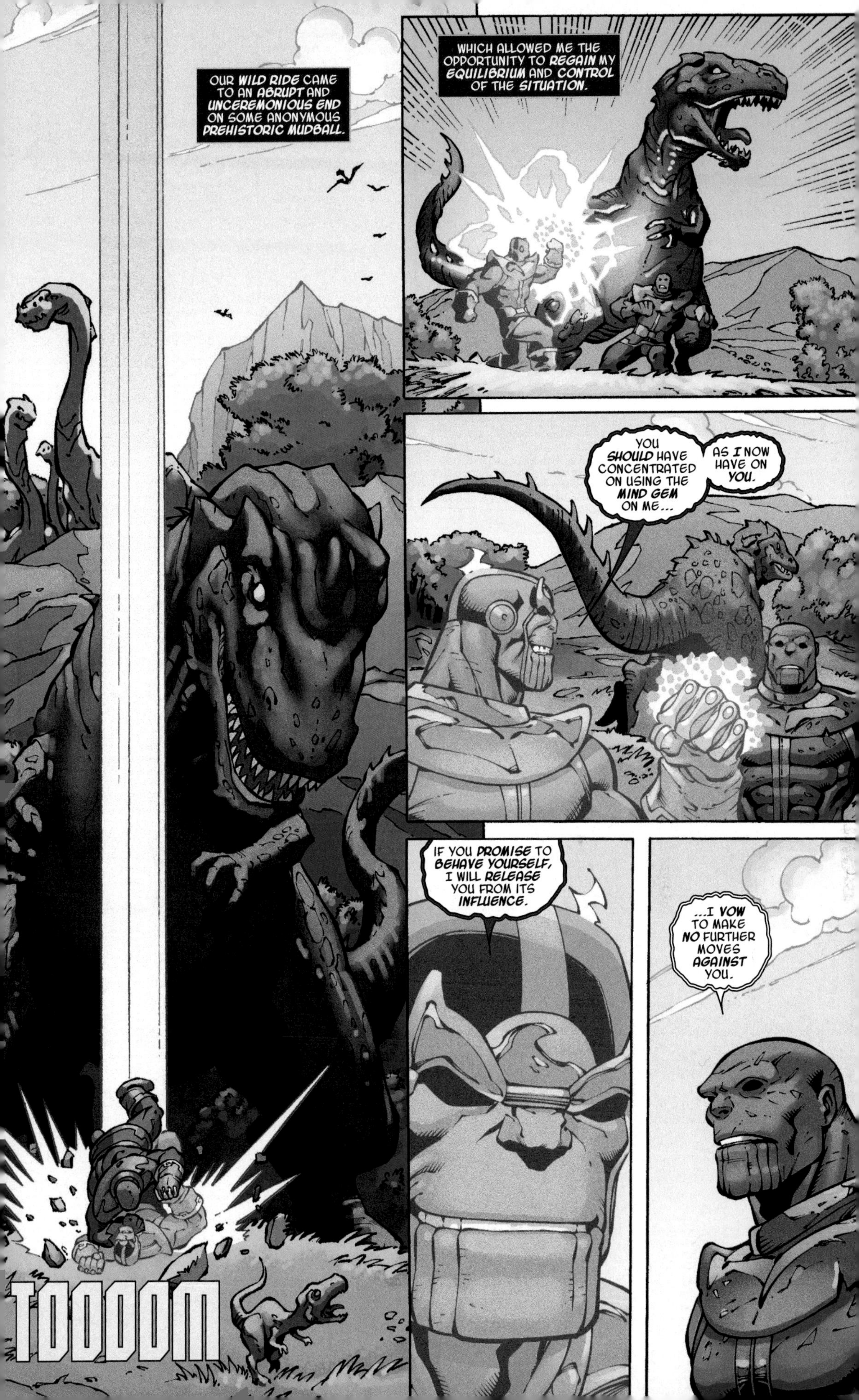
OUR WILD RIDE CAME TO AN ABRUPT AND UNCEREMONIOUS END ON SOME ANONYMOUS PREHISTORIC MUDBALL.
TOOOOM
WHICH ALLOWED ME THE OPPORTUNITY TO REGAIN MY EQUILIBRIUM AND CONTROL OF THE SITUATION.
YOU SHOULD HAVE CONCENTRATED ON USING THE MIND GEM ON ME...
AS I NOW HAVE ON YOU.
IF YOU PROMISE TO BEHAVE YOURSELF, I WILL RELEASE YOU FROM ITS INFLUENCE.
...I VOW TO MAKE NO FURTHER MOVES AGAINST YOU.

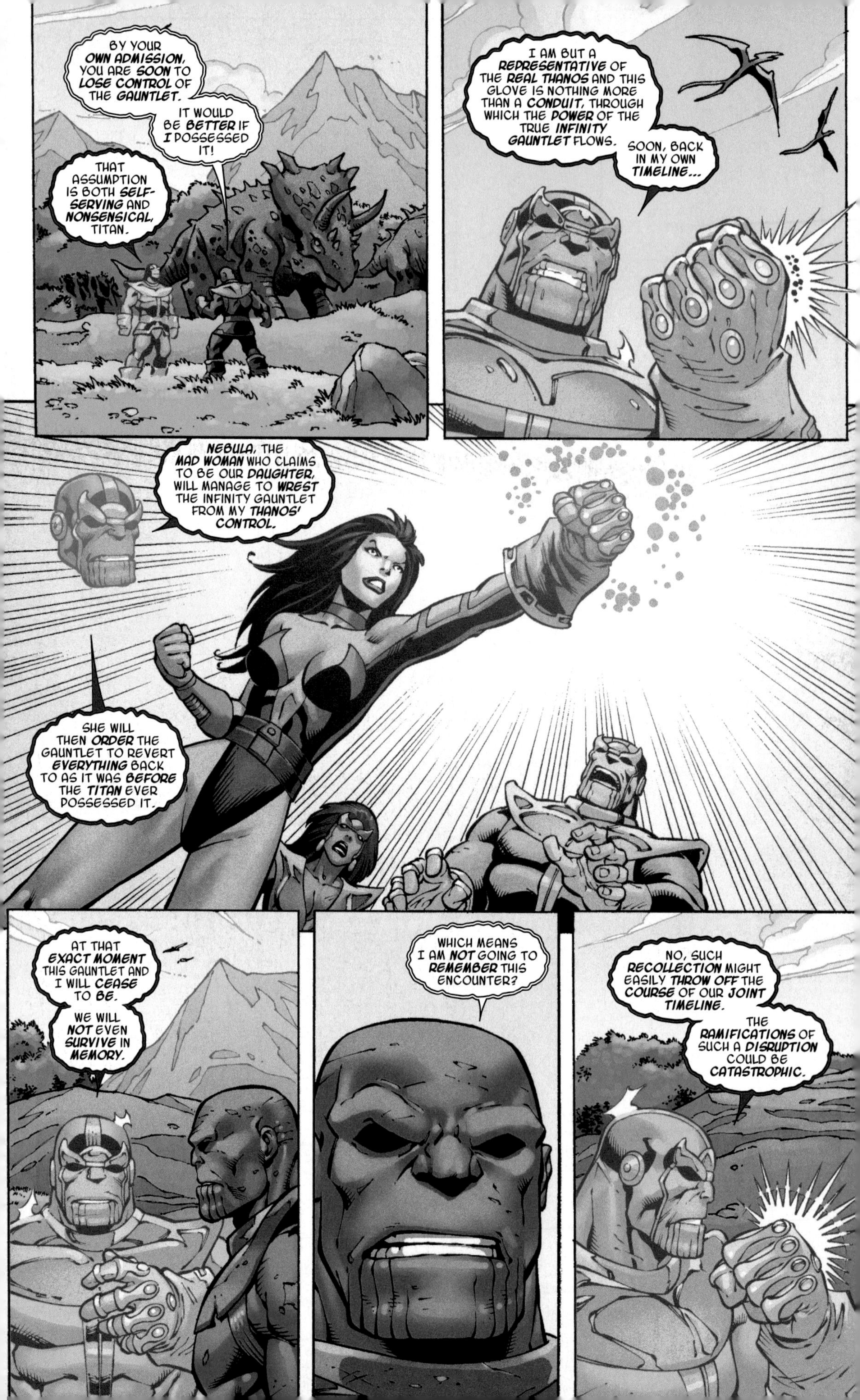
BY YOUR OWN ADMISSION, YOU ARE SOON TO LOSE CONTROL OF THE GAUNTLET.
IT WOULD BE BETTER IF I POSSESSED IT!
THAT ASSUMPTION IS BOTH SELF-SERVING AND NONSENSICAL, TITAN.
I AM BUT A REPRESENTATIVE OF THE REAL THANOS AND THIS GLOVE IS NOTHING MORE THAN A CONDUIT, THROUGH WHICH THE POWER OF THE TRUE INFINITY GAUNTLET FLOWS.
SOON, BACK IN MY OWN TIMELINE...
NEBULA, THE MAD WOMAN WHO CLAIMS TO BE OUR DAUGHTER, WILL MANAGE TO WREST THE INFINITY GAUNTLET FROM MY THANOS' CONTROL.
SHE WILL THEN ORDER THE GAUNTLET TO REVERT EVERYTHING BACK TO AS IT WAS BEFORE THE TITAN EVER POSSESSED IT.
AT THAT EXACT MOMENT THIS GAUNTLET AND I WILL CEASE TO BE.
WE WILL NOT EVEN SURVIVE IN MEMORY.
WHICH MEANS I AM NOT GOING TO REMEMBER THIS ENCOUNTER?
NO, SUCH RECOLLECTION MIGHT EASILY THROW OFF THE COURSE OF OUR JOINT TIMELINE.
THE RAMIFICATIONS OF SUCH A DISRUPTION COULD BE CATASTROPHIC.

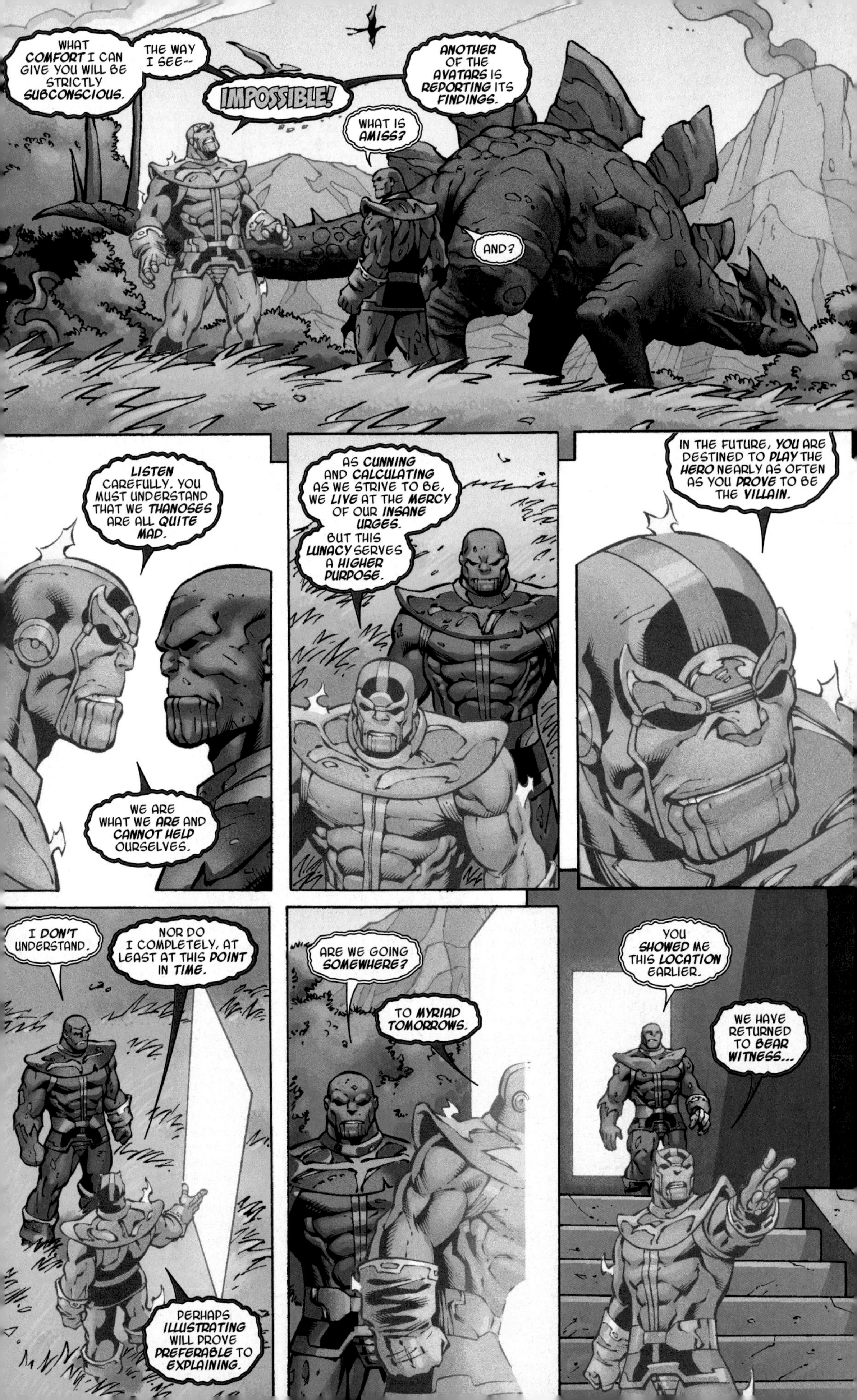
WHAT COMFORT I CAN GIVE YOU WILL BE STRICTLY SUBCONSCIOUS.
THE WAY I SEE--
IMPOSSIBLE!
ANOTHER OF THE AVATARS IS REPORTING ITS FINDINGS.
WHAT IS AMISS?
AND?
LISTEN CAREFULLY. YOU MUST UNDERSTAND THAT WE THANOSES ARE ALL QUITE MAD.
WE ARE WHAT WE ARE AND CANNOT HELP OURSELVES.
AS CUNNING AND CALCULATING AS WE STRIVE TO BE, WE LIVE AT THE MERCY OF OUR INSANE URGES.
BUT THIS LUNACY SERVES A HIGHER PURPOSE.
IN THE FUTURE, YOU ARE DESTINED TO PLAY THE HERO NEARLY AS OFTEN AS YOU PROVE TO BE THE VILLAIN.
I DON'T UNDERSTAND.
NOR DO I COMPLETELY, AT LEAST AT THIS POINT IN TIME.
PERHAPS ILLUSTRATING WILL PROVE PREFERABLE TO EXPLAINING.
ARE WE GOING SOMEWHERE?
TO MYRIAD TOMORROWS.
YOU SHOWED ME THIS LOCATION EARLIER.
WE HAVE RETURNED TO BEAR WITNESS...

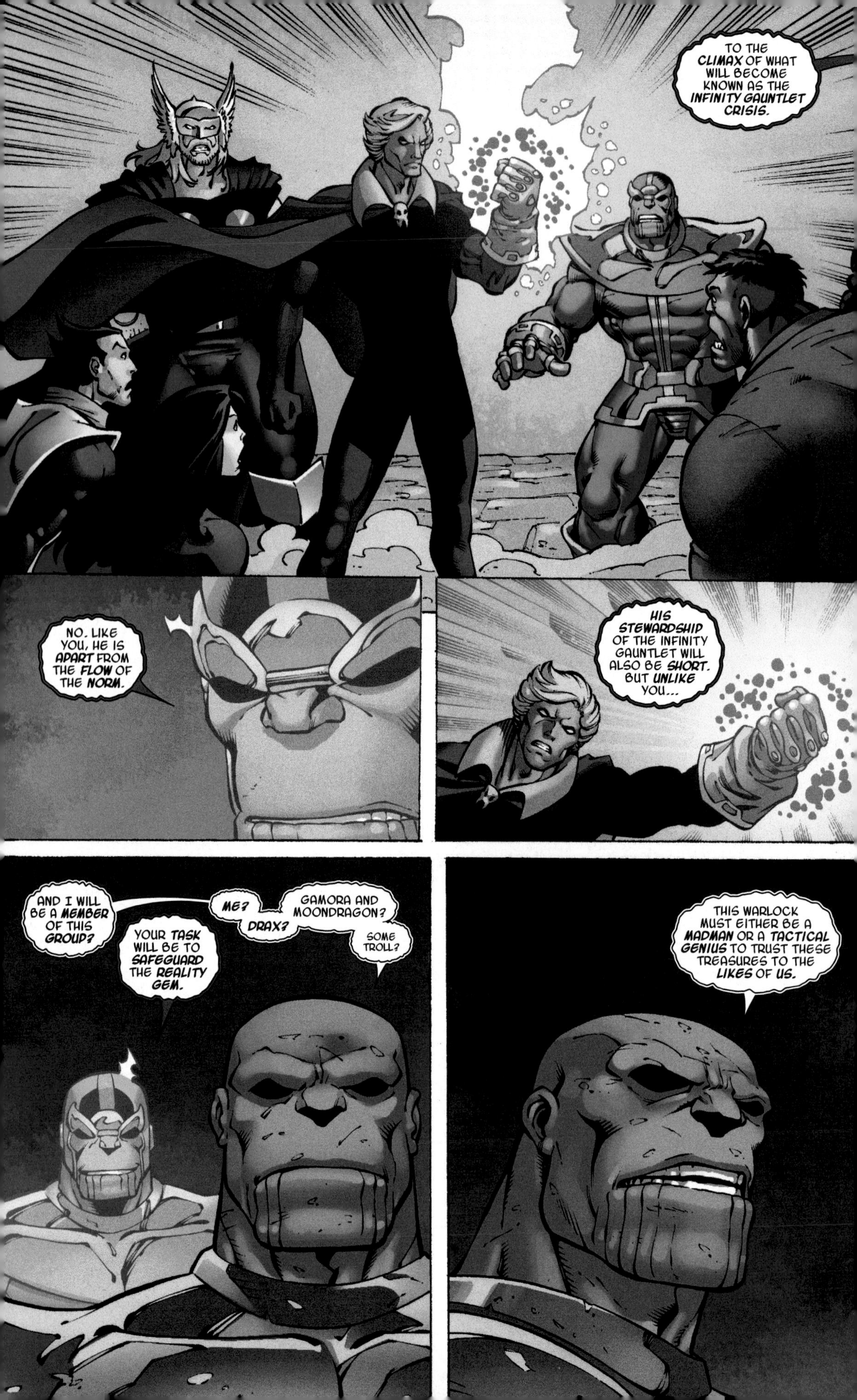
TO THE CLIMAX OF WHAT WILL BECOME KNOWN AS THE INFINITY GAUNTLET CRISIS.
NO. LIKE YOU, HE IS APART FROM THE FLOW OF THE NORM.
HIS STEWARDSHIP OF THE INFINITY GAUNTLET WILL ALSO BE SHORT. BUT UNLIKE YOU...
AND I WILL BE A MEMBER OF THIS GROUP?
ME?
DRAX?
GAMORA AND MOONDRAGON?
SOME TROLL?
YOUR TASK WILL BE TO SAFEGUARD THE REALITY GEM.
THIS WARLOCK MUST EITHER BE A MADMAN OR A TACTICAL GENIUS TO TRUST THESE TREASURES TO THE LIKES OF US.

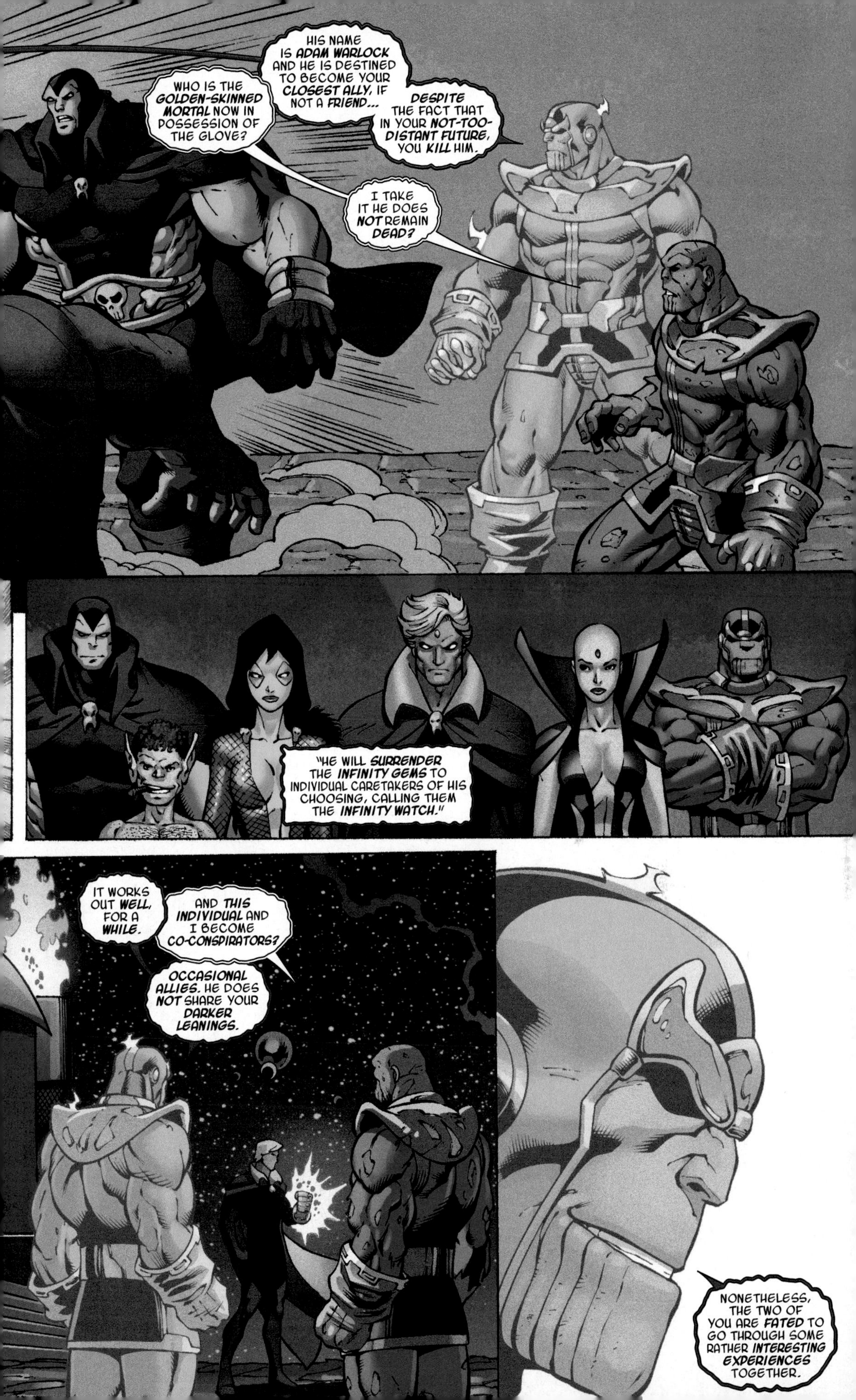
WHO IS THE GOLDEN-SKINNED MORTAL NOW IN POSSESSION OF THE GLOVE?
HIS NAME IS ADAM WARLOCK AND HE IS DESTINED TO BECOME YOUR CLOSEST ALLY, IF NOT A FRIEND...
DESPITE THE FACT THAT IN YOUR NOT-TOO-DISTANT FUTURE, YOU KILL HIM.
I TAKE IT HE DOES NOT REMAIN DEAD?
"HE WILL SURRENDER THE INFINITY GEMS TO INDIVIDUAL CARETAKERS OF HIS CHOOSING, CALLING THEM THE INFINITY WATCH."
IT WORKS OUT WELL, FOR A WHILE.
AND THIS INDIVIDUAL AND I BECOME CO-CONSPIRATORS?
OCCASIONAL ALLIES. HE DOES NOT SHARE YOUR DARKER LEANINGS.
NONETHELESS, THE TWO OF YOU ARE FATED TO GO THROUGH SOME RATHER INTERESTING EXPERIENCES TOGETHER.

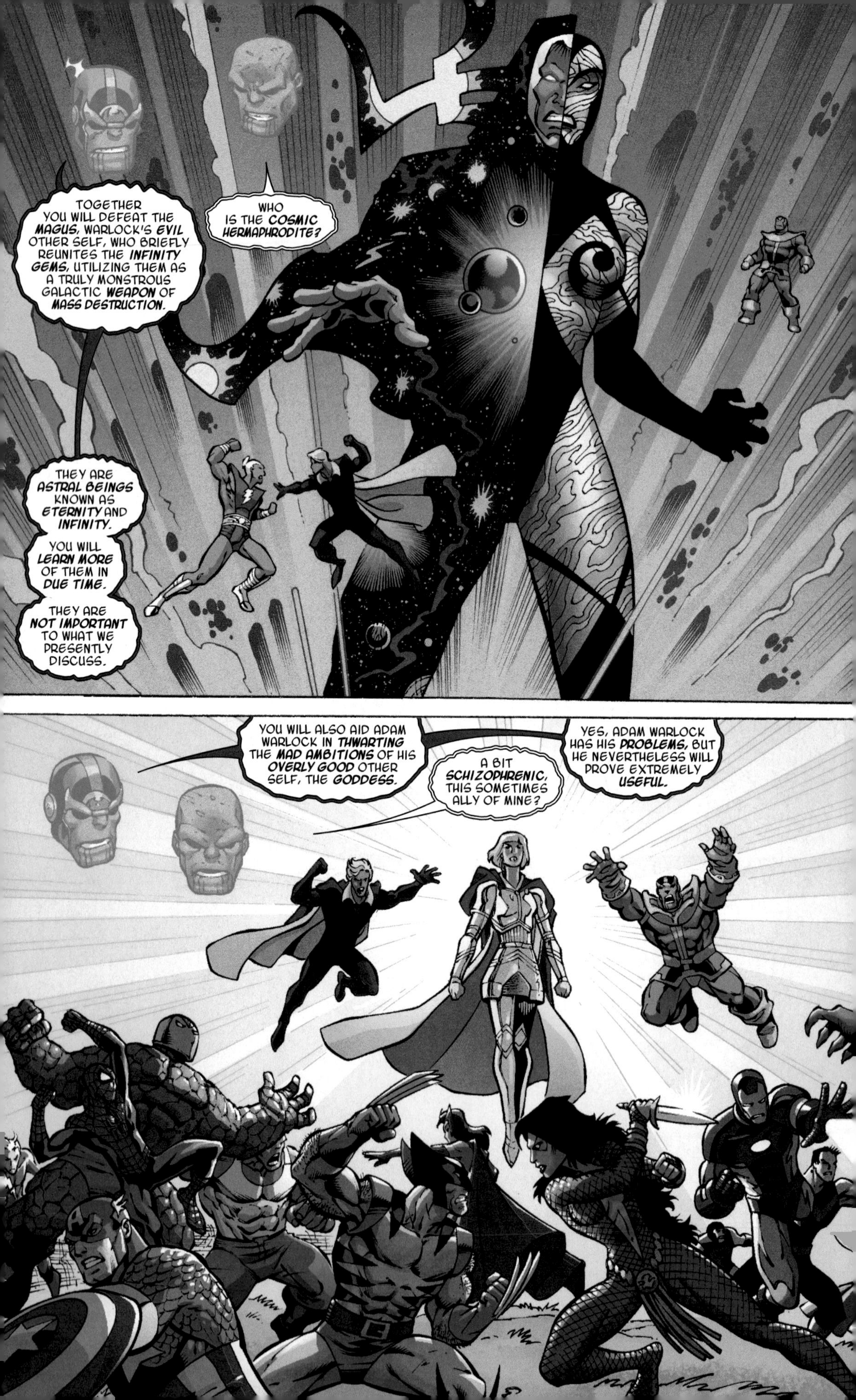
TOGETHER YOU WILL DEFEAT THE MAGUS, WARLOCK'S EVIL OTHER SELF, WHO BRIEFLY REUNITES THE INFINITY GEMS, UTILIZING THEM AS A TRULY MONSTROUS GALACTIC WEAPON OF MASS DESTRUCTION.
WHO IS THE COSMIC HERMAPHRODITE?
THEY ARE ASTRAL BEINGS KNOWN AS ETERNITY AND INFINITY.
YOU WILL LEARN MORE OF THEM IN DUE TIME.
THEY ARE NOT IMPORTANT TO WHAT WE PRESENTLY DISCUSS.
YOU WILL ALSO AID ADAM WARLOCK IN THWARTING THE MAD AMBITIONS OF HIS OVERLY GOOD OTHER SELF, THE GODDESS.
A BIT SCHIZOPHRENIC, THIS SOMETIMES ALLY OF MINE?
YES, ADAM WARLOCK HAS HIS PROBLEMS, BUT HE NEVERTHELESS WILL PROVE EXTREMELY USEFUL.

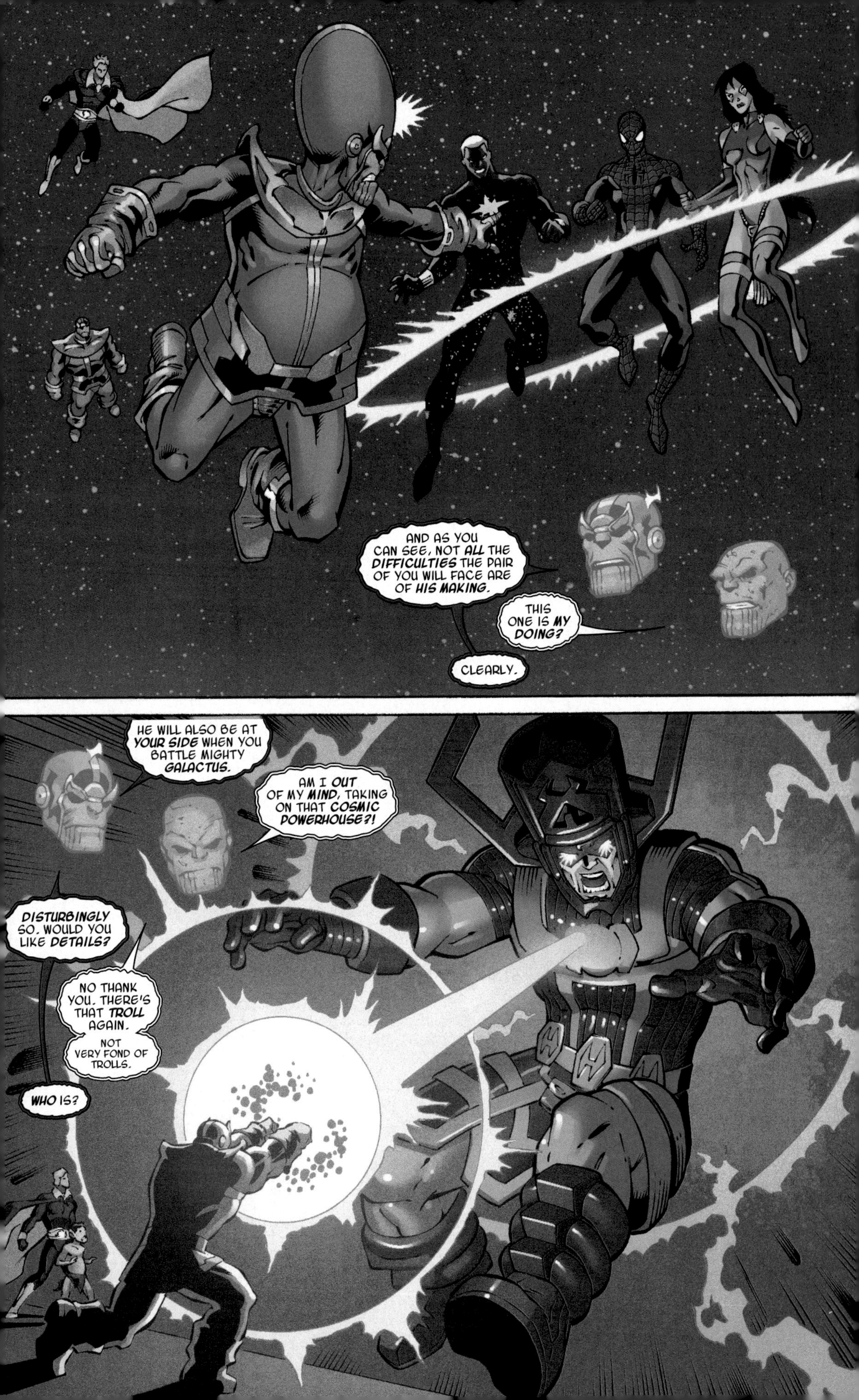

AND AS YOU CAN SEE, NOT ALL THE DIFFICULTIES THE PAIR OF YOU WILL FACE ARE OF HIS MAKING.
THIS ONE IS MY DOING?
CLEARLY.
HE WILL ALSO BE AT YOUR SIDE WHEN YOU BATTLE MIGHTY GALACTUS.
AM I OUT OF MY MIND, TAKING ON THAT COSMIC POWERHOUSE?!
DISTURBINGLY SO. WOULD YOU LIKE DETAILS?
NO THANK YOU. THERE'S THAT TROLL AGAIN.
NOT VERY FOND OF TROLLS.
WHO IS?

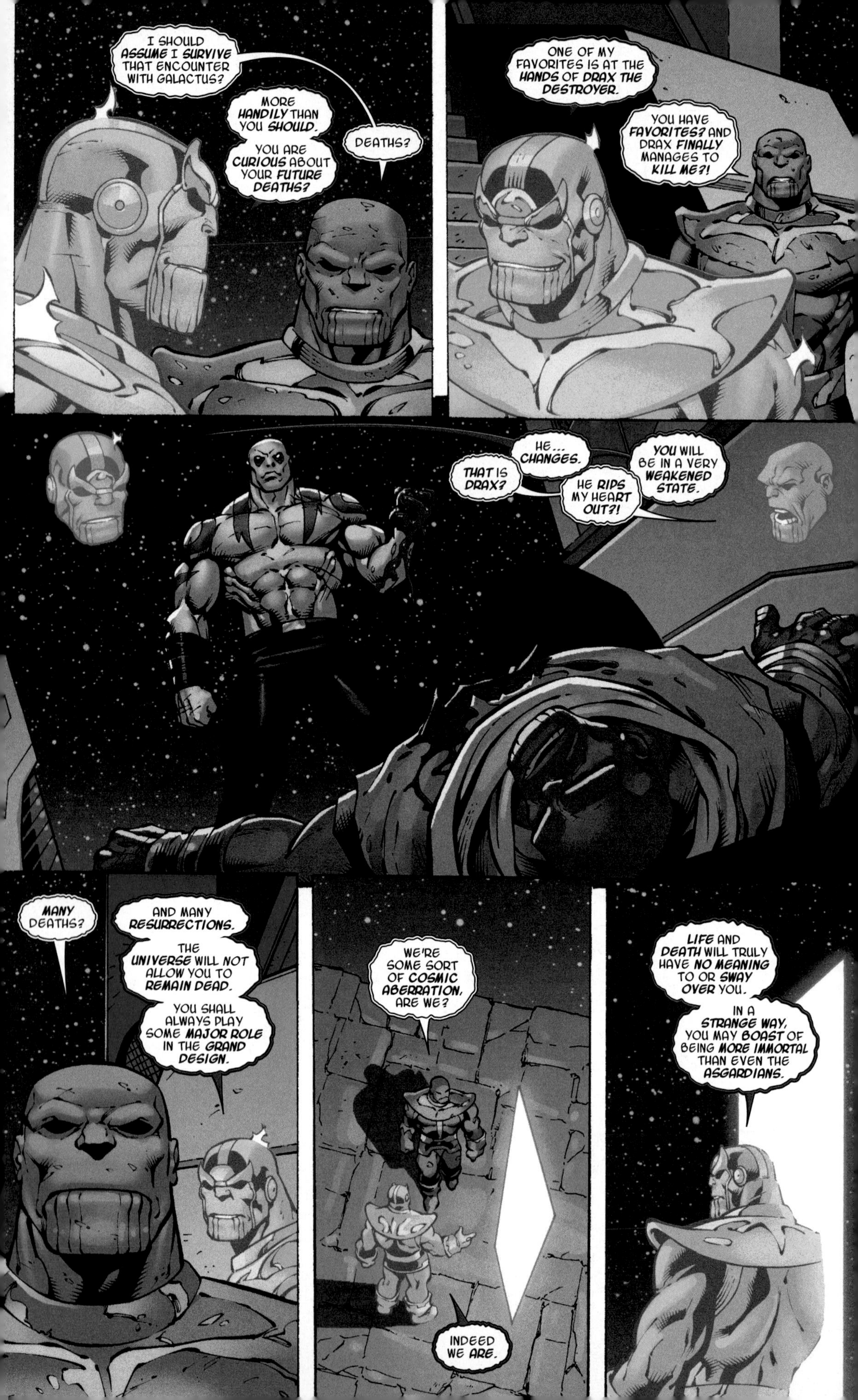
I SHOULD ASSUME I SURVIVE THAT ENCOUNTER WITH GALACTUS?
MORE HANDILY THAN YOU SHOULD.
YOU ARE CURIOUS ABOUT YOUR FUTURE DEATHS?
DEATHS?
ONE OF MY FAVORITES IS AT THE HANDS OF DRAX THE DESTROYER.
YOU HAVE FAVORITES? AND DRAX FINALLY MANAGES TO KILL ME?!
THAT IS DRAX?
HE... CHANGES.
HE RIPS MY HEART OUT?!
YOU WILL BE IN A VERY WEAKENED STATE.
MANY DEATHS?
AND MANY RESURRECTIONS.
THE UNIVERSE WILL NOT ALLOW YOU TO REMAIN DEAD.
YOU SHALL ALWAYS PLAY SOME MAJOR ROLE IN THE GRAND DESIGN.
WE'RE SOME SORT OF COSMIC ABERRATION, ARE WE?
INDEED WE ARE.
LIFE AND DEATH WILL TRULY HAVE NO MEANING TO OR SWAY OVER YOU.
IN A STRANGE WAY, YOU MAY BOAST OF BEING MORE IMMORTAL THAN EVEN THE ASGARDIANS.

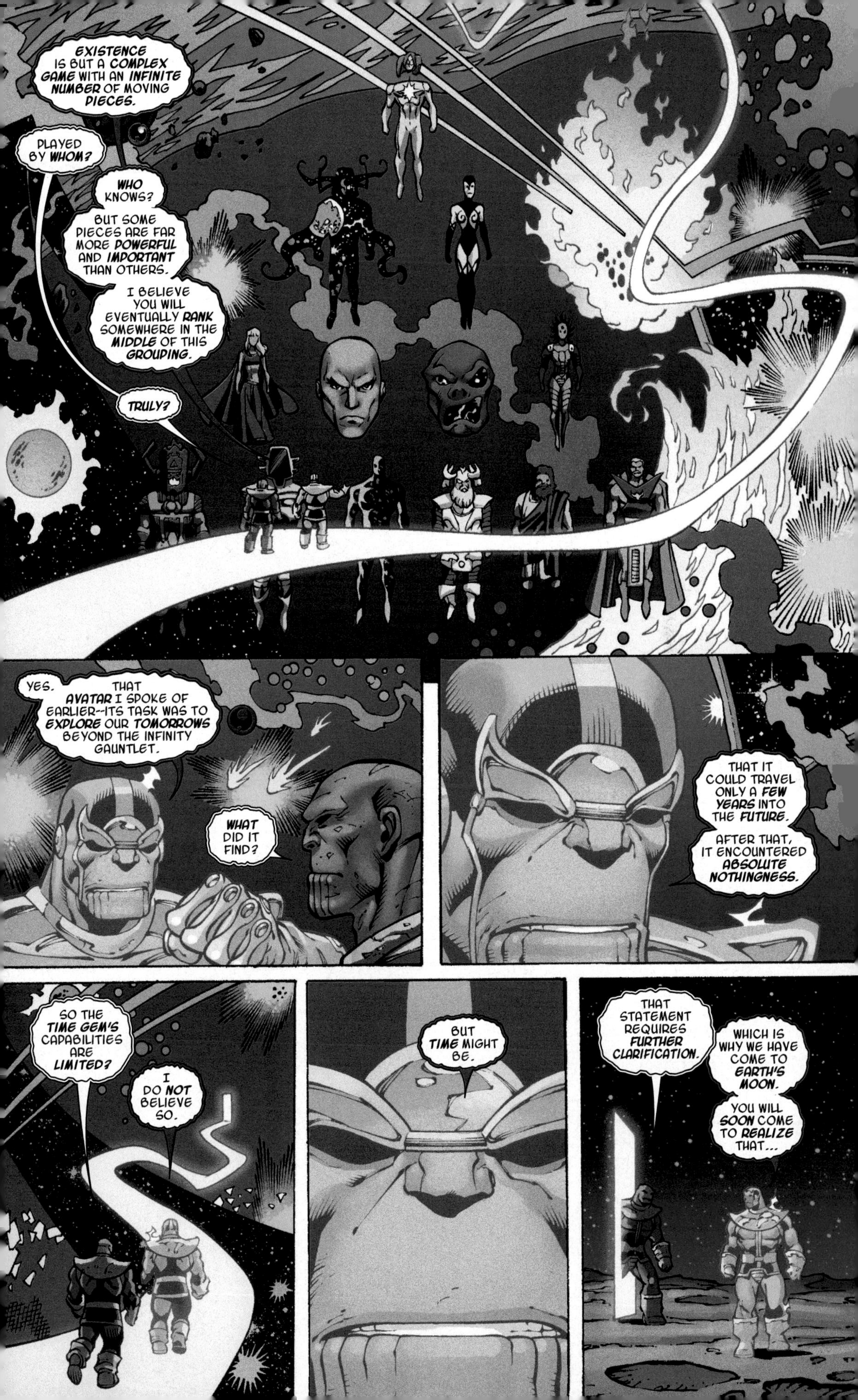
EXISTENCE IS BUT A COMPLEX GAME WITH AN INFINITE NUMBER OF MOVING PIECES.
PLAYED BY WHOM?
WHO KNOWS?
BUT SOME PIECES ARE FAR MORE POWERFUL AND IMPORTANT THAN OTHERS.
I BELIEVE YOU WILL EVENTUALLY RANK SOMEWHERE IN THE MIDDLE OF THIS GROUPING.
TRULY?
YES.
THAT AVATAR I SPOKE OF EARLIER--ITS TASK WAS TO EXPLORE OUR TOMORROWS BEYOND THE INFINITY GAUNTLET.
WHAT DID IT FIND?
THAT IT COULD TRAVEL ONLY A FEW YEARS INTO THE FUTURE.
AFTER THAT, IT ENCOUNTERED ABSOLUTE NOTHINGNESS.
SO THE TIME GEM'S CAPABILITIES ARE LIMITED?
I DO NOT BELIEVE SO.
BUT TIME MIGHT BE.
THAT STATEMENT REQUIRES FURTHER CLARIFICATION.
WHICH IS WHY WE HAVE COME TO EARTH'S MOON.
YOU WILL SOON COME TO REALIZE THAT...

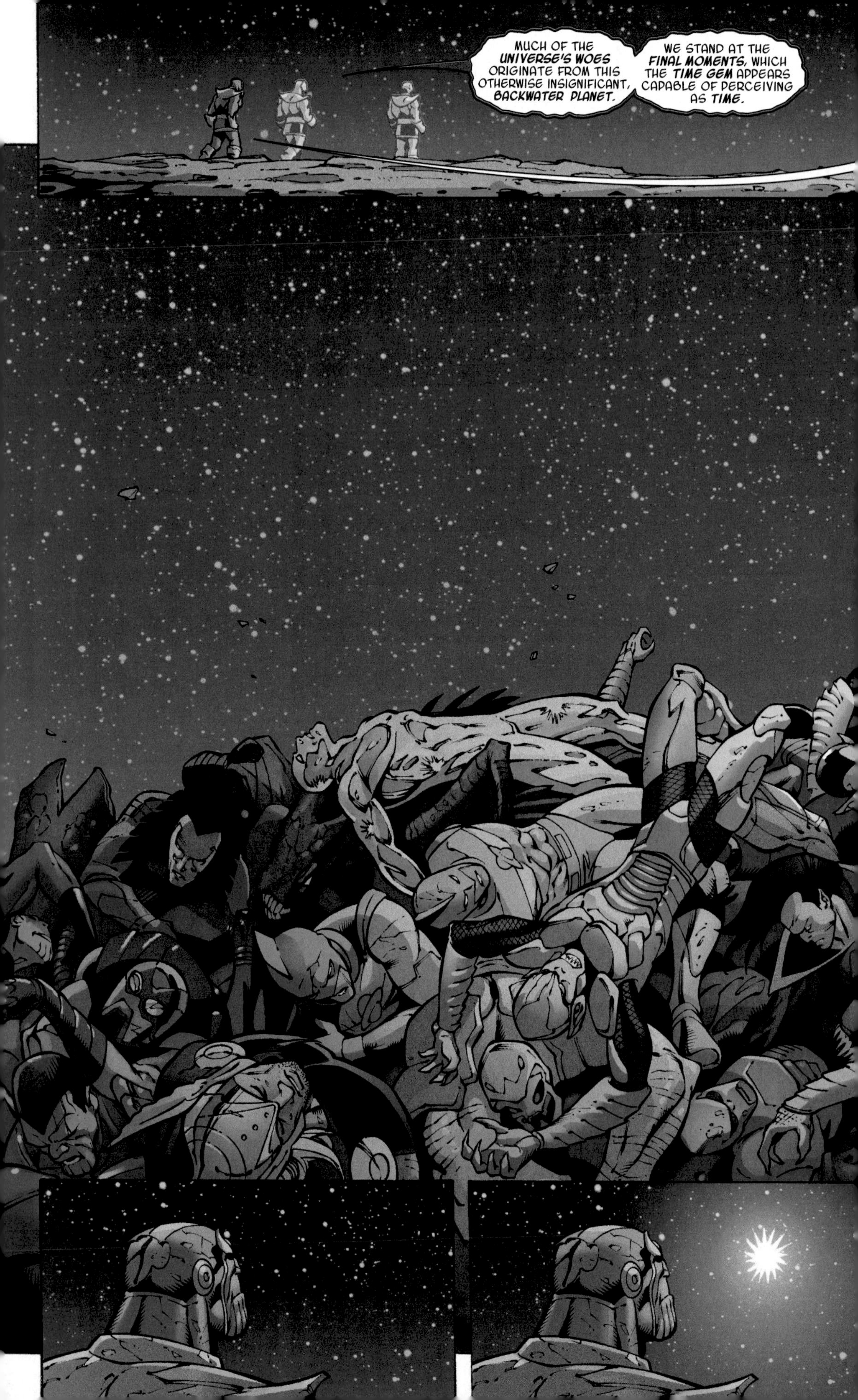
MUCH OF THE UNIVERSE'S WOES ORIGINATE FROM THIS OTHERWISE INSIGNIFICANT, BACKWATER PLANET.
WE STAND AT THE FINAL MOMENTS, WHICH THE TIME GEM APPEARS CAPABLE OF PERCEIVING AS TIME.

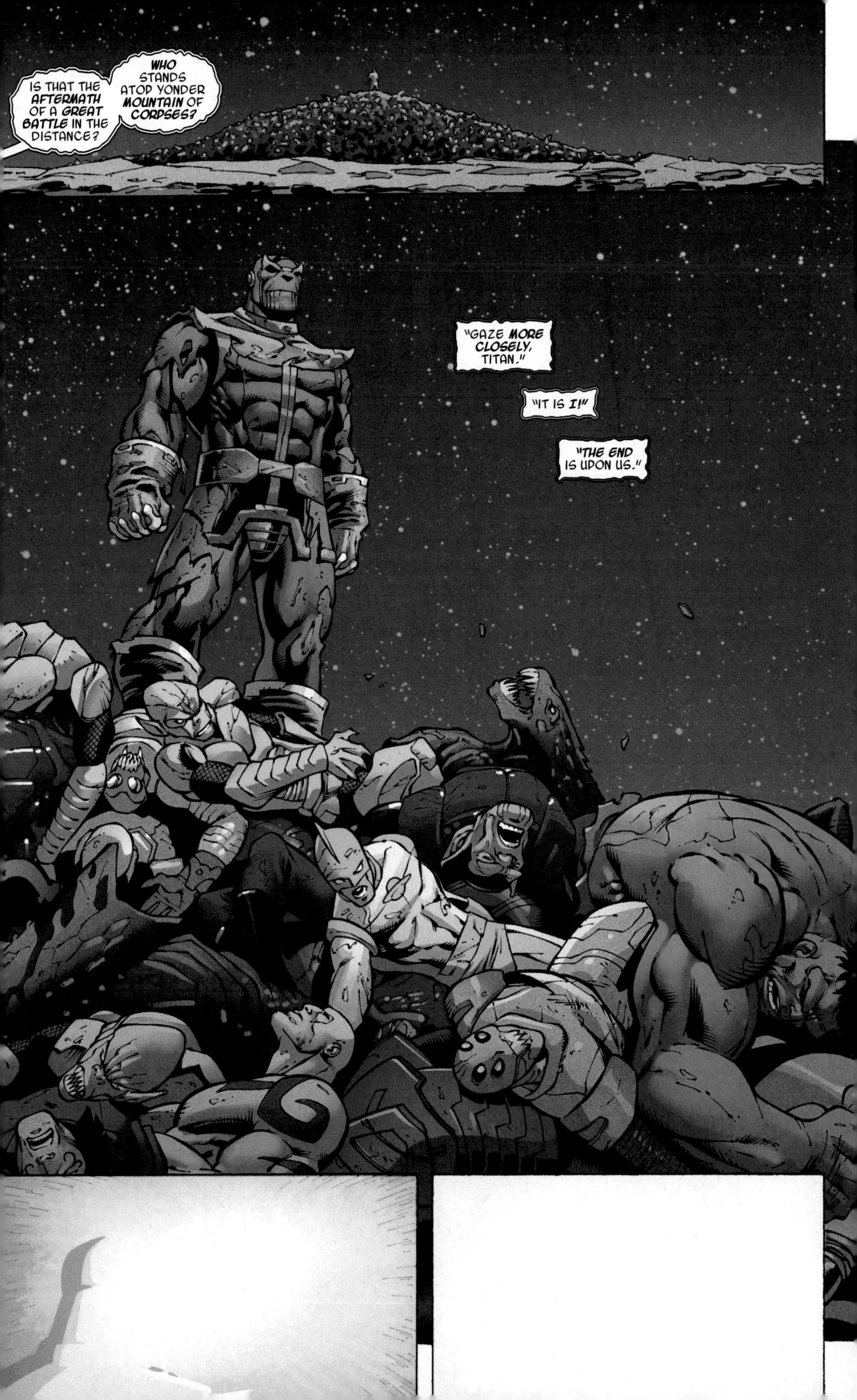

IS THAT THE AFTERMATH OF A GREAT BATTLE IN THE DISTANCE?
WHO STANDS ATOP YONDER MOUNTAIN OF CORPSES?
"GAZE MORE CLOSELY, TITAN."
"IT IS I!"
"THE END IS UPON US."

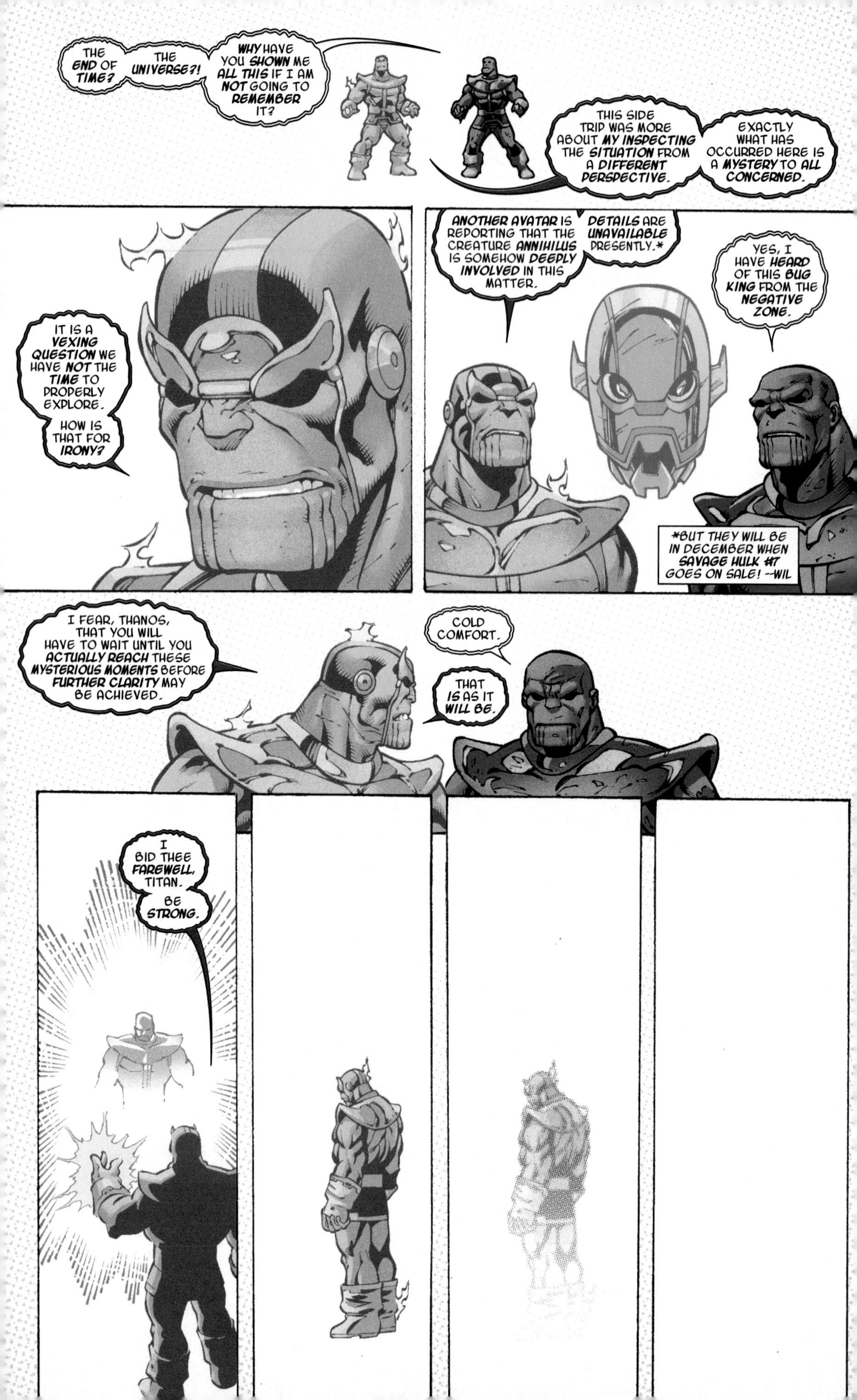
THE END OF TIME?
THE UNIVERSE?!
WHY HAVE YOU SHOWN ME ALL THIS IF I AM NOT GOING TO REMEMBER IT?
THIS SIDE TRIP WAS MORE ABOUT MY INSPECTING THE SITUATION FROM A DIFFERENT PERSPECTIVE.
EXACTLY WHAT HAS OCCURRED HERE IS A MYSTERY TO ALL CONCERNED.
IT IS A VEXING QUESTION WE HAVE NOT THE TIME TO PROPERLY EXPLORE.
HOW IS THAT FOR IRONY?
ANOTHER AVATAR IS REPORTING THAT THE CREATURE ANNIHILUS IS SOMEHOW DEEPLY INVOLVED IN THIS MATTER.
DETAILS ARE UNAVAILABLE PRESENTLY.*
YES, I HAVE HEARD OF THIS BUG KING FROM THE NEGATIVE ZONE.
*BUT THEY WILL BE IN DECEMBER WHEN SAVAGE HULK #7 GOES ON SALE! --WIL
I FEAR, THANOS, THAT YOU WILL HAVE TO WAIT UNTIL YOU ACTUALLY REACH THESE MYSTERIOUS MOMENTS BEFORE FURTHER CLARITY MAY BE ACHIEVED.
COLD COMFORT.
THAT IS AS IT WILL BE.
I BID THEE FAREWELL, TITAN.
BE STRONG.

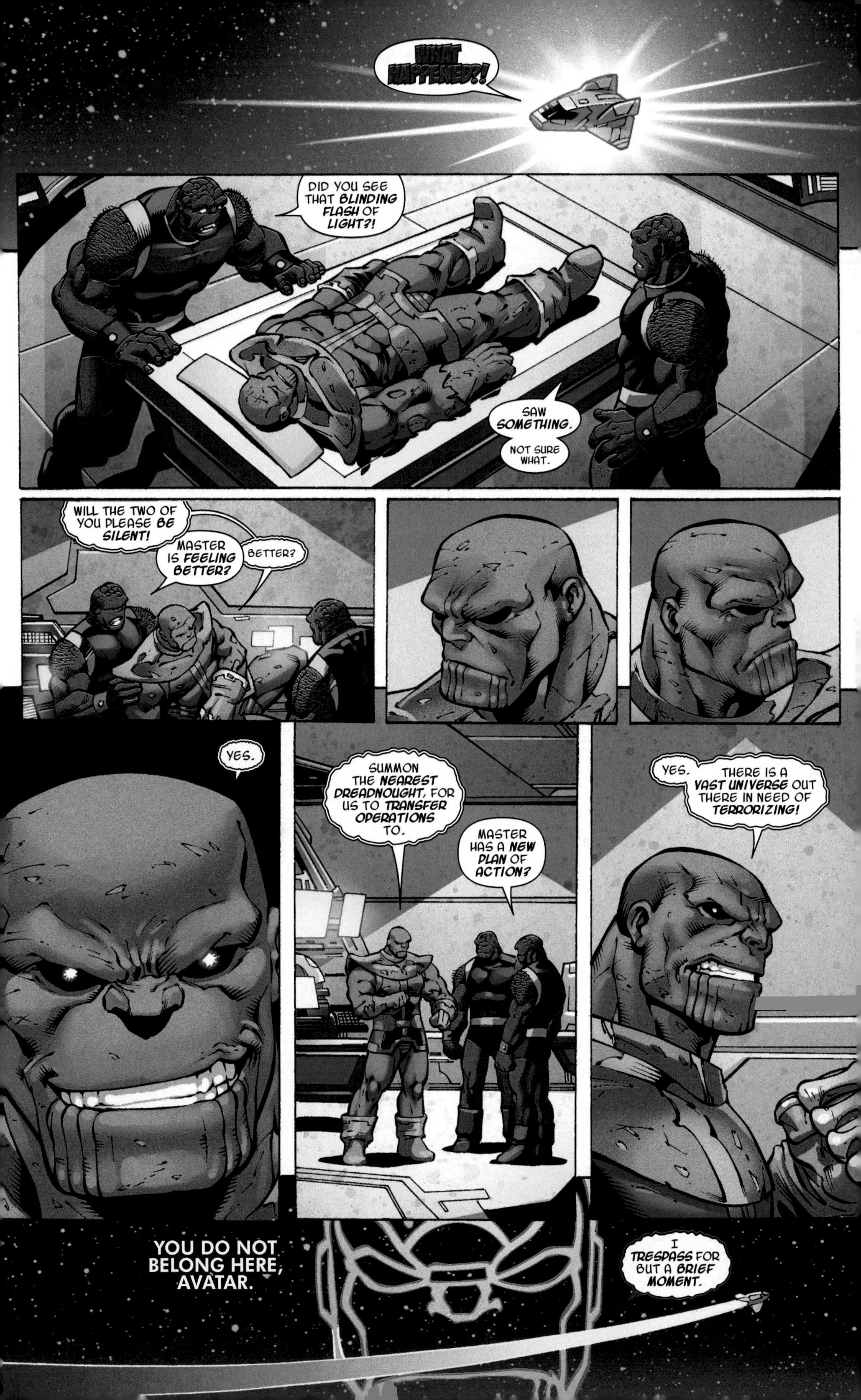
WHAT HAPPENED?!
DID YOU SEE THAT BLINDING FLASH OF LIGHT?!
SAW SOMETHING.
NOT SURE WHAT.
WILL THE TWO OF YOU PLEASE BE SILENT!
MASTER IS FEELING BETTER?
BETTER?
YES.
SUMMON THE NEAREST DREADNOUGHT, FOR US TO TRANSFER OPERATIONS TO.
MASTER HAS A NEW PLAN OF ACTION?
YES.
THERE IS A VAST UNIVERSE OUT THERE IN NEED OF TERRORIZING!
YOU DO NOT BELONG HERE, AVATAR.
I TRESPASS FOR BUT A BRIEF MOMENT.

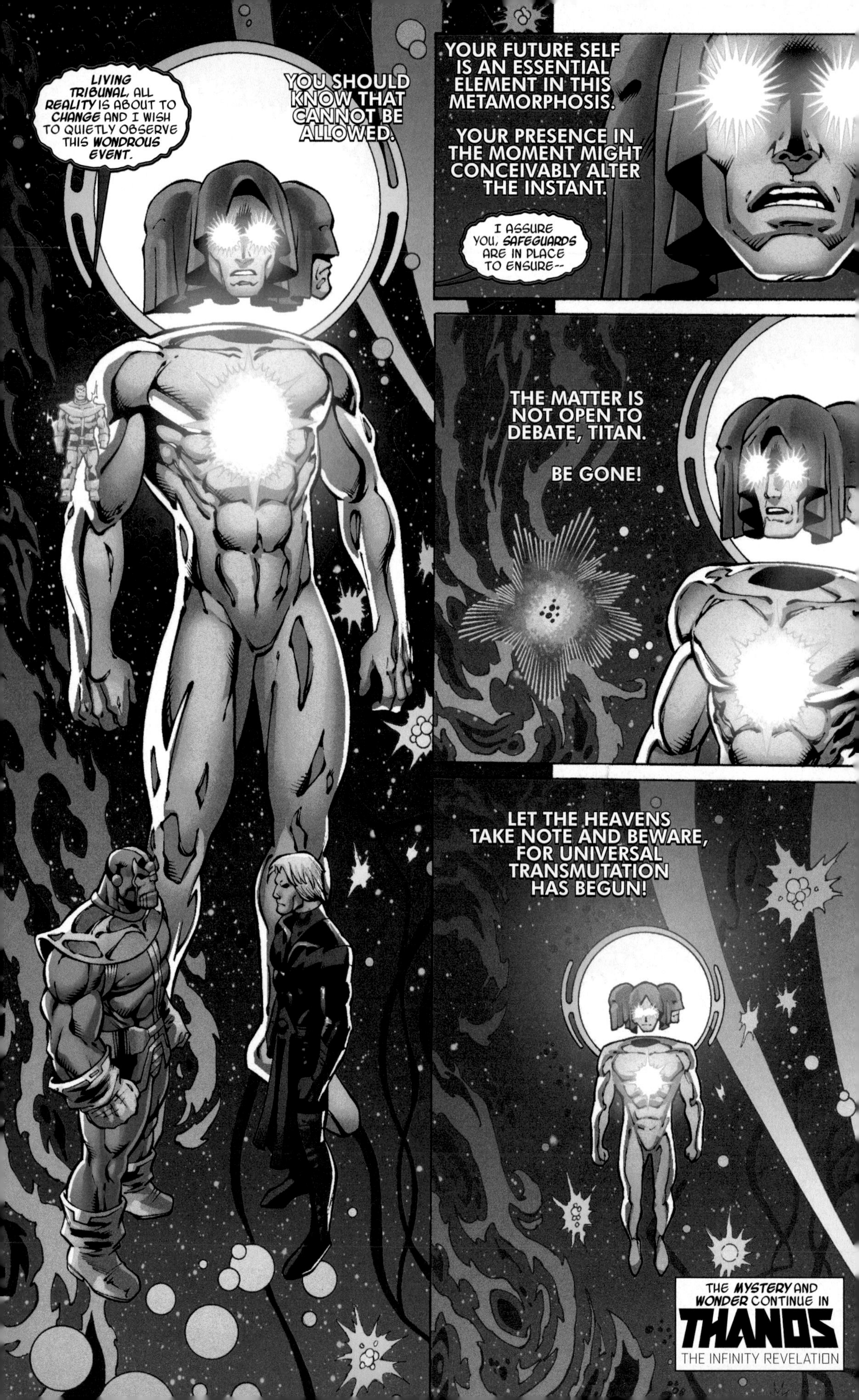
LIVING TRIBUNAL, ALL REALITY IS ABOUT TO CHANGE AND I WISH TO QUIETLY OBSERVE THIS WONDROUS EVENT.
YOU SHOULD KNOW THAT CANNOT BE ALLOWED.
YOUR FUTURE SELF IS AN ESSENTIAL ELEMENT IN THIS METAMORPHOSIS.
YOUR PRESENCE IN THE MOMENT MIGHT CONCEIVABLY ALTER THE INSTANT.
I ASSURE YOU, SAFEGUARDS ARE IN PLACE TO ENSURE--
THE MATTER IS NOT OPEN TO DEBATE, TITAN.
BE GONE!
LET THE HEAVENS TAKE NOTE AND BEWARE, FOR UNIVERSAL TRANSMUTATION HAS BEGUN!
THE MYSTERY AND WONDER CONTINUE IN
THANOS
THE INFINITY REVELATION

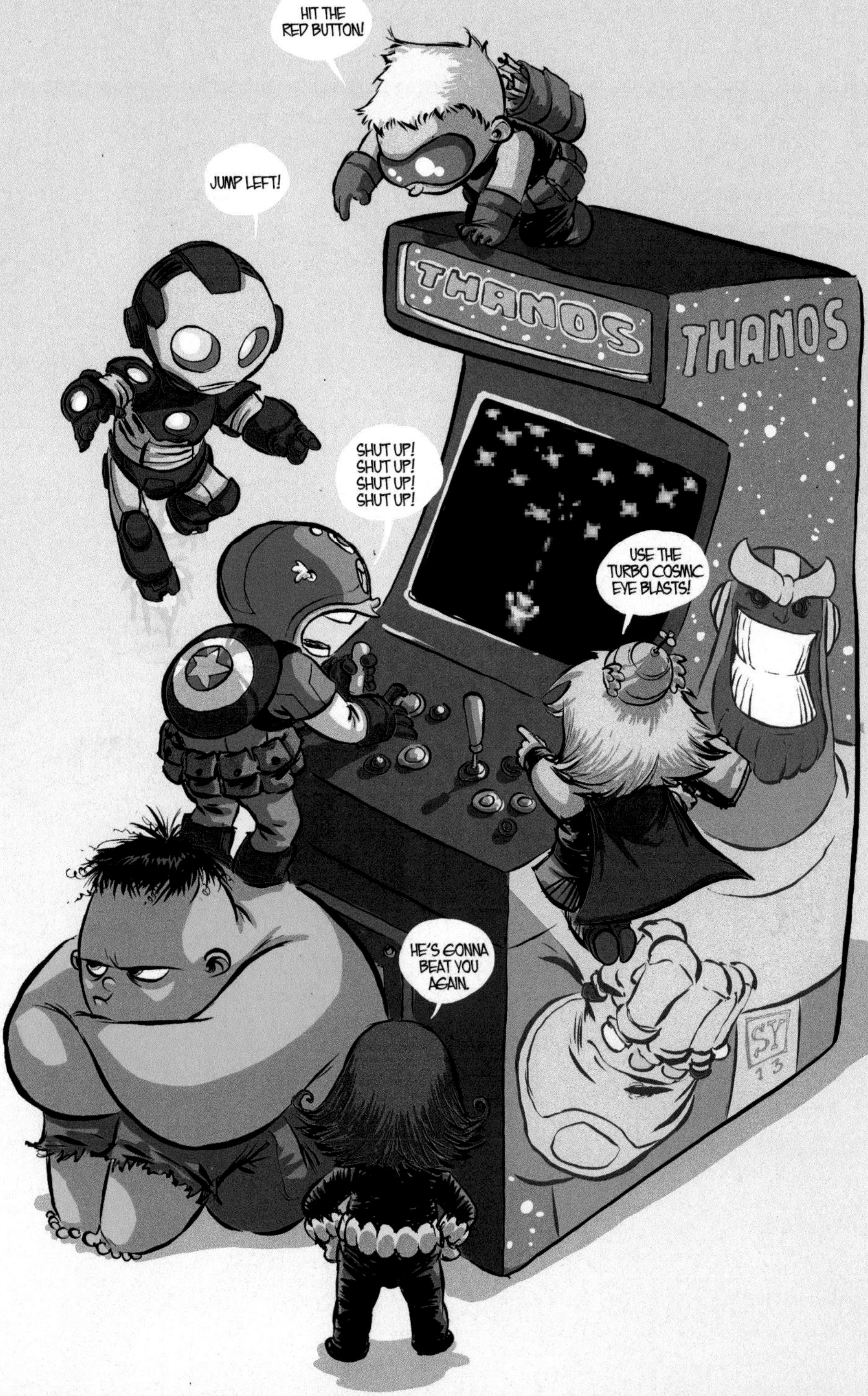
HIT THE RED BUTTON!
JUMP LEFT!
THANOS
THANOS
SHUT UP! SHUT UP! SHUT UP! SHUT UP!
USE THE TURBO COSMIC EYE BLASTS!
HE'S GONNA BEAT YOU AGAIN.
SY 13

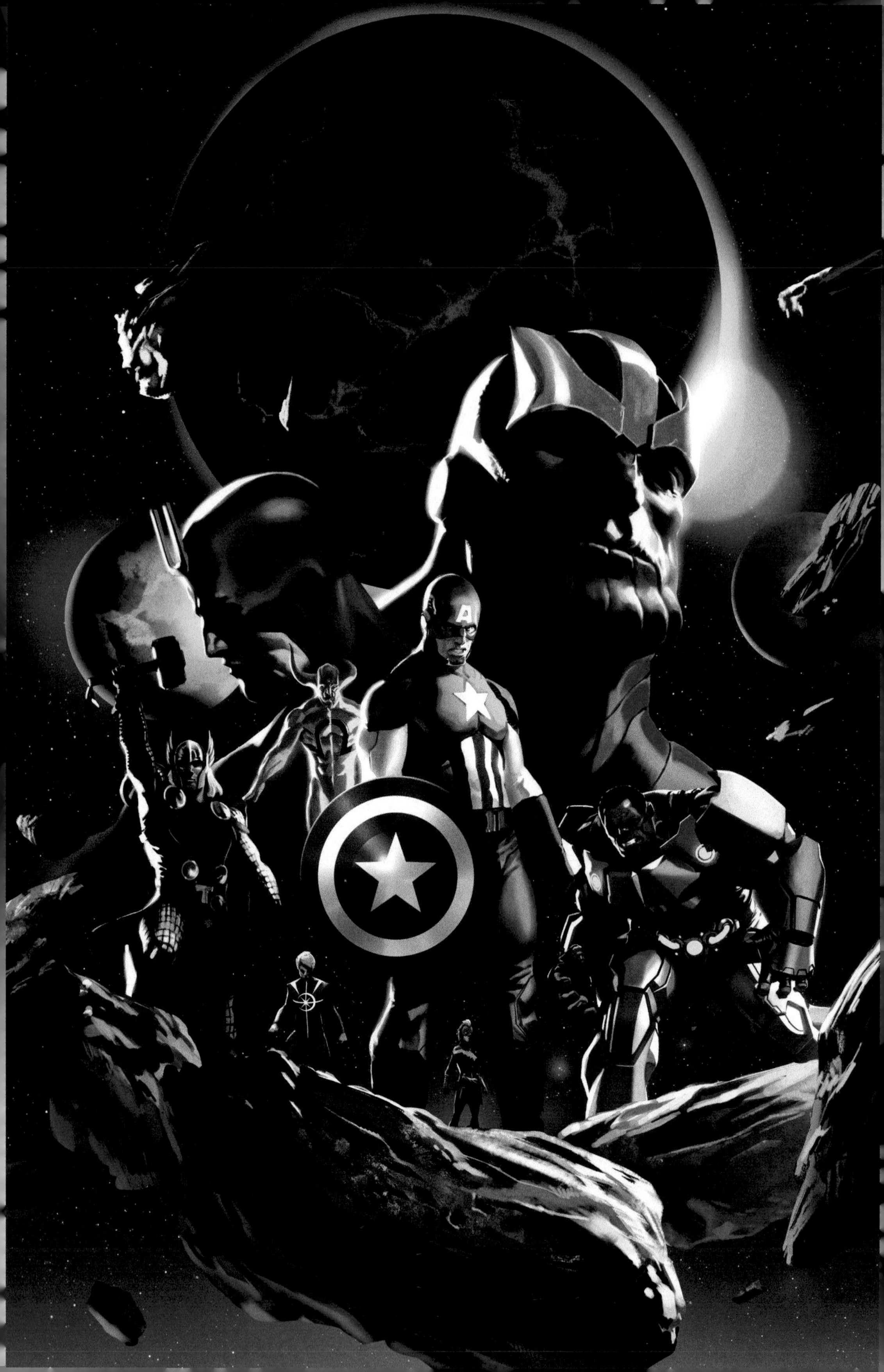

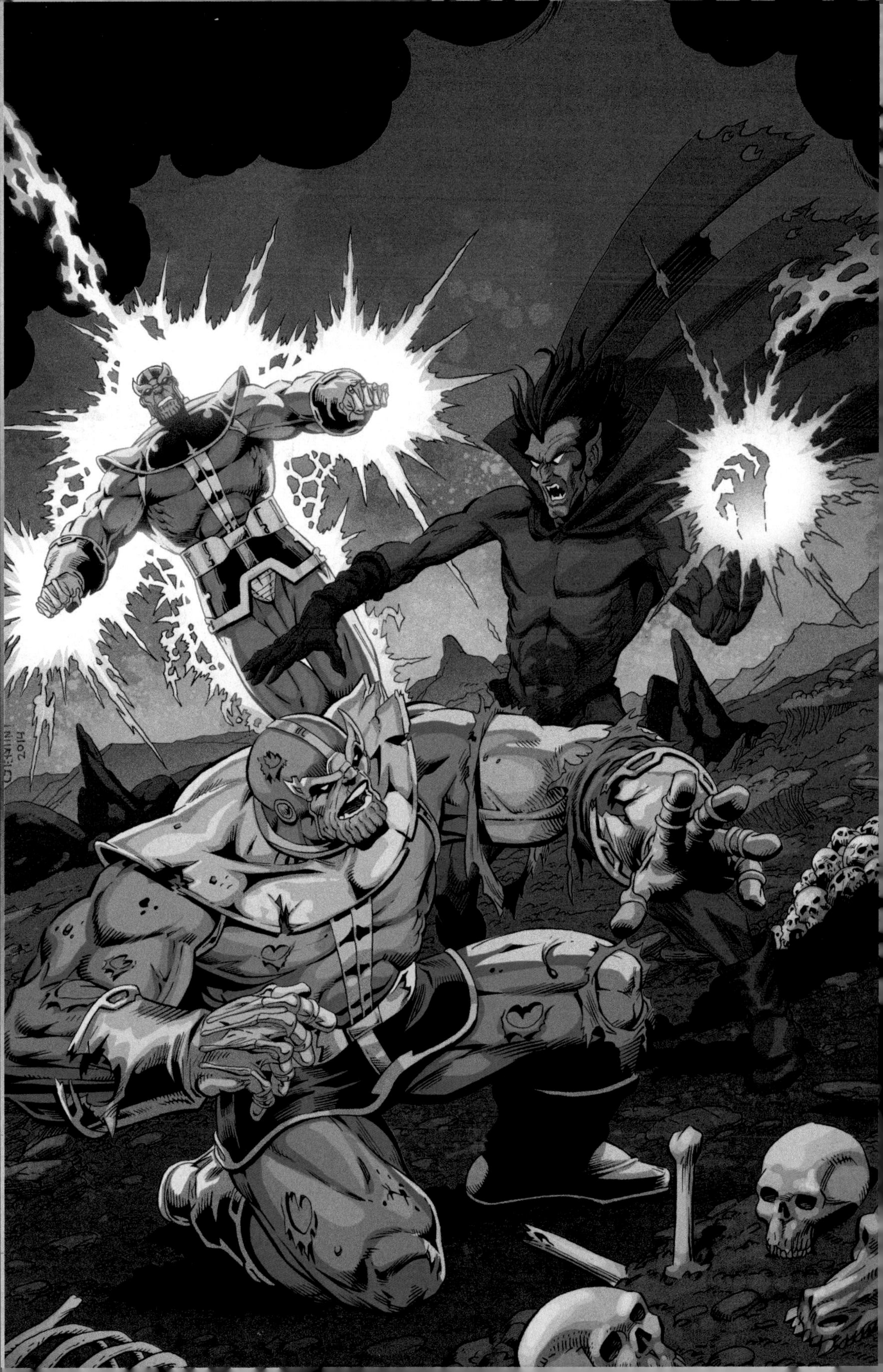

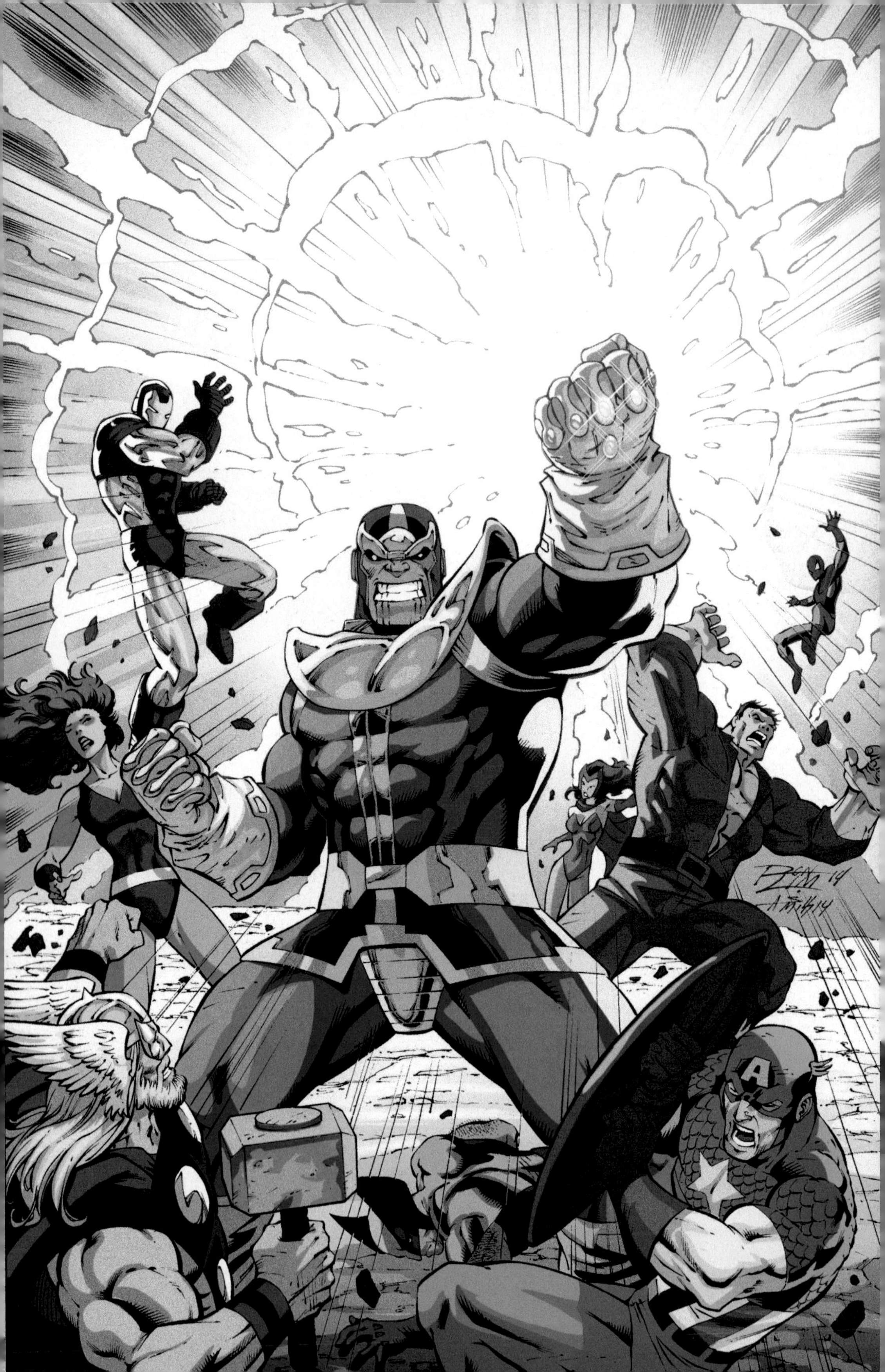